THE 2-IN-1 SERIES

EXPOSING DECEPTION & EMBRACING TRUTH

THE DEFINITIVE COLLECTION
UNPACKING THE CORRUPTION OF OUR GLOBAL FOOD SYSTEM
AND THE RISE OF VEGANISM

TODD SINCLAIR

First published 2023 by Intrepid Fox Publishing Ltd

INTREPID FOX PUBLISHING

20-22 Wenlock Road
London N1 7GU

Hardback ISBN 978-1-7392211-6-4
Paperback ISBN 978-1-7392211-7-1
eISBN 978-1-7392211-8-8

RebelVeganLife.com

Original Illustrations by Cathy Brear
Cover Design by Francesca Cook at Bloom & Bear Media

For curious and compassionate rebels
You have a home here

CONTENTS

VOLUME 2
THE PATH TO COMPASSION: HOW TO ALIGN WITH YOUR VALUES

FOREWORD

If you are curious about veganism, I can think of no better guide to this brave new world than Todd Sinclair's *REBEL VEGAN* series.

There is so much to recommend in this book, but ultimately, its most radical triumph is its reappraisal of vegan values and post-pandemic analysis of why veganism matters. In a welcoming safe space, we are all reminded of what we intrinsically know to be true. With compassion and diplomacy, Todd Sinclair highlights those vegan values that we all share. He shows us the way back to who we really are.

Being vegan reflects an aspiration to live as kindly as possible and to avoid causing unnecessary harm. It is a rejection of factory farming, which subjects billions of animals to intolerable cruelty, exploits disempowered workers, and destroys communities and the environment while producing foods that make us sick. Unfortunately, this inhumane and unsustainable system has spread around the globe.

The good news is that there is a burgeoning awareness about the harm caused by industrial animal agriculture, which is spurring an interest in vegan living. The COVID pandemic further exposed the lack of resilience and failures in our current food system, and the need for reforms. *Rebel Vegan* helps advance the discussion by focusing on ways we need to rethink our food systems and change our lifestyles to avoid future pandemics and create a sustainable, healthier future.

How we sustain and nourish ourselves has profound impacts on our planet and everyone who lives here. We can feed more people with less land and fewer resources, and prevent untold suffering by growing and eating plants instead of animals. Animal production takes up most of the world's agricultural land, including 90% in the United States, and is a leading cause of the Earth's most significant ecological threats, including the climate crisis.

Factory farming is polluting and depleting soils, draining rivers and aquifers, and destroying natural ecosystems and biodiversity. Only 4% of the mammals on earth today live in the wild, while 96% are domesticated or human. Scientists now warn that we are experiencing the planet's Sixth Great Extinction and living in the Anthropocene, a geological era of human dominance that will be marked in the fossil record with deposits of chicken bones and plastic.

Vegans are sometimes labeled as idealists or contrarians, but when you look at the evidence, being vegan is empirically grounded and aligns with our highest ideals. We can protect precious natural resources and save billions of dollars in preventable health care costs every year by shifting to a whole-foods plant-based diet. Avoiding animal products also serves our humanity, since most people oppose cruelty and are disturbed by how animals are raised and slaughtered for food. Consuming meat, dairy and eggs implicates us in violence and abuse, and if we can live well without causing unnecessary harm, why wouldn't we?

Within these pages, Sinclair takes you on a journey of discovery and empowerment. While many things in this world are outside our control, all of us can make a huge difference by making more mindful food choices. *Rebel Vegan* is an inspiring resource that helps empower people to eat and live in better alignment with our shared values and interests—while supporting a food system that can help heal our planet and ourselves.

Gene Baur

President and Cofounder

farm sanctuary

CONNECT WITH US

Facebook | Instagram | Twitter | FarmSanctuary.org

VOLUME 1

UNPACKING THE FACTS: WHY VEGANISM MATTERS

WHY VEGANISM MATTERS

"Nothing is more powerful than an idea whose time has come."
Victor Hugo

Welcome to an uprising.

REBEL VEGAN LIFE is a rallying call born out of love and respect for the planet, the animals, and ourselves. Together we will celebrate, uncomplicate, and demystify veganism. This humble book has hefty ambitions; to empower the rebel in us all by meticulously exposing some home truths so everyone can find their sweet spot on the dietary spectrum. Everyone's journey and battlegrounds are unique, so within this book are the keys needed to unlock your own individual plant-based life, feel confident with your choices, and be well-armored for this brave new world.

In the following pages, I will take you back in time on an unprecedented global history of veganism, as well as an in-depth exposé of our current food system and the urgent issues that, inadvertently, fueled the rapid rise of the modern vegan movement. Along the way, I will share shocking truths of why meat is so cheap but costs us dearly.

This fully revised second edition of *REBEL VEGAN LIFE* is updated for our rapidly shifting times and includes a whole new chapter on the future of food and veganism. It is crucial to be equipped for advancing technologies, to be open to change, and to be on the right side of history.

We are rebels with a cause.

"I predict that future generations will look back at our meat production and consumption with horror and disbelief. This book offers the motivation and means to be on the right side of history."

REBEL VEGAN

Whether you are a devoted vegan or just starting on this adventure, *REBEL VEGAN LIFE* covers everything you need to know about plant-based living. Within these pages, you will find the motivation and support needed to live with ease in the world as an informed and confident vegan. However, I recognize that your circumstances and story are singular, so this is not a one-size-fits-all book. We are rebels afterall, who celebrate your individuality and are committed to inspiring a version of vegan that works for you.

So, before we begin our journey, there's one important thing I need to point out. *REBEL VEGAN LIFE* is a judgment-free zone. Too often, discussions about veganism can lead to conflict and censorship. My purpose is not to demonize people who consume animals, or even those who work in the farming industries—that was me once as I come from a family of farmers. We all know, from personal experience, that good people can make choices that cause harm. And, let's be honest, the word "vegan" has the power to put people's backs up. It has sadly become a divisive word that is seen by many to be an extreme or even ascetic lifestyle.

Yet, at its core, veganism is about embracing the simple, yet timeless, principles of compassion and justice. There should be nothing severe or scary about becoming more aware and kind. So, you won't find any guilt-tripping, patronizing, or stereotyping here, and everyone is welcome at this table. I am not the vegan police, and promise not to raid your fridge!

REBEL VEGAN LIFE not only offers a radical take on veganism with our openness and all-embracing philosophy, but also our fresh perspective. Ultimately, our most groundbreaking act is reappraising the importance of vegan values and lifestyle for these unforeseen times, creating the first post-pandemic analysis of why veganism matters. So, while bringing the debate up to date, we also make the issues relevant and actionable for this brave new world.

The Vegan Society officially defines the term veganism as:
"...a philosophy and way of living which seeks to exclude— as far as is possible and practicable—all forms of exploitation of, and cruelty to, animals for food, clothing or any other purpose; and by extension, promotes the development and use of animal-free alternatives for the benefit of animals, humans and the environment."[1]

With that in mind, *REBEL VEGAN LIFE* does not preach one way of living. This isn't a cult, it's a philosophy. You don't blindly apply a set of rules—you interpret and adapt them to suit your unique situation. As you read this book, you can choose the issues that inspire or motivate you on your journey. The foremost definition even allows that veganism goes "as far as is possible and practical." This relaxed openness provides accessibility and lots of room within the vegan space.

So, if you are open to new ideas and hearing the truth about a lifestyle shrouded in misinformation, then this is the book for you. After all, how can you make an informed choice without a clear picture of the situation?

We all live in a polarized and baffling time that has us swimming in contradictory information and 'fake news'. And the vegan debate has become a battleground for many in politics, the media, and even within our homes. But please feel secure to let your guard down here—this is a safe space to explore new ideas, be challenged, and find a connection with your true values.

I believe that knowledge is power, but we have been kept in the dark about the reality of animal farming. We have been sold a lie. The truth has been hidden or distorted by the farming industries and their pervasive marketing throughout multiple generations. Almost weekly, headlines are heralding new 'science' or studies that promote meat-eating as healthy or sustainable. However, it's vital to check the small print, as most of these 'studies' are discreetly funded by the meat or dairy industries and produced to muddy the waters and keep the public buying their products. It's deliberately confusing and seductive as we are always looking for good news about our bad habits.

I have spent long months wading through these swamps of spin or disinformation and filtering out the industry-backed studies as a means to curate authentic research and establish common themes. From these murky waters, I bring together and cite the most recent peer-reviewed science so it's digestible and demonstrate what independent studies have shown time and again, that animal products are both unnecessary and dangerous to our health and environment. Many powerful industries do not want you to read this book, but sometimes, as *Rebel Vegans*, you have to swim against the tide.

Ultimately, our mission is to empower everyone in making informed choices, finding alignment in our shared values, living our healthiest lives, and enjoying fabulous food. I strongly believe that any change you make from a place of compassion will be beneficial, even profound, and help secure a stronger future for us all.

Wherever you are on the diet spectrum—mindful meat-eater, pescatarian, vegetarian, vegan-curious, or fully plant-based—I celebrate the fact you are here, reading this book and taking steps to lead a kinder and more sustainable life.

Vegans and non-vegans are not on opposite sides. We are in this together, sharing the planet and its resources, and striving to make better choices within our circumstances.

MY VEGAN JOURNEY

Like most of you, I wasn't brought up in a vegan home. In fact, I was born and raised on a dairy farm in eastern Canada, so have lived at each end of the dietary spectrum and experienced both sides of the story.

I knew farming was not for me, so I broke away at a young age and have spent much of my life traveling the world, searching for my purpose, learning from different cultures, and exploring all the diverse diets on offer.

Then one fateful day I became very ill in Vietnam, and my traveling life came to a screeching halt. I sought refuge with my monk friends in a Buddhist monastery in the cool hills of northern Vietnam. There, my old friends nurtured me back to health on a lacto-vegetarian diet. For someone who had always considered dairy and meat to be a key part of a healthy, balanced diet, it was a revelation and gave my life a new direction.

I didn't convert to Buddhism, but I did become a vegan devotee.

I have been vegan for over six years now, and I have never felt healthier, happier, or more aligned with my choices and impact on the world. There is a sense of contentment and confidence in choosing foods that are right for both my body and the planet. This book was born out of my own struggles and triumphs as I transitioned to a fully plant-based lifestyle. *REBEL VEGAN LIFE* is a love letter to the new vegan in all of us. I hope it challenges and inspires you in equal measures in building your best life.

This is a critical time to consider a lifestyle change as we build a new normal in a changing world. As we leave behind several years of Covid restrictions and the world has opened up again, many of us are searching for new ways to live our lives. We no longer view the world and how it works as locked in or unchangeable. It's time to reimagine and create new systems and lifestyles that puts our health, ethics, and sustainability at the forefront. We can be the change we want to see.

We've known for years that the way we produce certain foods harms our planet. And now, thanks to articles in the British Medical Journal, we know that the food industry is at least partly responsible for the severity of Covid-19.[2] How we live, how we eat, and how we relate to our environment matters now more than ever.

Embracing veganism is the most powerful step you can take to make a positive impact and help alleviate many of the most pressing issues facing our survival as a species: chronic diseases, antibiotics resistance, future pandemics, deforestation and loss of biodiversity, environmental collapse, and, of course, animal exploitation and extinction. Every time we stop to eat a meal, we have the potential to generate these important and radical changes and be part of the solution. So, instead of perpetuating the problem, we have the capacity to be a force for good and contribute to building a better world for future generations. This means making thoughtful decisions based on compassion and justice for the planet, the animals, and ourselves.

I think we can all agree that the world is changing and we will have to change with it. The information in the following chapters will fortify you to stay battle-ready and motivated to come out as vegan, in whatever way that works best for you.

So welcome to the table, fellow rebels.
Let's veganize our lives.

1

RECLAIMING OUR HISTORY

"Knowledge is power.
And power should always
be used with compassion."
REBEL VEGAN

There is a common misconception that veganism is a modern-day fad that will have its moment and fizzle out in due course like other trendy diets. So, as a history geek, it was important for me to seek out neglected narratives to find our brave ancestors and reclaim our overlooked but proud past. Consequently, I set out to trace and piece together our vegan family tree.

And their rebellious voices came echoing back through the centuries. I think their courage and activism can inspire a sense of purpose in us all; empowered by being part of a historical and global movement.

History is essential to understanding and appreciating who we are. It provides us with a powerful awareness and sense of purpose. That's what is so magical when you realize you connect to others who came before you. They become our forefathers/mothers and a divine source of strength that you can draw on whenever you need that boost. We become part of the story.

First and foremost, the rejoinder to the fad-diet myth is a resounding NO. Veganism is far from a fad. The latest research[1] into our early ancestors shows we weren't the meat-eating predators depicted by traditional history books or the Flintstones. Another clue lies in religious scriptures, which advocate against violence of all kinds, including violence towards non-human animals. Even ancient Greek philosophy is full of arguments against eating other animals.

With that said, the answer is also yes. The vegan diet is trending. There is no denying that veganism has enjoyed a resurgence in present times as a response to the growing and frightening crisis we face today. As we open our minds to explore plant-based living, it is useful, and indeed powerful, to stand back and get some perspective on what is an age-old philosophy. Modern veganism is a type of rebalancing. It offers an answer to our world's current challenges.

The start of the vegan movement is often dated to the invention of the word "vegan" in 1944.

Although that's when Western society first acknowledged it as a lifestyle option, ethical eating has its roots in both prehistory and ancient history.

THE MYTH OF THE HUNTER-GATHERER

It was famed anthropologist Raymond Dart who, after discovering the first fossil of one of our ancestors in Africa, planted the notion of the meat-eating prehistoric man. He described our ancestors as: "*...carnivorous creatures that seized living quarries by violence, battered them to death, slaking their ravenous thirst with the hot blood of victims and greedily devouring livid writhing flesh.*[2]"

Talk about making early humans sound barbaric!

We have been fed an alpha-male fairytale of brave, muscled cavemen thrusting spears and killing large game for food. The emphasis has been firmly on the "hunter" element of our ancestors. It is time to revisit this, bring in some modern findings, and reclaim our lost history.

Do you remember the Flintstones? They have a lot to answer for. We imagine cavemen hunting mammoths and saber-tooth tigers, but there is little evidence that this happened on any scale. Don't trust those upper-Paleolithic cave paintings. You might have been told that these depict traditional hunting scenes, but you should know that it is now thought our cavemen ancestors were overly creative and had an inflated ego. An increasingly accepted theory is that cave paintings are depictions of grandiose visions or hallucinations, rather than actual events. This hypothesis has gained wider acceptance and has been advanced many times in the last decade, most recently by the Journal of Archeology, Consciousness and Culture.[3]

Given that humans cannot tear flesh or hide by hand, it is very likely that our earliest ancestors only turned to animal flesh out of necessity, when their usual staples were unavailable. They were opportunistic hunters of meat, only taking the easy kill.[4]

These ancestors began fashioning crude stone tools around 2.5 million years ago.[5] They had two main priorities: survival and reproduction. Their primary focus on a daily basis was gathering food. Working in small groups, they would go into the woods, rivers, and grasslands to see what could be found to eat that day.

When the tools and rudimentary weapons entered the scene, did we turn into big-time hunters? Early humans caught bugs, tree squirrels, fish, rabbits, and other small wild animals.[6] But the vast majority of their diet consisted of native, wild plants, such as roots, fruits, nuts, seeds, and vegetables. We were not exclusively herbivores, but we definitely weren't carnivores either. Our diet was similar to our closest relatives—the other large primates. Seeing as we share over 96% of our DNA with chimpanzees,[7] it's no great leap of faith to assume we probably shared the same diet back in the day.[8] All primates (which includes us humans) are omnivorous. Our closest animal relatives evolved and still eat primarily plants (fruits, flowers, leaves, nuts, seeds, and grasses) supplemented by small animals (birds, birds' eggs, lizards, small rodents, frogs, and insects).

**Let's put it another way:
do we look like carnivores to you?**

Would you have survived in the wild? This is a question that the Ancient Greek philosopher Plutarch wrote about in his essays on eating meat. Look at the structure of our bodies. Do we have hooked beaks, sharp talons, or jagged teeth? Do we even have enough stomach acid to break down a diet made up mostly of flesh?

2,000 years ago, Plutarch argued what modern science has since explained, that the softness of our body, our small mouth, flat teeth, and our digestive system are not designed by nature to hunt. If we were carnivorous animals, we would hunt like tigers or lions. We would use our fangs and our claws to tear down a gazelle, a boar, or a lamb. We would eat it while it was still alive, the way predatory animals do.

Oh, wait, we don't have fangs or claws. And as for eating our prey as the life flutters out of them, Plutarch asks: "*If you have qualms about eating the flesh while life is still present, why do you continue, contrary to nature, to eat what possesses life?*"[9]

It is a powerful question, worth pondering. Our meat must be dead, sanitized, boiled, roasted, fried, and seasoned with spices or herbs (plants!) to make it palatable. Or, as Plutarch puts it, in order that: "*...the palate may be deceived and accept what is foreign to it.*"

Even if we go down the road of the sophisticated carnivore—making up for what we lacked in physical ability with weapons—the picture of a meat-centric diet still doesn't add up. Hunting is hard work. It is dangerous. The dedicated Hada and Kung bushmen of Africa, who hunt with bows and arrows, fail to get any meat more than half the time. Wild animals aren't just hanging around waiting to be caught.

The truth is hunter-gatherers did not eat meat that often. According to research published in National Geographic[10], hunter-gatherers received approximately 30% of their annual calories from meat, and this wasn't even a consistent measure. In fact, they endured lean times when meat was limited to less than a handful of meat a week. There is no denying that our early ancestor's activities included some hunting, but it was not the method by which they obtained most of their protein or nutrition.

So, what was?

Well, it turns out that "man the hunter" was backed up by "woman the forager." According to anthropologists, almost 70% of the hunter-gatherer diet was made up of plants, including tubers, nuts, roots, fruits, and grains. The story that hunting and meat-eating made us human is flawed. The truth is our ancestors might have turned to meat at times, but they survived on a predominantly plant-based diet.[11]

Based on this, you could say that a plant-based diet is far from a fad—it is actually millions of years old. In fact, we vegans have a rich past. Our diet has been a cause for debates that have echoed through the centuries. Veganism is as old as recorded history, and it has kept us alive and enlightened throughout the ages.

WORLD RELIGION AND VEGAN VALUES

"Around the time that homo-sapiens were elevated as divine status by humanist religions, farm animals stopped being viewed as living creatures who could feel pain and distress, and instead came to be treated as machines. They spend their entire lives as cogs in a production line, and the quality and length of their lives is determined by the profit and losses of business corporations."

Yuval Noah Harari on animal agriculture[12]

Our early ancestors had a spiritual relationship with their fellow animals. Cave paintings and ancient art give us a clue that animals were closely linked with divinity. So it is hardly surprising that the earliest people to adopt what is now known as a vegetarian or vegan diet were religious and spiritual followers.

The world's most practiced religions have all advocated against cruelty towards animals. They each have their own teachings and scriptures surrounding animals and their place in the world. Animals have traditionally played a role in religious ceremonies, meals, and sacrifices. Some religions consider animals sacred, while others consider them a source of food, but for the most part, they have a deep respect for all that God created, including animals and plants. However, just like the concepts of love, forgiveness, and unity can be turned around to encourage wars (like the Christian crusades of the Middle Ages), religion has sometimes been used as justification for harming animals. We are witnessing the result of this disregard for life in the environmental and animal welfare crisis we are currently facing. Let's take a closer look at what the world's principal religions say about animals.

JUDAISM - ORIGINATED IN 2085 BC

Judaism believes animals are part of God's creation. It therefore calls for the proper treatment of animals and asks humans to avoid causing pain to any living creatures. One of the Jewish codes of law mandates that animals should be treated with compassion, and that a Jew cannot pass by an animal in distress or animals being mistreated, even on the Sabbath.

It is forbidden, according to the law of the Torah, to inflict pain upon any living creature. On the contrary, it is our duty to relieve the pain of any creature, even if it is ownerless or belongs to a non-Jew.

Code of Jewish Law[13]

HINDUISM - ORIGINATED IN 1500 BC

Hinduism believes all creatures have a soul and that they are part of the supreme soul—the god-like energy that brings all things into being. Occasionally, some animals are sacrificed in Hindu ceremonies, but the animal must be treated with great care leading up to the event. Treating animals with kindness and respect is an integral part of a Hindu's way of life, and many followers are vegan or vegetarian.

I have visited Hindu temples in Indonesia with animal gods like Nandi the bull. The most impressive is at the 9th century temple at Prambanan on the island of Java, where a huge carved stone bull Nandi stands guard. Although commanding, it is in a sitting position, emphasizing its calm discipline and dignity. It is seen as a timeless lesson about controlling power to protect harmony that seems just as relevant and urgent to today's world.

BUDDHISM - ORIGINATED IN 560 BC

Buddhism is based on the Vedic Scriptures written in 1200 BC. These scriptures promote the concept of ahimsa, or "non-violence." Ahimsa is the virtue of inflicting no harm to any living being, so that your spirit stays pure. Many teachings clearly advocate staying away from eating meat. So as not to become a source of violence, followers of Buddhism are encouraged to be catalysts of compassion by not eating meat. To them, meat is for wild and violent beasts.[14]

Five ethical teachings govern how Buddhists live. One of these teachings prohibits taking the life of any person or animal. Followers of Buddhism usually follow a lacto-vegetarian diet. This means they consume dairy products, but exclude eggs, poultry, fish, and meat from their diet.

The Buddha himself is known to believe that eating meat destroys great compassion, and advises his disciples to avoid the consumption of meat, just as they would avoid the flesh of their own children.

CHRISTIANITY - ORIGINATED IN 30 AD

Christian teachings state that everything in the universe owes its existence to God, and therefore this can provide a basis for opting for a vegan diet. Many leading notable Christians treated animals with high regards and compassion. For example, St Francis of Assisi is known to have preached to the birds, while St. Anthony of Padua preached to fish.[15] Genesis 1 states God created all creatures and made them good. Psalm 145 states God has compassion and provides for every living thing. Luke 12.6 mentions that not a single sparrow is forgotten in God's sight.

The book of Genesis states: *"God said, 'See, I have given you every plant yielding seed that is upon the face of all the earth, and every tree with seed in its fruit; you shall have them for food. And to every beast of the earth, and to every bird of the air, and to everything that creeps on the earth, everything that has the breath of life, I have given every green plant for food.' And so it was."* [16]

Many interpret these verses as that God created the world vegan. But it goes further. The Bible also speaks of God's intentions, his idea of a "peaceable kingdom" is one where: *"The wolf shall live with the lamb, the leopard shall lie down with the kid, the calf and the lion and the falling together, and a little child shall lead them. The cow and the bear shall graze, their young shall lie down together; and the lion shall eat straw like the ox."* [17]

The Bible tells of a world where no animals are killed for food. While many Christians believe that all God's creatures can feel pain and suffering, and should therefore be treated with kindness, others view this from a different standpoint—the standpoint of human dominion. Christian texts have been interpreted so wildly that even meat eaters can justify their dietary choices.

This justification comes in the form of downgrading animals by suggesting that God created animals solely for the use of humans, and that animals were inferior because they had no soul. However, Jesus himself made comments that imply animals are endowed with a soul and to be cherished. When he was sending his disciples out into the world to spread the gospel, he told the disciples to preach to them. Mark 16:15 *"And he said unto them, Go ye into all the world, and preach the gospel to every creature.*[18]*"* It is clear that at the root of Christianity is love for everything that God has created. Is there any better way to show love and respect for these creations than by following Jesus' lead?

ISLAM - ORIGINATED IN 610 AD

Islamic religion calls for using animals when necessary, but cruelty towards an animal is considered a sin. In his teachings, prophet Muhammad states that mercy towards animals will be rewarded, and that both animals and humans should be treated with kindness.

All these religions, rooted as they are in respect for what God or a higher power has created, may not directly advocate a vegan diet, but do ask their followers to be mindful of how they treat other sentient beings. Today we would call that a cruelty-free lifestyle. In other words, living a life based on compassion and justice; the core values of veganism.

Perhaps religious teachings fall short of advocating complete abstinence from meat, because they were written at a time when using animals for food did not have the environmental and social implications it has today, and when we lacked the structural, technological, and pharmaceutical knowledge to create the extremes of industrial farms that is the norm across the world today. Regardless, they tell their followers that cruelty towards animals is wrong. They all agree that when an animal must be killed or be of service for transport, it should be treated with respect and kindness. For example, the Torah states:

> *"Since the desire of procuring food necessitates the slaying of animals, the Torah commands that the death of the animal should be the easiest. It is not allowed to torment the animal by cutting the throat in a clumsy manner, by piercing it, or by cutting off a limb while the animal is still alive."* [19]

Before we developed monotheism, the pagan world celebrated and cherished animals. Multi-god religions tend to connect humans and their environment. There are gods of nature, gods of wine, and gods of animals. Some gods were part animal, such as the Egyptian goddess Isis (often depicted as a cow, or with the horns of a cow[20]), or the Greek god Chiron (half man, half horse[21]). Instead, over the years, monotheistic religions appear to have elevated man above his environment and other living things, leading to the crisis we face today. Animals have become commodities, here for the sole purpose of being used by man. Consequently, we turn away as the horrific atrocities are committed against them.

Something has gone terribly wrong. Somewhere along the way, we have forgotten these teachings and lost our way.

ANCIENT GREEK PHILOSOPHY AND VEGANISM

Ancient Greece, which we most often associate with wine-fueled orgies and a plethora of horny gods, was actually the setting for a fiery debate on the topic of justice for animals. Early veganism was actually referred to as *"abstinence from beings with a soul."*[22]

One of the first Greek philosophers to promote a vegan lifestyle was Pythagoras. Born in 569 BC, he is best known for being a classical superstar and the founding father of mathematics, music, astronomy, and philosophy. His teachings influenced Plato and Aristotle, and he was an early champion of women's rights and education.

As if that wasn't enough, he was the first philosopher on record to promote animal welfare and an ethical diet. He believed that all creatures are created equal and should therefore be treated with respect. He also believed that eating meat caused people to become more violent towards each other.[23]

Due to his teachings, the first self-proclaimed vegetarians called themselves "Pythagoreans." These original *Rebel Vegans* were not about self-denial or vague spiritual concepts. Following in his footsteps, they advanced a grounded theory on the treatment of animals. They believed that any being that experiences pain or suffering should not have pain inflicted on it unnecessarily. Because to Pythagoras, vegetarianism, pacifism, and humane treatment of other sentient beings are all part of a path towards both personal contentment and world peace.[24]

Five hundred years later, another respected philosopher and Delphi priest, Plutarch (who was inspired by Pythagorean philosophy), went on record to defend animals and debunk some of the arguments that are still being used today, 2000 years later, in defense of meat-eating. It's a case of history repeating itself.

And there are more. Apollonius of Tyana, as a Pythagorean, opposed animal sacrifice and lived on a frugal, strictly vegetarian diet.[25] Plotinus, a Greek philosopher who avoided any products or medicines made from animals, considered interconnectedness and ethics inseparable. He said: *"If my soul and your soul come from the soul of the All and that soul is one, these souls must also be one, allowing us to feel one another's feelings."* [26]

We have come so far in modern times, with technology and our conquest of space, and yet in some ways we have stood still or even regressed. When it comes to our humaneness and compassion for other animals, we still have much work to do. You, as a *Rebel Vegan*, are helping put kindness back on the map.

"All beings tremble before death. All fear death. When you consider this, you will not kill or cause someone to kill. All beings fear before danger. Life is dear to all."

Dhammapada - Buddhist Scripture

THE FIRST ANIMAL RIGHTS ACTIVIST?

PLUTARCH'S ESSAYS ON VEGANISM 66 AD:[27]

"For the sake of a little flesh we deprive them of the sun, of the light, of the duration of life to which they are entitled by birth and being.

We declare, then, that it is absurd for them to say that the practice of flesh-eating is based on nature. For that man is not naturally carnivorous is, in the first place, obvious from the structure of his body. A man's frame is in no way similar to those creatures who were made for flesh-eating; he has no hooked beak or sharp nails or jagged teeth, no strong stomach or warmth of vital fluids able to digest and assimilate a heavy diet of flesh. It is from the very fact, the evenness of our teeth, the smallness of our mouths, the softness of our tongues, our possession of vital fluids too inert to digest meat that nature disavows our eating of flesh.

If you declare that you are naturally designed for such a diet, then first kill for yourself what you want to eat. Do it however, only through your own resources, unaided by cleaver or cudgel of any kind or axe. Rather, just as wolves and bears and lions themselves slay what they eat, so you are to fell an ox with your fangs or a boar with your jaws, or tear a lamb or hare in bits. Fall upon it and eat it still living, as animals do. But if you wait for what you eat to be dead, if you have qualms about enjoying the flesh while life is still present, why do you continue, contrary to nature, to eat what possesses life?

Even when it is lifeless and dead, however, no one eats the flesh just as it is; men boil it and roast it, altering it by fire and drugs, recasting and diverting and smothering with countless condiments the taste of gore so that the palate may be deceived and accept what is foreign to it."

We should learn from our forefather, The First *Rebel Vegan*.

VEGAN LEADERS AND RULERS

Egyptian Pharaoh Akhenaten (1353-1336 BC): *banned animal sacrifice because he believed it was a sin to take away any given life by the god Aten. Interestingly, Akhenaten has been described as revolutionary and as "the greatest idealist in the world." No doubt this is at least partly due to his approach to animal rights.*[28]

Japanese Emperor Tenmu (673-686 AD): *banned the consumption of domesticated animal meat (horses, cattle, dogs, monkeys and birds) between April 1st and September 30th of each year as a nod to Buddhist teachings.*[29]

"Animals should not be consumed but should be viewed as prized gifts from God. That is the way of a whole human being."
Abraham Lincoln[30]

"Eating flesh is unproved murder."
Benjamin Franklin[31]

"The life of a lamb is no less precious than that of a human being. The more helpless the creature, the more that it is entitled to protection by man from the cruelty of man."
Mohandas Gandhi

RENAISSANCE AND ENLIGHTENMENT

During the Renaissance period between the 14th and 17th century, new vegetarian ideology or debate was rare. Meat was a scarce luxury, available only for the rich.

During this time, Greek philosophies from thinkers like Pythagoras were rediscovered and became influential again. Later in this period, the notion that animals feel pain, and therefore deserve consideration, was being debated. Luigi Cornaro was a Venetian nobleman and dietitian, who lived to an unheard of age of ninety-nine years. He spoke out about the excesses of the elite classes meat consumption and promoted a vegetarian diet. Desiderius Erasmus, a Dutch humanist, Thomas More, a social philosopher, and Michel de Montaigne, one of the best known philosophers of the French Renaissance, were appalled by the brutal practices associated with blood sports, writing with passion about the plight of animals. Leonardo da Vinci, the superstar of the Renaissance Movement, is also on record as denouncing meat-eating.

"I have since an early age abjured the use of meat, and the time will come when men will look upon the murder of animals as they look upon the murder of man."
Leonardo da Vinci, 1512

The Enlightenment period of the 18th century marked a dramatic shift and a new view of man's place in the order of creation—above all animals—as masters of the universe. The renowned philosopher René Descartes advanced the notion that non-human animals do not have souls and introduced the concept of animals as machine-like creatures. However, not all were in alignment with this. John Locke, a British philosopher, argued that animals are, in fact, intelligent. Among western religions, there was a re-emergence of the idea that eating animals was an aberration of God's will and human nature. Other famous vegetarians of this period include poets Alexander Pope and John Gay, the royal physician, Dr. John Arbuthnot, and the creator of the Methodist movement, John Wesley[32]. Dr. George Cheyne was a pioneering physician of his time, well-known for going vegetarian to recover from obesity-related health problems. He was an early advocate of the lacto-vegetarian diet. Although the medical community criticized it at the time, his book *An Essay of Health and Long Life* was a huge success.[33] Around this time, British philosopher Jeremy Bentham is known for comparing animal suffering to that of humans.

"The question is not 'can they reason?' Nor 'can they talk?' But 'can they suffer?'"
Jeremy Bentham[34], 1789

The 19th century saw many radical thinkers promoting vegetarianism. Dr. William Lambe, for example, was a prominent figure in both the medical and literary worlds, and would influence Dr. John Newton, who later set up The Vegetarian Society. The romantic poet Percy Shelley was convinced of the health benefits of a meat-free diet, and was vegetarian. He made a political point with his diet choices, pointing out that inefficient use of resources meant that meat production was one of the reasons for food shortages among the neediest people.[35]

A BRAVE NEW VEGAN WORLD

"We can see quite plainly that our present civilisation is built on the exploitation of animals, just as past civilisations were built on the exploitation of slaves, and we believe the spiritual destiny of man is such that in time he will view with abhorrence the idea that men once fed on the products of animals' bodies."

Donald Watson, in the first issue of The Vegan News, 1944 [36]

In 1809, with the modern age gathering pace, animal welfare was reclaimed as a religious and social issue. That year, Reverend William Cowherd, in northern England, made a link between vegetarianism as an expression of Christian faith. His Bible Christian Church caused a stir when he began using biblical references to make the case against meat-eating. This church, together with members of a progressive educational college, Alcott House and the Northwood Villa Infirmary, formed the Vegetarian Society in 1847. Three years later, William Metcalfe, a disciple of Reverend Cowherd and member of the Bible Christian Church, emigrated to the US with members of his congregation and established the American Vegetarian Society,[37] and the new designation 'Vegetarian' made its debut in North America. It would be another 100 years before 'Vegan' would be coined, but the seeds were sown in this transatlantic crossing to a brave new world.

A short two decades later, in the 1830s, the concept of vegetarianism was starting to gain attention and cause debate. During this time, technological leaps meant agriculture was becoming more intensive, and the rise of larger scale animal farming was beginning to raise questions about the ethics of eating animals. This early vegetarianism advocated excluding animal products in clothing and other areas of life, and was therefore comparable to veganism. However, when the Vegetarian Society was established, anxious at seeming too strict, they shied away from formally excluding eggs and dairy in their manifesto.

At the dawn of the new 20th century, between 1909 and 1912, members of the Vegetarian Society had heated discussions about animal welfare and whether vegetarians should eat eggs and dairy products. In 1923, the editor of the Vegetarian Messenger wrote: *"We feel that the ideal position for vegetarians is abstinence from animal products and that most of us are, like other reformers, in a transitional stage."* [38]

Then, as the Vegetarian Society was at war, the editor wrote in 1935: "*The question as to whether dairy products should be used by vegetarians becomes more pressing year by year.*"[39]

The schism opened up further when the secretary of the Leicester branch, Donald Watson, challenged this position and their indecision. At the time, Donald had been a vegetarian for seven years, but, after witnessing the brutal conditions on his uncle's farm, he had begun to question the ethics of dairy. Having experimented with a diet free from all animal products and found it "varied, appetizing, and in every way satisfactory," he and Elsie Shrigley, a fellow activist, suggested that a subgroup of non-dairy vegetarians be formed within the Vegetarian Society.[40] When their request was refused, they decided to set up a new society and quarterly magazine. Through rebellion and conviction, the vegan movement was about to be formally launched onto the world stage.

And so, on a sunny Sunday afternoon in 1944, Donald Watson, Elsie Shrigley, and four other rebels met in the Attic Club in London to discuss the birth of a groundbreaking organization. And the first thing on the agenda was to settle on a name for this brave new movement. Among the options were "dairyban," "vitan" and "benevore." I don't know about you, but I'm glad they settled for vegan, which was the winning pick, as it contained the first three and the last two letters of "vegetarian." Donald Watson said it marked "the beginning and the end of vegetarian." A typically bold statement from our founder, especially when you consider the first Vegan Society newsletter went out to just twenty-five subscribers.[41]

However, the initial response was promising and attracted more than 100 supporters, including a celebrity endorsement from vegetarian playwright George Bernard Shaw[42] who pledged to abandon eggs and dairy. This rebel movement had begun in earnest and would only gather momentum in response to the escalating atrocities of industrial farming in the last half of the 20th century.

It wasn't until 1949 that the official definition of veganism was established: "A philosophy and way of living which seeks to exclude—as far as is possible and practicable—all forms of exploitation of, and cruelty to, animals for food, clothing or any other purpose; and by extension, promotes the development and use of animal-free alternatives for the benefit of humans, animals and the environment. In dietary terms, it denotes the practice of dispensing with all products derived wholly or partly from animals."[43]

Although veganism remained very much a little-known niche movement throughout much of the 20th century, the counterculture movements of the Sixties and Seventies increased its popularity. More and more young people were traveling to places like India and discovering spirituality, yoga, mindfulness, and peaceful lifestyle options.

What's more, the Sixties also marked the rise of fast-food outlets and the rapid growth of infrastructure and technologies needed to supply an increasing demand for cheap meat. These brutal advances helped focus the rebels in the underground vegan movement to find their voices and promote the urgency and necessity of veganism.

Fast-forward to the time of writing, 2022, and veganism is on the up, in a big way. But it isn't a victory... yet. Never before have we consumed as much meat, dairy, and eggs as we do today. Even so, the vegan movement has exploded in the last decade. In the US, the number of vegans rose from 4 million to 20 million between 2014 and 2018, a 600% increase. In the UK, the number of people identifying as vegan has quadrupled since 2014, going from 150,000 to 720,000.[44]

Despite this unprecedented growth, veganism would have to grow at the same rate for 30 years before the whole world became vegan. Globally, it's estimated that there are around 79 million vegans—that's just 1% of the world's population.

The Economist termed 2019 *"The Year of The Vegan."* What has happened in recent times to spur this on? Why has there been a sudden surge in veganism in the 21st century?

There is no straight-forward answer, but I think it is part of a domino effect caused by many factors all coming together at once. A huge component of this is the internet, and the fact we have access to information like never before—we have encyclopedias at our fingertips. Millennials and Generation Zs have run with this. Social media has been a tool to spread the message far and wide, creating digital communities of *Rebel Vegans* who all share this shared passion on Instagram or TikTok. Of course, it has its dangers and pitfalls, but one can't deny it has been key to challenging us all to rethink our eating habits. I am hopeful it might just save the world. In many ways, social media has replaced direct action as the way to bring about social change.

Organizations like *Anonymous for the Voiceless* would not be half as active without social media and the internet to share their message and show what happens behind the locked doors and barbed wires of slaughterhouses. However, it is vital that these movements go beyond the internet as spreading awareness online is only the first step.

It seems we are just starting to take our collective heads out of the sand—this is only the beginning. It's been a long process. In 2005, *Earthlings* aired for the first time, narrated by Joaquin Phoenix—an almost-too-hard-to-watch documentary shining a light on humankind's dependence on animals for economic purposes, and the exploitation happening across five areas: food, entertainment, medicine, clothing and the pet industry. In 2011, the film *Forks Over Knives* gave us a sobering look at the effect of meat and dairy on our health, linking it to the obesity and heart disease crises.

Cowspiracy hit our screens in 2014, with its focus on the environmental impact of animal agriculture and statistics that had many who watched it committing to at least reducing their meat consumption. Suddenly, veganism was becoming sexy. Hollywood stars were funding documentaries about it. Celebrities were coming out and sharing their vegan diets.

"I do recommend a vegan diet because you wake up and feel great!"
Jennifer Lopez

For many in the west, veganism stopped being something extreme or annoying and started looking like a desirable lifestyle option—the colorful breakfast Buddha bowls on Instagram probably helped.

Simultaneously, the climate crisis has been getting more and more airtime. It has been at the center of global conversation for most of the 21st century. Unfortunately, there has been little political drive for real change. The internet exposed these political flaws and inspired people—particularly young people—to take matters into their own hands. This is hardly surprising, as they will face the consequences of previous generations' blasé attitude to ecology. Greta Thunberg is perhaps the best example of a young activist with the knowledge and passion to inspire others to join the cause.[45]

Although decreasing carbon emissions and fossil fuels are at the center of this issue, the vegan movement stands firmly alongside this, given that agriculture is responsible for a significant part of high carbon emissions and loss of biodiversity. We are an integral part of the solution. No climate survival remedy is possible without a huge shift in the way we eat. This is something we'll explore further in the chapter on the environment as a driving force of veganism.

With all this information at our fingertips, many have become increasingly outraged and frightened at the effects of our diets. But you know what? We have not seen anything yet. The climate crisis, as mind-numbingly frightening as it is, remains pretty abstract, especially for many of us in the Western world. Warmer summers almost sound like a pleasant side effect of unrestrained consumerism. As for the health crisis, it's easy to imagine that this is just something that happens to people with no self-control. Covid however, forces us to really look at how we live, how we eat, and how this impacts both the world and us as individuals.

Could this global health disaster actually help us rebalance the way we live?

Are we humble enough to learn these lessons and driven enough to make changes? I sincerely hope so.

We still have a chance to turn the tide. The resurgence of veganism in the last few years is a direct response to the more pressing crises we face, crises that we will cover in more detail in the next few chapters. And now Covid has come along and shone a light on a problem that scientists have been talking about for years, but that hasn't really hit the headlines: antibiotic-resistant viruses, how meat damages our immune systems, and how it opens the door to further epidemics like the one the world is only recovering from.

So, back to where we started: Is veganism a modern-day fad?

The answer is no.

Our earliest ancestors evolved on a mainly plant-based diet, both from necessity and limited hunting ability. Ethical eating and compassion for animals have been part of our earliest religions and philosophies—respecting other beings was considered a way of respecting God and living in harmony with the natural world. For the last seven decades, veganism has become a much-needed and formidable movement, spurred on not only by animal welfare but also due to the fact that our current meat-centric diets threaten our very existence.

This is what we are fighting for. As part of the vegan movement, you are a rebel, joining the fight for justice and compassion.

NOT NATURAL BORN KILLERS

FIVE REASONS WHY HUMANS AREN'T DESIGNED TO EAT MEAT

1. We don't like blood. 99.9% of humans cannot stand the sight of blood and intestines, nor the sounds of an animal dying. Most of us can't stomach the bloody reality of eating an animal.

2. We lack the physical tools. Real carnivores have large canine teeth and sharp claws that can tear flesh from prey. Humans have small, dull canines and short, soft fingernails. Humans also have flat molars like herbivores, to grind plant foods like fruit and vegetables.

3. Our digestive systems can't take it. Carnivores have short digestive tracts that allow meat to pass quickly through their system. The human digestive tract is much longer, which gives the fiber and nutrients in plant foods enough time to be broken down and absorbed.

4. We don't have the right stomach acid. Carnivores have strong stomach acid that can break down raw meat and kill any bacteria present. Human stomach acid is similar to plant-eating animals. It is strong, but not strong enough to kill some bacteria found in meat. This is why we must cook meat to eat it. But cooking meat at high temperatures creates substances (heterocyclic amines and polycyclic aromatic hydrocarbons) that cause DNA mutations and increase the risk of cancer.

5. Meat makes us sick. According to the American Heart Association, meat eaters have a 32% higher risk of developing heart disease than vegetarians[46]. If we are meant to eat meat, then why does it make us sick?

2

MEAT CORRUPTION

AN INDUSTRY BASED ON LIES

"The world will not be destroyed by those who do evil, but by those who watch them without doing anything."
Albert Einstein[1]

We have touched on how the vegan movement has grown and is building momentum, but why has it become so urgent and essential at this moment?

Before we dive deeper into the motivational driving forces, let's take a look at our current food system and the mess in which we find ourselves. To find our way out, we have to understand why we find ourselves at this critical point in history.

There are forces at play keeping us stuck in a situation that threatens our survival. Where once we could only kill a handful of animals with our rudimentary spears, the meat industry has, over the last 250 years, grown into a monster that threatens to kill us all.

We need to wade through the murky waters of the current food system to understand why the meat industry has grown into a beast that threatens our survival. Much of it has to do with what happened after the Second World War. Industrialization, government subsidies, and even the scientific community created the perfect storm and the necessary conditions for this sector to expand to such a degree that it is now one of the most powerful industries in the history of the world: a sector worth an annual two trillion dollars[2] and producing 340 million tons of meat per year.[3]

Another reason this industry has grown exponentially is that it keeps us coming back for more, with a little help from governments, health institutions, and clever marketing.

How could the vegan movement not spread as a response to this? After all, every force has its opposite. As the meat industry grows, so does the counterforce, a movement dedicated to protecting animals and the planet from the effects of our human "progress." Being a *Rebel Vegan* has never been so urgent—we need rebellious spirits more than ever.

I like to keep faith that since we created this mess, we can clean it up. But time is running out. We are facing many tipping points, and veganism has never been so essential.

We can see this clearly with the industrial and agricultural revolutions. Both are celebrated as wonderful events without which we would all still be living in mud-huts, scratching a meager sustenance from barren fields. While it isn't all bad (I recognize the blessings and advantages of our globalized world—my local corner store has exotic fruits and vegetables from around the globe, and I am grateful for that), these revolutions have come at a high price. I'm no longer sure we got a good deal in the bargain.

FROM FORAGERS TO FARMERS

Twelve thousand years ago, the Agricultural Revolution[4] happened and dramatically changed forever the trajectory of the lives of, and relation between, humans and animals. From a human population of under four million scattered tribes, this proved a turning point that enabled our population to soar into the billions as we settled and tamed nature and its wild animals.

Foragers became farmers, going from a nomadic hunter-gatherer lifestyle to a more settled way of life that included growing cereal and domesticating animals. This shift from nomadic to settled continued and spread across the globe. Domesticated animals did not just provide an additional source of food, they also made large scale farming possible (a bull pulling a plow goes much faster than a man on his own). This created increasingly stable populations and a move towards the type of settlements we know today: towns and cities.[5]

The agricultural revolution is often viewed as the time when our wild nomadic ancestors finally began to become "civilized." But there are question marks over whether this was all that positive. The latest retelling of our human history, *Sapiens* by Yuval Noah Harari, offers a different perspective. Yes, farms meant more food was available, but this additional food didn't necessarily mean a better diet nor a better life. Farmers were at the mercy of their crops and had a less varied diet than their nomadic foraging counterparts. This agricultural revolution also triggered the appearance of a completely new life-form on earth—the domesticated animal. As the centuries passed, the tables turned and this life-form became the new norm. Today, 90% of all large animals are domesticated.

Far from being an unprecedented improvement, the agricultural revolution created new kinds of suffering which have grown steadily worse with each passing century. Animals are the biggest victims of history. We have captured, mutilated, enslaved, and continue to kill them. Except we no longer do it out of necessity, like a lion kills a gazelle.

We do it for profit.

FROM FARMERS TO FRANKENSTEINERS

The first agricultural revolution of 12,000 BC paved the way for the industrial revolution that began in 1840. This saw us leaving behind traditional methods, such as crop rotation that restored and maintained soil quality, to adopting the modern practices we have today. In the mid-18th century, two British agriculturalists, Thomas Coke and Robert Bakewell, introduced selective breeding and inbreeding to reduce genetic diversity. Bakewell was the first person to breed cattle to be used exclusively for meat.

This was an interesting time. In the Western world, religious teachings were on shaky ground. This was a period of intellectual and religious upheaval. People began to question whether there really was a God, and whether everything on this earth was indeed a divine creation that needed to be respected and cared for. Plato's view of the universe as an intelligent living being[6] was being eroded by a new theory, that of a mechanical universe. It sparked the rise of the modern metropolis, factories, and the individual over the collective.

This philosophy of an unthinking, mechanical universe where things act according to strict laws of nature creates the perfect backdrop for the industrial revolution and the global economic shifts that followed. At this time, René Descartes argued that the only creatures to have been endowed with a consciousness were humans, which left animals stripped of a soul and the ability to feel. Conveniently, this made it acceptable to treat them in whatever way humans deemed necessary or beneficial.

As atheism grew in popularity, even human beings stopped being endowed with a divine soul. We went from being children of a higher power to biological happenings, here purely by accident. Darwin's "survival of the fittest" theory conspired to place humans at the top of an animal hierarchy, from which we could express our dominion over other creatures. Ironically, we have now taken it to such an extreme that we face a situation where our treatment of animals threatens our survival on this planet.

This set the scene. The wheels of progress were in motion, and there seemed no turning back.

In the early 1900s, around half of the population were farmers or lived in rural communities. Farms produced various crops, and different animals were present together and used in complementary ways (for example, keeping horses and using the manure to fertilize soil). Animals typically had access to the outdoors. Most of the work was done by human or animal labor.

In the 1950s, technology and specialization began to take over. Big farms grew larger, while smaller farms were often bought up and incorporated into these bigger farms. Industrialized farming quickly became the norm. Fields of diverse crops gave way to monocultures of genetically identical crops—particularly corn, wheat, and soy. Milk, egg, and meat production became separate from crop production. These facilities housed a single breed of animal during one period of its lifespan. Selective breeding meant animals were being bred for a single outcome, such as increased milk production, rather than being part of the life of the farm.

Chemical and pharmaceutical advances conspired to make things both more brutally efficient and less humane. Synthetic fertilizers and chemical pesticides were introduced in the early 1900s, became widespread in the 50s, and then enjoyed exponential growth. Today, we use 5.6 billion pounds of pesticides globally every year, with devastating consequences for our health and the environment.[7] Pharmaceuticals also became commonplace in the newly industrialized production of milk, egg, and meat. Experiments in the 1940s and 50s found that antibiotics made animals gain weight faster, and by 2009 80% of the antibiotic drugs sold in the US were used in livestock production.[8]

What drove this push for bigger farms? It wasn't just that new technology enabled these operations. Economics and government were at play. Government policies encouraged farmers to scale up. In the late 1950s, for example, the US secretary of agriculture, Ezra Taft Benson, called on farmers to "Get big or get out." These days, we have a situation where the majority of food production and agriculture is carried out by a small handful of large companies. In the US, 82% of the earnings from cattle slaughter are split between four corporations.[9]

Some will have you believe this is how we get better products and cheaper prices. For the most part, the opposite is true. With fewer competitors, dominant companies have more power to influence prices in their favor. They can also dictate how food is produced and can lobby the government to enact policies that suit them.

It was never about creating better consumer products, but about achieving a higher profit margin at the cost of much suffering.

THE ROLE OF SCIENCE

Alongside this exposition in technical know-how, scientific know-how also grew in leaps and bounds. Unfortunately, progress in the wrong hands can have devastating consequences.

In traditional societies, such as ancient Egypt, the Roman Empire, or medieval Europe, humans had a very limited understanding of zoology, biochemistry, and genetics. As a result, their powers of agricultural manipulation were limited. Chickens ran around pecking worms out of the ground. Cows were kept ten or twenty to a barn, and grazed during the day. If an entrepreneurial peasant had chosen to lock a thousand chickens inside an airless coop, the result would have been a deadly bird flu that probably would have wiped out the chickens and the villagers—no doctor, shaman or priest would have been able to prevent it.

But modern science knows the secrets of animal disease. Vaccinations, antibiotics and pesticides supported the technological advances that gave us automatic feeders and air-conditioning systems. We were suddenly able to cram tens of thousands of chickens in tiny coops and produce eggs and meat with chilling efficiency.

We could do this thanks to the scientific study of animals, which looked at animals not as sentient beings, but as commodities—there to be managed and manipulated for our benefit, not theirs.

Our technological advances allowed us to intensively farm animals with little risk to ourselves, or at least so it seemed to begin with. Some market this as a critical moment, which enabled us to "feed the world."

- We were able to cross breed seeds to create plants that produced higher yields or were resistant to the latest pesticides and herbicides.
- We could halt crop rotation and spray the soil with chemical fertilizers instead.
- We could create larger and larger animal farms, using grains and antibiotics to make animals bigger, while minimizing the space they needed to live and to eat.
- We became a caricature of God, behaving as though the natural world and the animals in it were mere commodities whose sole purpose is to serve us.

The relentless march of history had dark clouds gathering on the horizon.

SUBSIDIES: THE GAME CHANGER

Why have the meat and dairy industries grown so big and powerful since the Second World War? How did we get from the quintessential farmer with his herd of cows graving in green fields, to feedlots where thousands of cattle are fattened on a diet of grains and soy?

Government subsidies is the most succinct answer. Simply put, your taxes are being used to prop up the animal industry, sell us a lie, and drive the illusion of cheap meat.

It can be jarring that I grew up within the same industry that I am now fighting. I have flashbacks and remember hearing updates on subsidies, and it's the broader shifting political scene that supported us. I took it as standard that subsidies were an integral part of the system and required to feed the world.

So when I started investigating the murky world of government farm subsidies, I was appalled and angry. I think you will be too.

SO WHAT EXACTLY IS A SUBSIDY?

A subsidy is a financial grant, funded by public tax money, and offered by the government to private businesses or public institutions. Its purpose is to reduce production costs so the industry receiving the subsidy is in a stronger financial position.

Subsidies to the agriculture industry are entrenched and far-reaching, yet rarely talked about. Our governments don't want us to know the extent to which we fund animal agriculture. The argument is they are useful for protecting a nation's food supply, particularly supporting farmers through unforeseen events, like extreme weather. However, it has become very political, hidden, and often used in harmful ways.

What if I told you that your tax money provides one million dollars every minute to prop up agriculture? And it isn't going to the small-scale farmers.

Most subsidies go to large animal farms and mono-crops like soybean and corn, which are used to feed cattle on factory arms. Meanwhile, only 1% of this amount goes towards measures that could help protect the environment from the detrimental impact of animal farming.[10]

THE REAL PRICE OF MEAT

According to studies, the US government spends up to $38 billion every year subsidizing the meat and dairy industries. Less than 1% of that sum is allocated to fruit and vegetable production.[11]

So we have a system where our tax money—which is meant to be spent on improving public services and society—is being used to drive down the price of meat. As we'll see in the next chapter, meat has a lot to answer for when it comes to ecological collapse, social issues, chronic disease and zoonotic viruses—not to mention the suffering of billions of animals every year.

This is fast becoming an urgent conflict of interest and one that isn't discussed enough. We hear governments all over the world telling us there's no money for welfare, no support for the homelessness, not enough funding available for education, free healthcare, and climate protection. Yet at the same time, our governments covertly make extravagant handouts to the meat and dairy industries. This means that all of us, regardless of our lifestyle choices, end up contributing to animal farming and all its consequences. So, whatever our beliefs or values, we are, in essence, funding and supporting animal cruelty, environmental degradation, and increasing the likelihood of future pandemics.

Then there are the hidden costs of meat such as our healthcare costs and the environmental clean-up needed from industrial farming. Add all this up and those fast food burgers don't seem so cheap!

In Europe, subsidies are so huge that each head of cattle gets a subsidy worth $2.20 per day. This means that a European dairy cow's annual income is higher than half the world's population.[12] *And of course, the cow isn't benefiting from this, the meat industry is.*

In the UK, 90% of the annual profit of livestock farmers comes from government subsidies. For comparison, only 10% of the annual profit of fruit farmers comes from subsidies.[13]

In the US, animal farmers were awarded $12 billion in subsidies in 2018 and $16 billion in 2019.[14] *At the same time, $5 billion was cut from social programs like food stamps.*

Globally, we're eating more meat than ever before. Whereas the average per capita consumption of meat was around 50 pounds (23 kilos) per person in 1961, this had almost doubled to 95 pounds (43 kilos) per person in 2014.[15] In the US, per person consumption of meat averages at 273 pounds (124.1 kilos) per year, up 40% since 1961.[16] It's not just that more meat is being produced. We have also been sold the idea that meat is good for us.

Meat has always been something aspirational. Once, only the richest people could afford to slaughter an animal for food. Meat was a symbol of prosperity. Henry IV of France is said to have made the impractical promise of "a chicken in every pot." I say impractical because the infrastructure and technology simply were not available to make his grand gesture a reality. It would be over a century until technological advances meant farmers could grow bigger animals, kill them more efficiently, and preserve the flesh. That's where we are today; where meat is available and affordable in every port.

There was a sort of psychological tipping point after the Second World War, a kind of "beef madness." Soldiers were sent to war with rations of tinned meat. When the war ended, what better symbol of freedom in a new world than meat on every soldier's plate? From an unattainable luxury, meat became the new daily bread. Now, we feel entitled to eat meat three times a day if we so wish. And yet we are still locked into an old way of thinking that associates meat with prosperity, progress, and even health.

Still, something doesn't quite add up. In early times, people could not afford meat but could afford vegetables or they grew their own. Now this has been turned on its head. We live in a world where a hamburger costs pennies, while vegetables, particularly those grown organically, are almost prohibitively expensive.

Logically, this makes no sense. After all, it takes more resources to produce meat. The animal has to be born, then kept alive for years before being killed and processed. It needs to be fed, watered, medicated, transported from feedlot to slaughterhouse, from slaughterhouse to meatpacking plant, etc. Whereas a carrot is just a seed planted in soil that grows over a few months, then it is picked. A carrot does not need to be fed 25 pounds of grain a day, as is the case for cows. Clearly, not all the costs are being carried forward into the price of the final product.

So, how does it work?

Meat is big business, and it is profitable. But what if this profit is artificial? What if meat only makes good business sense because government subsidies are propping it up?

Well, guess what? It is.

A lot of your tax money goes straight to big agriculture to keep meat prices artificially low.

FOOD DISPARITY[17]

Price of a hamburger in a fast food outlet: $0.99
Price of a 16-ounce pack of organic kale: $4.56

Price of 5 pounds of chicken drumsticks in Walmart: $4.76
Price of 1 pint of organic blueberries in Walmart: $4.16

It's easy to see which products we are being encouraged to buy.

LOBBYING: Meat is the New Cigarette

When we see the price of meat, dairy, and eggs and think they are cheap, the truth is their price does not reflect reality. For the price to be so low, tax money has been diverted from other, worthier causes, either social or environmental. This is how you can pay $4 for a tray of blueberries, while a burger can cost you as little as $0.99.

This kind of price-fixing is one of the reasons the meat industry is so profitable and so huge, but there are other reasons too. The industry itself drives business by keeping us coming back for more. Its strong ties to government mean it can change the nutrition narrative to make animal products seem an essential part of a balanced diet.

I not only believe that farm subsidies must end, but that there should be a tax on animal products to reflect their true cost on society. Just as we accept that other harmful products like tobacco and alcohol should be taxed, it is perfectly logical that the same must happen to meat and dairy. Currently, we are giving billions to these industries despite them causing countless unnecessary deaths and huge ecological devastation. We need to reclaim our public raised funds and support our local communities. We need to rebel and demand a smarter use of our taxes.

The dying days of the tobacco industry provide a perfect example of how our systems of government can work against our interests. We need to be vigilant and learn these lessons as the powerfully connected meat industry has huge influence and a bottomless marketing budget.

In 2000, a World Health Organisation document reviewed formerly secret internal tobacco industry documents and found evidence of a fifty-year conspiracy to resist smoking restrictions and restore smoker confidence.[18] Tobacco lobbyists did this by spreading misinformation and buying scientific experts to create controversy or to question established facts (including studies whose statistics could be manipulated to show that smoking did not increase the risk of lung cancer). They also pre-empted strong legislation by suggesting instead voluntary codes and weaker laws, not to mention corrupting public officials.

These documents demonstrate that the industry's goal was not to act ethically and responsibly towards consumers and their health, but rather to protect its profits at all costs. It sounds a lot like what the meat industry is doing—funding campaigns to restore consumer confidence and promoting a narrative that disputes the effects of meat on climate change.

These days, it is unlawful to advertise tobacco products.

"The sausage is the cigarette of the future."
CEO of Germany's oldest producer of meat cold cuts[19]

I believe meat is the new cigarette. Meat advertising should go the same way, but we're not there yet. Currently, governments still pay for campaigns that promote meat-eating. More on that in a moment.

When it comes to lobbying, it is not all bad. NGO's (non-governmental organizations) such as Greenpeace, World Wildlife Fund, and Climate Action Network (to name but a few), are busy lobbying the government to fight climate change via ecological farming and changes in policy. The same goes for NGOs pushing for social rights, gender equality, and others. The problem is their budget is a drop in the ocean compared to the billions that the food industry and other corporate interests have at their disposal.

It's David and Goliath. We are at a tipping point and we need to be championing the underdog.

Part of moving towards a more sustainable or vegan way of life is to become aware of how our behaviors and thoughts towards animal products are manipulated by an industry that profits keeping us in the dark.

There are three ways the meat and dairy industry seeks to influence and control our dietary behaviors. The first is information campaigns, the second is labels, and the third is clever advertising.

INFORMATION CAMPAIGNS

The food industry uses government-funded information campaigns to share the merits of their products, usually in response to opposing campaigns that shine a light on the problematic issues of meat and dairy on health and the environment.

These campaigns are rooted in denial of the problems. Take the environmental aspect, for example. We'll dive into it in the next chapter, but suffice it to say that scientists agree our current meat-centric diet is unsustainable. Instead of acknowledging their part in this, the agriculture industry pretends there's no problem.

The same goes for the health element of eating animal products. Information campaigns focus on meat's health benefits, in complete opposition to the many studies that show eating meat increases the risk of chronic disease. For example, the World Health Organization's report that demonstrated a link between meat and certain cancers (again, we will look at this more closely in the next chapter).

A good example of pro-meat campaigning is the European Union's 2020 "Proud of EU Beef" campaign, which was funded by 3.6 million euros of public money and incited European citizens to increase their consumption of meat.[20] This campaign was not based on science, but rather aimed to "highlight the benefits of the product" and "make the consumer feel identified and supported in its choice," adding that "consumers who choose to eat red meat should feel at ease should they wish to reaffirm their choice for this product."[21] The question that springs to mind is why should consumers be targeted in this way when the evidence points to meat production being incompatible with the EU's climate targets? Interestingly, the EU's European Green Deal, designed to reduce greenhouse gas emissions by at least 55% by 2030, fails to mention agriculture on its list of proposed policies.[22] This highlights how the political sphere is willingly deaf to the warnings of science.

This is not only an EU problem, but a global one. In the United Kingdom, the British Meat Processors Association launched a new website in 2020 aimed at debunking information that encourages consumers to reduce their meat intake, with a particular focus on promoting the "environmental benefits of eating beef and other animals."[23] In 2021, the UK's Agriculture and Horticulture Development Board (AHDB) spent £1.5 million of public money to fund their "Eat Balanced" campaign, a partnership between the pork, beef, lamb, and dairy sectors (which doesn't sound super balanced to me). The AHDB's head of marketing made no secret about what this campaign was about: *"We wanted to create a campaign that feels uplifting and reassuring for consumers who are increasingly being told by the media to reduce their meat and dairy consumption."*[24]

There you have it: this is about reassuring the public that eating meat is absolutely fine, regardless of the truth.

And when it comes to dairy? I think most of us can remember the "Got milk?" campaign, all those famous faces with their milk-taches, looming huge on billboards, extolling the virtues of milk and even chocolate milk as "a high-quality protein was scientifically shown to help repair and rebuild muscles." I wonder what science they are referring to because I'm sure there are healthier post-workout options than a drink filled with sugar, preservatives, and artificial sweeteners. And what about the "Milk Life" campaign, which focused on showing the type of active, happy life you can have when you drink plenty of dairy? The campaign conveniently forgot to mention that this is the very opposite of the life of a dairy cow. It conveniently failed to come clean about the fact that some of the whey and casein proteins in milk have been linked to cancer.[25]

Your tax money funds these campaigns. This money could be used to support people in need, fund green energy infrastructure, and provide social welfare initiatives.

Instead, it is used to help the meat industry promote its products with little regard to their negative effects on our health or the environment.

MANIPULATING DIETARY GUIDELINES

But the industry goes further, lobbying for changes to dietary guidelines to keep meat on our plates, even when the research indicates we would be healthier with less. This means that, despite a report by the World Health Organisation classing processed meat as a Class 1A carcinogen and red meat as a Class 2A carcinogen, meat remains a government-approved dietary staple, and people are encouraged to have at least two to three portions of animal foods every day. Perhaps it doesn't come as a huge surprise, since the USA's dietary guidelines are written up by the United States Department of Agriculture in collaboration with the United States Department of Health and Human Services (in that order!).

These dietary guidelines have been issued in the USA every five years since 1985. Interestingly, since that time, has health improved? No. What's wrong with guidelines? It's not that they fall completely short of telling us what's best for us. To some degree, it is common sense that too many processed foods and insufficient exercise contribute to excess weight and chronic disease. And even the "MyPlate" guidance at first appears to offer some reassurance—it tells us to fill half our plate with vegetables and fruits, to focus mostly on whole grains, and to limit sugar.

So far, so good. But the problem arises when you dive deeper into the recommendations.

MyPlate is rather vague when it comes to quantities. When we look at the approved "Healthy US-Style Eating Pattern—Amounts from Food Groups," it all becomes much clearer, but not in a good way.

What is interesting is these recommendations have barely changed in the last three revisions of the US Dietary Guidelines (covering 2010–2025). A huge fanfare is made each time about new recommendations and their health implications, but the truth is they are still pushing the type of diet where meat and dairy take pride of place.[26]

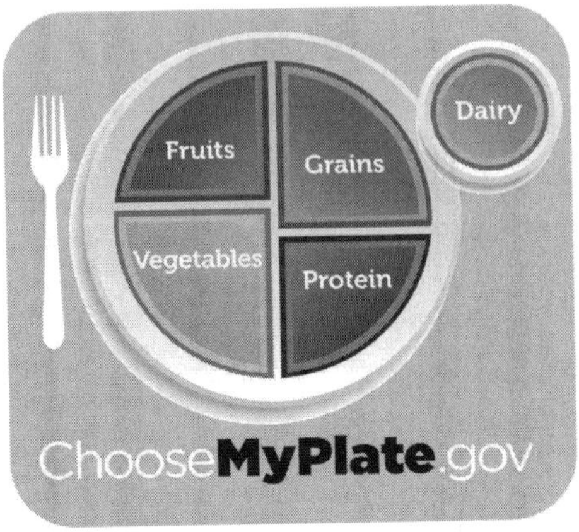

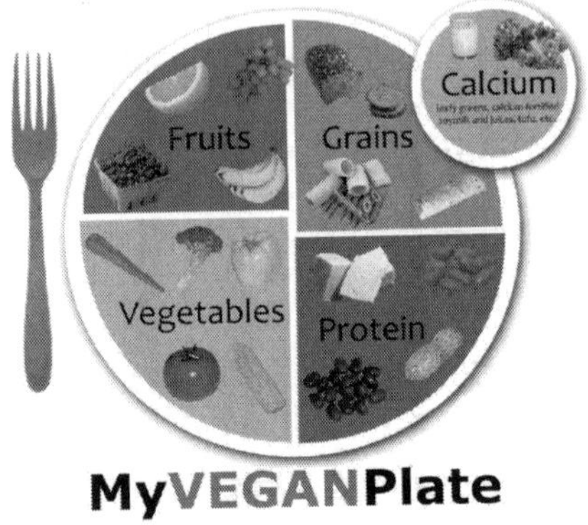

FOOD GROUP: PROTEIN

Amount recommended: 5.5 oz (156 grams) per day from meat, poultry, eggs, fish, nuts, seeds, and soy products.

Problem: Despite telling people to "vary their protein source", the guidance fails to give people the proper information to do so without reverting to animal products. It does so firstly by not including beans and legumes as protein foods (they are in the "Vegetable" food group instead, which leads to confusion), secondly by promoting "meats, poultry, eggs" as the preferred source of protein, and thirdly by recommending a weekly intake of 26 oz (737 grams) of meat, poultry and eggs, 8 oz (227 grams) of fish, and just 5 oz (142 grams) of nuts, seeds and soy products.

FOOD GROUP: VEGETABLES

Amount recommended: 2.5 cups per day

Problem: They've unhelpfully included beans and legumes in the vegetable category, which means they do not appear in the protein category, where they actually belong.

FOOD GROUP: DAIRY

Amount recommended: 3 cups per day

Problem: Recommending that people eat more dairy than vegetables is highly flawed and doesn't match the MyPlate guidance at all. What happened to fill at least half your plate with vegetables?

LABELS

Labels and packaging are another way the meat industry keeps us coming back for more. Clever wordplay and misleading classifications—such as "ethically sourced", "natural", and "humanely raised" on product packaging—often has little to do with the way the animals were raised, and more to do with making the product appear as reassuring and appealing as possible. The same goes for quaint images of farmers in dungarees and happy cows in lush green fields. Take a look at the box section in **Appendix 1** to see examples of labels you might come across and what they really mean.

ADVERTISING

Big business makes a significant effort to understand the mentality that drives consumption. The meat industry is no different, but it has to work even harder in the face of the mounting evidence against it. Marketing is an art form and a science that has been fine-tuned and refined for a century. Adverts, infomercials and campaigns are carefully designed to press certain buttons and get us to buy whatever is being sold. They either target our fears or stimulate our desire, then present their product as a solution or antidote.

When it comes to advertising animal products, the industry relies on our natural desire to fit in, our need to feel we're doing the best for our bodies and the comfort we derive from cultural traditions. Check out the box section in **Appendix 2** to learn how the industry manipulates our wants to sell us their products.

SO, WHY IS THE MEAT INDUSTRY STILL SO POWERFUL?

It isn't just the industrialization of our food supply and advances in science that have allowed this industry to grow. The largest producers of meat and dairy have also had a hand in making sure they receive substantial government subsidies that make their business profitable, even in the face of decreased interest and increased environmental costs. What's more, they manipulate the nutritional guidance policy to keep their products firmly on our plates. At the same time, they fund studies and run ad campaigns designed to reassure consumers into buying products that are bad for health and bad for the planet.

They are using tactics last used by the tobacco lobby in the 1970s and 80s. As the next chapter will show, these are survival tactics by an industry that knows it is no longer tenable.

3

MEAT THE FUTURE

A WATERSHED MOMENT FOR VEGANISM

"The secret of change is to focus all of your energy, not on fighting the old, but on building the new."
Socrates

There are ominous storm clouds gathering over the food industry. New technological advances are taking shape on the horizon that have the potential to bear upon us upheavals not seen since the Agricultural Revolution 12,000 years ago.

The cultured meat revolution is nearly upon us and experts are forecasting it is only a matter of years, not decades, before we will all be able to walk into our local supermarket and choose between three types of meat: plant-based meat, animal-based meat, and cruelty-free, cell-based meat. There are over 30 well-endowed start-ups around the world racing to produce every conceivable form of lab-grown meat from pork to lobster. In 2020, the Singapore Food Agency was the first of its kind to approve the sale of lab-grown meat commercially. It was the first time that actual meat was ever produced and consumed that did not come from a slaughtered animal.[1]

This is a turning point in human history and a watershed moment for the vegan movement. Its impact will transform our industries, society, and behavior. It will also come with many uncomfortable challenges that deserve much more consideration and discussion. We can't put our heads in the sand. This is a storm of biblical proportions that we need to prepare for.

The scientist's grand claim is that these rapidly developing technologies will marry our cultural taste for meat with a production method that bypasses animal suffering and reduce environmental pollution. And, at first glance, lab-grown meat seems an ideal solution. But many concerns and unanswered questions hang over this controversial revolution, both ethical and practical.

U.S. INTERNATIONAL CANADA ESPAÑOL 中文

The New York Times

Business Opinion Tech Science Health Sports Arts Books Style Food Travel Magazine

The End of Meat Is Here

If you care about the working poor, about racial justice, and about climate change, you have to stop eating animals.

May 21, 2020

CLEAN MEAT REVOLUTION

"An anti-speciesist, I look forward to meat cultured with no animals killed.
Richard Dawkins

There is a part of me that gets a kick out of Silicon Valley's recent rebranding of lab-grown or cell-based meat as "clean meat". I see it as an admission of sorts as it infers that old-fashioned, animal-based meat is somehow dirty or evil and, therefore, inadvertently, we are getting the masses to accept the long-standing political position of veganism.

It is entirely probable that future generations will be marketed and sold clean meat as the optimum eating experience and increasingly look at outdated farmed-meat as contaminated or uncouth. I have heard from reliable sources that many of the leading scientists driving the clean meat revolution are vegan themselves. They believe they are working for the same things that generations of animal rights activists have been fighting for.

However, I have found it a very divisive issue within the vegan community. Some within my large international Facebook group say they wouldn't feed it to their (vegan) dogs! Others seem anxious that veganism will become obsolete once this technology takes over the food systems. There may even be a sense of anger or failure that this technology will lead to the radical changes that the animal rights movement failed to achieve. In contrast, many others welcome it and see it as a way to make everyone vegan without even changing their dietary habits.

THE HISTORY OF THE FUTURE OF MEAT

Cell-based or lab-grown meat is an exciting emerging technology that uses lab-grown animal cells to create meat products, without animal slaughter or resource waste. Stem cells are placed in bioreactors that trick them into growing strands and muscle fibers that combine to create a piece of meat biologically identical to the meat tissue from the original animal. Fat and other ingredients can then be added to give the meat texture that matches traditional meat.

It began in Maastricht, The Netherlands, where a burger was created from cultured cells. At the time, it was only intended as a proof of concept[27] and cost 250,000 euros[28] - that's one expensive burger!

In the last five years, the sector has grown from almost nothing to over fifty companies, all racing to bring lab meat to supermarket shelves. It is still a specialized product and expensive to make, but it won't be long before it reaches restaurants and supermarkets.

In December 2020, Singapore authorized the first sale of cultured meat. In fact, there is a restaurant where you can eat cultured chicken made by the Californian start-up Eat-JUST.[29] According to forecasts, the lab meat market will be worth 11.13 billion dollars by 2041.[30] Could it spell the end of traditional meat production? I certainly hope so.

"We shall escape the absurdity of growing a whole chicken in order to eat the breast or wing, by growing these parts separately under a suitable medium."
Winston Churchill, 1931[2]

GREAT EXPECTATIONS

I understand how this breakthrough is both exciting and unnerving. Potentially, our relationships with animals, the earth, and food are about to change forever. On a purely practical level, it has the potential to save billions of sentient lives a year and help avert the ecological collapse of our planet. We could be the last generation to raise and kill animals to eat, which is a momentous milestone in our evolution.

However, I still harbor unresolved concerns with lab-grown meat[3]. A niggling bone of contention is it props up the status quo's mentality by perpetuating the myth that animal products are intrinsically desirable or necessary for humans. Instead of fighting the good fight, winning the argument against meat-eating, we are acquiescing that humans will always want or need meat. That is something the vegan and animal rights movements have been challenging since the ancient Greek philosophers.

And there are other areas where we should be having a wider debate. 'Clean meat' is not the perfect solution, as it is often promoted. The labs themselves require a lot of electricity, which means carbon emissions unless they can be powered by wind, solar, or other green alternatives. And the product itself cannot be said to be completely animal-free, because the stem cells need to be harvested from a donor animal. They can be harvested painlessly, but even so, lab-grown meat cannot strictly be classified as vegan.

But does this mean we should reject it completely or judge those who want to try it? Let's remember that veganism is about choosing more compassionate options. Clean meat, given that it does not necessitate the mutilation or slaughter of any animals, is a cruelty-free option. It may not be perfect, but it goes a long way to helping us move away from an industry responsible for so much suffering and devastation. For the first time in living memory, this industry is under threat, losing its dominance. Should vegans not claim this as a victory?

So, although conflicted, I am trying to be pragmatic and strip it back to the crux of the dilemma and the aim of our movement. Veganism is about compassion and justice. More than 200 million sentient beings are killed each day to satisfy humanity's appetite for flesh. And cutting down rainforests and razing natural habitats to grow crops to feed these increasing numbers of animals so we can eat them is hugely inefficient and unsustainable. Our shared mission—vegans and non-vegans—must be to build a fair future for all where we are can feed 9 billion people in a way that doesn't cause more unnecessary suffering or destroy the planet. This may be the revolutionary reset that is needed.

When lab-grown meat takes over from traditional farmed-meat, will this mean the end of veganism? Is our fight over? Some predict that we may live in a less divided, post vegan/animal agriculture world. Personally, I don't think clean meat will reduce the relevance or potency of the vegan message. It is a common misconception that veganism exists solely to oppose the brutality of factory farming. Significantly, the moral issues around consuming animal products are not purely focused on the severity of our farming traditions or food systems. This reductive view allows people to avoid looking deeper at the mentality that fostered and accepted factory farming and our seemingly insatiable desire for meat. There is still a long battle ahead.

A vegan lifestyle should always be the foremost goal for individuals and society. I don't think this technology can ever alter the reality that a plant-based diet is better for us than meat—wherever it comes from. Just look at all the elite athletes transitioning to plant-based, which has nothing to do with the animals and how they are treated and culled. Ultimately, optimum performance and nutrition can only be fully achieved from a meat-free, plant-based diet.

My thoughts are that clean meat will provide an easy transition for current meat-eaters, alleviate their unease or cognitive dissonance, save millions of animals lives, and reduce the waste that the meat industry produces. Additionally, it should remove all the drugs used in the current intensive animal industry, which eventually end up on our plates. But it still faces the greatest hurdle—scalability and price.

Once clean meat takes off on an industrial scale (and surely this is something that the meat industry should be spending their billions on), then a huge number of the ecological issues will also be resolved, or will at least be well on the way to resolution. Finally, we can bring our habitation of the planet back into unity rather than opposition. Surely that has to be a win-win for all of us. Could we end up with a compassionate vegan world, but just not how we imagined it?

"It's not a faith in technology. It's faith in people."
Steve Jobs[4]

A VICTORY FOR VEGAN VALUES

Our taste for meat is not hard-wired but a practice we are taught from birth. From childhood, eating meat is normalized and (literally) rammed down our throats. It's an unspoken belief system that is all-pervasive and powerful. Indeed, in a perfect world, this is what should be challenged and changed, the conditioning, not new ways to produce meat to make it 'clean'.

We are being sold this new technology as an easy way out of the mess we created over the last century. But this rebalancing or magic remedy of cell-based meat can be solved more effectively by simply reducing our meat consumption. That should be where we are putting our focus: harnessing our cultural appetite for meat, not mastering new technologies. By just embracing vegan values, we could help solve most of the threats facing our world and build a strong and just future for all its inhabitants.

I appreciate how increasingly seductive this technology will become. But it sets a dangerous precedent by taking the quick-win and relying on technology to solve all our problems. Where will it all end, with the ever-increasing consumption of lab-grown meat? A guilt-free gluttony!

Change and comfort seldom coexist, and it would likely prove futile to fight this leap into the unknown. But, possibly, by learning to work in tandem with this emerging technology, we can lead by example to stimulate a new awareness and more complete solution to the issues we face. Our message is still as vital as ever.

Ultimately, I am a vegan realist. There is no perfect solution—and no perfect veganism. The vegan movement started this revolution, made the world take notice of the atrocities of the meat industry, and forever altered the future of the food industry. But a clear victory is a way off. Our rebel's rallying cry is still needed to promote and protect vegan values. We've won the argument—not the war.

If nothing else, let's at least celebrate that we acted with compassion and integrity, made our voices heard, and helped shape a better world for future generations.

That's the *Rebel Vegan* way!

4

REBEL WITH A CAUSE

THE DRIVING FORCES ON YOUR VEGAN JOURNEY

"There is a driving force more powerful than steam, electricity and nuclear power: the will."
Albert Einstein[1]

I have already mentioned that we are not just another vegan book. And there are dozens of books on this topic. I should know, I've read most of them! They're helpful, but they're missing something: a deep dive into the why. For any long-term change, there must be a solid foundation of understanding. We need to fully grasp the different values, or driving forces, that support our determination to change our behavior and create a better world. Knowledge is power, and it's vital for lasting change.

The reality of our food systems and what is happening under our noses might both disturb and alarm you. It can get ugly, so it's natural to turn away and ignore it. In order to cope, most of us stick our heads in the sand, or look the other way. I did for most of my life. This avoidance is a natural response to having to exist within a system that creates immense injustices on all levels—animal, environmental, and societal.

But there comes a point when something pierces our blissful ignorance. It could be a chance conversation with another vegan. It could be a news report about the Amazon rainforest being willfully burned down. It could be getting a diagnosis that forces a lifestyle rethink. It isn't easy when our accepted beliefs are shaken up and challenged, but if we want to change, if we want to create a better world, we need to go deeper to understand how certain foods get on our plate and their impact on the wider world.

Being a *Rebel Vegan* means being bold and brave enough to take this deeper dive. *Rebel Vegans* seek the truth, know the power of change, and cherish the role they have to play in creating a kinder world for themselves and others. To do this, you need to open yourself up to facing some shocking truths and starting this radical journey.

Underpinning the standard Western diet[2] is an unspoken ideology that meat is natural, normal and healthy, even necessary. We grow up with and are indoctrinated into this belief system, and only occasionally question it. Increasingly, over the last few years, the animal industry has made the headlines in a significant way. There was Cowspiracy's exposé of beef's environmental impact in 2014, the World Health Organization's Meat and Cancer report in 2015, David Attenborough's Blue Planet series in 2017. But these stories follow the same cycle. The information comes out, making the farmers angry, and giving false hope of change to the animal activists and environmentalists. Then there follows a day or two of commentary which makes good viewing for news channels, as they pit these two sides against each other in heated debates. And then... nothing. We put our heads back in the sand, and carry on with life. The supermarket aisles remain full of beef, rainforests continue to be torn down to plant cattle feed, meat-packing plants continue to be manned by exploited workers and meat continues to be promoted as a staple of a healthy balanced diet.

WHAT IS THE STANDARD AMERICAN DIET (SAD) / STANDARD WESTERN DIET?

SAD, also known as the standard Western diet, is a pattern of eating generally characterized by high intakes of meat, dairy products, eggs, fried foods, refined grains, and refined sugars, with low intakes of vegetables, fruits, whole grains, legumes, nuts and seeds.

Having said that, these continuous warnings and alarming reports touch a nerve with some people, and they want to be part of the change. The animal industry is so pervasive and impacts our personal and social lives, and indeed our very survival on Earth. For that reason, the driving forces that bring people to question this unspoken belief system or ideology are many. This is what we will explore throughout this chapter.

What is your driving force for dipping your toe into veganism? We all have one. What originally brought me to veganism was a health scare. For others, it is about animal welfare. For you, it might be that you want to leave a safe, green, and thriving world for your children and grandchildren. Whatever it is, it's something that made you stop dead in your tracks and think; wait a second—maybe I don't want to do this anymore. Maybe there is a better way.

That's why knowledge is powerful. Knowledge is the first step. It gives you the motivation to make changes and informed choices that are really aligned with your ethics and values.

I believe that the survival of our inner and outer environments depends on us weaving veganism into our lives. When it comes to human health, animal welfare, the planet, our water, soil and air, few things are worse than eating meat. It's an uncomfortable truth, but the mountain of evidence is growing every year and becoming indisputable. This chapter will break down exactly why. Get ready to push aside all the increasingly desperate industry-funded "studies" that confuse and misinform, and instead dive into the driving forces that can inspire a healthy vegan life.

"We are rebels for a cause, poets with a dream, and we won't let this world die without a fight."
Nobel Prize winner Albert Camus[3]

Disclaimer: These next chapters are not always a comfortable read. I appreciate these chapters can challenge or disturb, but this knowledge can also change your life. I've tried my best to be concise, to give as much information as needed without being gory. It will be life-changing, but also confronting so fasten your seatbelts.

My aim is to give the most relevant, up-to-date information on each driving force so that you can stand proud as a *Rebel Vegan*, and go out into the world feeling confident in your lifestyle choices.

The first driving force is animal welfare, and the question this section will answer is - is it really that bad? Maybe not. This then begs the question of why there's been such a flurry of so-called Ag-Gag laws passed around the world in recent years (we'll dive into this in a second). I will say for now that if slaughterhouses and feedlots had glass walls, we would all feel very different about meat. This topic is particularly challenging and can be divisive, but can also motivate and inspire the strongest drive for change.

The second is our planet, and the question: Since we've eaten meat throughout the ages, why is it suddenly an ecological problem? I have brought together the most respected and up-to-date science and research to detail how intensive animal agriculture impacts our air, our land and our oceans.

The third is our health: Is the meat industry really having that big of an impact on our individual and global health? Alarming increases in lifestyle-related diseases like diabetes, obesity and heart disease, as well as the rise of medicine-resistant superbugs and the creation of zoonotic viruses, put our wellbeing in danger from all angles.

The fourth driving force is our society: What does intensive animal farming have to do with social welfare? It's a question that came up when I began researching this book and exploring how we are growing millions of tons of grains, and yet almost three billion people are either going to bed on an empty stomach or facing food insecurity.[4]

In the next four chapters, I have brought together the most current and compelling research to inspire lasting change. Depending on where you are on your vegan journey, you may or may not want to read all of this information chronologically or in one sitting. That's fine. I designed the following driving forces chapters so you can dip in and find what resonates, moves, and motivates you to make a change. Sometimes the truth hurts, so please take it at your own pace.

In my experience, you discover who you really are when you open yourself up to new ideas and push yourself to the edges of your comfort zone. Living authentically is worth the initial unease/ discomfort.

LET'S FASTEN OUR SEAT BELTS AND START THIS JOURNEY.

5

LIVESTOCK

ANIMAL WELFARE

"One day the absurdity of the almost universal human belief in the slavery of other animals will be palpable. We shall then have discovered our souls and become worthier of sharing this planet with them."
Martin Luther King Jr

"Veganism was the next logical extension of Martin Luther King, Jr's, philosophy of non-violence."
Coretta Scott King, activist and widow of MLK Jr[1]

FARMBOY VEGAN

This has been one of the most difficult chapters to research and write, not just because of having to revisit disturbing memories and details, but because I feel as though I am betraying my background. I feel an element of guilt. After years of avoidance, I had to confront the complicity of my family's business and my heritage.

On the surface, my childhood had something idyllic about it. I grew up in the lush, open spaces of the Canadian countryside. I drove a tractor before I drove a car. I was surrounded by fields dotted with beautiful black and white Holstein cows. Their calves became my first playmates. It was like living in a children's book. But, dig deeper, and some of the story was unsuitable for young readers.

Only today, from a distance, can I get some perspective and see the whole story and understand the suffering. And I suppose I suffered from my own cognitive dissonance. I remember staring into the calves' big eyes, stroking the soft fringe between their ears, watching in delight as they played and cuddled together, and the funny way they loped around the field on legs they were still learning to coordinate. Conversely, I also remember helping to cut off the bulls' testicles, driving to a slaughterhouse, hearing the orphaned calves crying all night.

One summer, I worked for a neighboring farmer and had to clean out the chicken sheds. Every so often, a hen would escape. Instead of opening up the top hatch of the long row of battery cages and risking more chickens escaping, the neighbor would grab the free bird by its neck, rip its head off with his bare hands and throw it on the manure pile. It may seem shocking, but my child's eyes quickly accepted it. It was just part of life on the farm.

I have immense respect for my family's hard work. My ancestors came to Canada from Scotland, cleared the land, and built up the farm through five generations. They cared deeply for their animals. My grandfather would be up before dawn every morning to feed and look after the cows. If an animal was poorly, he would stay up all night with it. Lucky, the dog, would round up the cows twice a day for milking, and their straw was changed every night.

Once, my dad raced home because one of our horses was pregnant and struggling to deliver her foal. He was so concerned to get back that he broke the speed limits and didn't even stop for the police, who put on their sirens and chased him all the way back to the farm. He sped around our house, jumped out of the truck, raced into the barn, and delivered the new foal, all while the anxious local police called in backup and started a stakeout to surround our barn.

I saw farming at its best; my ancestors were small-scale farmers who were devoted to and proud of their land and animals. But alongside this devotion was an assumption that these animals were there to provide for and serve us. Although our animals were valued, they were still 'livestock' and a commodity. They were robbed of their individuality and freedoms, and ultimately had their lives cut short.

This is why I feel a real sense of conflict writing this book, especially with this chapter. My complicity seems obvious now. I somehow switched off, disconnected, and lived and breathed this belief system. I grew up entrenched in the mindset that this was the natural normal order of things. The abuse didn't register as such, it was just the way things were.

It was only later, after I experienced the health benefits of a plant-based diet and began doing the research, that everything caught up with me and it all suddenly felt so wrong. Memories came flooding back and nightmares haunted me. I could hear the newly orphaned calves crying through the night. I committed to a cruelty-free lifestyle and became a *Rebel Vegan*.

My family's farm was a traditional, family-run, mixed-use farm. They rotated crops, the cows grazed in the fields and slept on straw in big wooden barns. But I've noticed the landscapes changing over the years when I make my annual trip back to my people. Gradually, over the years, large-scale industrial farms have replaced family farms. When I drive through the countryside of my childhood, I don't see cows grazing. The fields are empty of animal life. The old barns are unloved and falling apart. Instead, I see the huge, prefabricated sheds that house livestock in hidden and unimaginable conditions.

How animals are treated on industrial farms is one of the most urgent ethical questions we face today. Over 77 billion sentient beings—animals with emotions, feelings, and consciousness—live and die in horrific conditions right under our noses. Farming is no longer a family-friendly story.[2]

THE REAL VICTIMS OF HISTORY

"Non-violence leads to the highest ethics, which is the goal of all evolution. Until we stop harming all other living beings,
we are still savages."
Thomas A. Edison[3]

This section is not about trying to shock. It is about finding truth and justice. It's about doing the right thing. When we think about historical crimes, we always think of atrocities inflicted by humans on other humans. What about animals? Are they not the main victims of history and human progress?

It isn't just that humans bring animals to life simply to kill them—it is that humans cause them unimaginable suffering throughout their short lives. They are classed as livestock and have become product units in a profit-driven business. They are no longer individuals.

WHAT IS A SENTIENT BEING?

Philosophers first coined the word sentience in the 1630s to describe an ability to feel. In modern Western philosophy, sentience is the ability to experience sensations (including light, darkness, pain and pleasure, as well as emotions like love, or suffering).[4]

Sentience is simply the capacity to experience feelings and sensations. A sentient being will avert suffering, seek out comfort, revel in affection, enjoy being part of a community or pack. They are aware of danger and value their lives. Although this could sum up a much-loved family cat or dog, it is equally true of cows, pigs, and even marine animals.

The growing scientific evidence of animal sentience has contributed to the ethical debate over farming animals and using animal products for food or fashion

One of the main excuses for the mistreatment of animals is that they are inferior: not as intelligent as humans, not as conscious, not as complex or refined. This thinking is flawed, and it is rooted in beliefs that put man above all other things. The truth is that humans would be nowhere without animals, or without nature—we should cherish, support and maintain them. As it stands, we treat both as commodities there to be profited from. One way we commodify—and disconnect from—animals is by giving them different names. Chickens become poultry. Cows become cattle. Calves become veal. Pigs become pork. This helps us distance ourselves from the living, breathing being that died to end up, cellophane-wrapped and sanitized, on the supermarket shelf.

"There is no fundamental difference between man and animals in their ability to feel pleasure and pain, happiness, and misery."
Charles Darwin

Science has long confirmed that animals are sentient beings. All religions recognize this to a degree, and the Greek philosophers we mentioned earlier knew it too. We have reconfirmed it scientifically, in modern times. The Cambridge Declaration of 2012, drafted by the world's leading group of neuropharmacologists, neuro-physicists, neuroscientists, states that the absence of a neocortex (the part of the brain in humans attributed with complex thinking, like language) does not stop an animal from experiencing affective states such as love, pain, compassion, fear and even shame.

Evidence shows that animals have the neural capabilities to experience conscious states, as well as the capacity to exhibit intentional behaviors. Anyone who has had a pet or even interacted with one, or has observed animals in their natural habitats, knows this to be true. However, most of us go through life with this cognitive dissonance between our natural inclination to love animals and our tradition of eating them.

It has become increasingly and alarmingly evident that animals are intelligent beings with complex social and emotional needs, and that these basic needs cannot be met in a factory farm setting. The goal in these places is simply to get them from birth to slaughter and extract maximum revenue from them as efficiently as possible. They are treated as a product, rather than a living, breathing being. If this sounds like a dystopian horror show, that's because it is. I have lived it and still have the nightmares to show for it.

Here's what the agricultural revolution gave humans: the systems, drugs and scientific know-how to keep animals alive while ignoring their psychological, emotional, and social needs. Vaccinations, medications, antibiotics and hormones, pesticides, automatic feeders, automatic milking machines—all these make it possible to cram thousands of animals together in a tiny space to produce meat, eggs and dairy with horrifying and brutal efficiency.

But is it really that bad? When we soul-search, we have to admit that we do not want to inflict physical pain on another creature, so we shy away from the images that this throws up for us. Our desire to turn away from the truth is in part what makes it possible for these things to take place under our noses. We grow up with rose-tinted spectacles when it comes to what happens on a farm.

I had an animal farm set by Fisher-Price. I remember the little animals with their smiling faces, the little plastic fences, sheds and trees. It was deceptively reassuring to recreate the real farm behind my house into this bright, cheery, genteel world. Big agriculture, or 'big ag', depends on this. They know that we do not want to think about the pain behind the product, so they hide their practices behind reassuring logos and soothing slogans. But if it was all fine, if there was nothing to hide, nothing to see, nothing to report, then why do we need Ag-Gag laws designed to hide and protect farming practices?[5]

> *"The fate of farm animals is not an ethical side issue. It concerns the majority of Earth's large creatures: tens of billions of sentient beings, each with a complex world of sensations and emotions, but which live and die on an industrial production line."*
>
> **YUVAL NOAH HARARI, author of Sapiens**[6]

COVER-UPS AND TERRORISM ON THE FRONT LINES

Ag-gag laws first came into force in the US in the 1990s, as a way to stop underground activists associated with the Animal Liberation Front movement. They have since spread like wildfire and been enacted in Australia, Canada, and many European countries. These laws make it a crime to take photos or videos of an industrial farm without the owner's consent. In 2002, the Animal and Ecological Terrorism Act was enacted to "prohibit entering an animal or research facility to take pictures by photograph, video camera, or other means with the intent to commit criminal activities or defame the facility or its owner." Those found guilty of committing this offence were put on a terrorist registry. What is interesting here is the "defame the facility or its owner" element. To me, this is an admission that what goes on behind the barbed wire of our industrial farms is so wrong and unpalatable that it "defames" the people responsible for it. It is a cover-up and an acknowledgement of guilt.

In 2006, the Animal Enterprise Terrorism Act was passed in the USA, prohibiting any person from any behavior "for the purpose of damaging or interfering with the operations of an animal enterprise," including conduct that could damage or cause "the loss of any real or personal property." An interesting question is about the use of the term "terrorism" to describe the acts of passionate activists whose mission, ironically enough, is to shed light on the terror suffered by animals. Whether you agree with their methods or not, these are people who have been unable to turn away from the reality of what is happening in factory farms.

Similarly, in 2019, Australia passed the Right to Farm Bill, which criminalizes anyone who damages property, releases livestock, or encourages others to unlawfully enter animal facilities.[7] It is worth pausing on the bill's title. Nobody is threatening farming in itself, it's the "right" to abuse and slaughter that is being contested. The activists are not taking videos of farmers innocently going about their business of planting carrots or lovingly tending to their animals. In fact, many farmers are shocked when they see the horror show inside factory farms.

The truth is, without undercover reporting, we would have no idea what really happens in these animal facilities. According to the non-profit organization Government Accountability Project, this type of whistleblowing is essential. To suggest that there are proper channels by which "law-abiding" whistle-blowers can report abuse ignores the fact that employees who complain about conditions tend to either be intimidated into silence or fired.[8]

We need to ask, why are our governments supporting the limiting, concealing and suppressing of this information? Do they think we can't handle the truth? Do we not have the right to know how our food is produced? Or is the traditional image of farming so dear to us that we are collectively willing to turn a blind eye?

Let's buckle up and explore what these Ag-Gag laws are actually protecting. What are we not allowed to see? The brief descriptions that follow can be confronting, but I have been mindful not to be gratuitous. My mission is to tell the truth in as respectful a way as possible, while not diluting the facts. It was a tough balance to strike. For the brave, I recommend a deeper dive with the documentary Earthlings (you can find a free link to this in the Resources section).

AFO AND CAFO

ANIMAL FEEDING OPERATION AND CONCENTRATED ANIMAL FEEDING OPERATION[9]

An AFO is a term used by the US Environmental Protection Agency (EPA) to define enterprises where animals are kept and raised in confined conditions.

AFOs process animals, manure, urine, dead animals, and production operations on a small area of land. Animals in AFOs and CAFOs do not graze—feed is brought to them.

A CAFO is a large AFO,
one with more than 1,000 animal units.

One animal unit is defined as being equivalent to 1,000 pounds of live animal weight, which equates to:

1,000 beef cows,
700 dairy cows,
2,500 pigs (over 55 pounds each),
125,000 broiler chickens,
OR 82,000 laying hens.

MEAT THE TRUTH:

"Animals run no risk of going to hell,
they are there already."
Victor Hugo of Les Misérables

WHAT REALLY HAPPENS ON MODERN FACTORY FARMS

Farm animals are intelligent, gentle beings with complex personalities and strong social ties. However, today's factory farms do not allow them to express their natural behaviors. Instead, they are mistreated, neglected, and mutilated before being sent to a violent death.

COWS

Cows are consumed as beef and veal, kept as dairy producers, and used for products such as leather and manure. In their natural habitat, cows will live up to 22 years.[10] In the industrial farming industry, dairy cows live on average 4 years, while cows grown for beef are slaughtered after only 18 months.[11]

COWS RAISED FOR BEEF

Cows raised for beef usually start their life on a ranch or farm. Within a few days of being born, male calves will be restrained and a hot iron will be pressed into their flesh to identify them. Their horns will either be gouged out or burnt off. I recall helping with this as a boy and wanting to run away from the cries. They will be castrated, either by ripping or cutting the testicles from the scrotum, or by clamping down on them so they atrophy.

All this is done without pain relief. I vividly remember helping with this procedure on our farm. The bulls were put in a holding pen, and a contraption was used to place a strong elastic band around their scrotum. The band stayed in place until the bull's balls dried up and dropped off. This was done in order to make the bull produce more meat.

After about a year, they are shipped to auction, and then sent—sometimes hundreds of miles away—to feedlots, also known as concentrated animal feeding operations (CAFOs), where they are crowded together by the thousands. Instead of their natural diet of grass and hay, they are fed corn and soy, as well as the remains of other animals (see What Do Factory Farmed Animals Eat box section). This is designed to fatten them up quickly, but places undue strain on their digestive systems. The unnatural feed causes their stomachs to bloat to such an extent that it makes it hard for the cows to breathe. This is worsened by the air quality, which in CAFOs is saturated with ammonia, methane and other gasses from the buildup of animal waste. The fumes cause the cows to develop chronic respiratory conditions.

The squalid, unsanitary and crowded conditions create the perfect breeding ground for bacterial infections, so hormones and antibiotics are used to keep the animals alive and get them to their slaughter weight as quickly as possible. This is less about the animals' health more about profit. They are kept alive but do not experience a life worth living.

Once they have reached their kill weight, cows are sent to slaughterhouses. They are herded into trucks, where they will go without food, water, or rest for the journey, which sometimes takes days. Many will collapse from heat exhaustion. In the winter, cows can freeze to the side of the trucks and have to be pried off with crowbars. When they arrive at the slaughterhouse, many will be too sick to walk. These will have ropes or chains tied to their legs and will be dragged off. The cows that can still move are terrified and do not want to leave the truck. Workers prod them in the face and body with electric prods or beat them with chains to get them to move.

After being unloaded, cows are forced into a pen and shot with a captive bolt gun. This is meant to stun them and render them insensitive to pain. However, the lines move fast and workers are poorly trained, so many cows are still conscious when their throats are cut and are alive for as long as seven minutes after this. One longtime slaughterhouse worker told the Washington Post, "They blink, they make noises. The head moves, the eyes are wide and looking around... They die piece by piece."[12]

COWS RAISED FOR DAIRY

"My oat milk saves all the cows in the yard."

Cows, like all mammals, only produce milk after pregnancy to feed their young. To produce milk for our consumption, cows must give birth to one calf per year. Three months after giving birth, they are artificially inseminated again. If the cow does not conceive after her first insemination, or does not produce enough milk after her first calf, she is sent to slaughter.

If a dairy cow's calf is female, she will spend the first 8 weeks of her life isolated in a small pen before becoming part of the dairy industry. If it is male, he will be shipped to the veal industry, where he will spend 18 to 20 weeks gaining weight in a crate typically no bigger than 22 inches (0.56 meters) wide and 58 inches (1.47 meters) long, where he must lay in his own faeces and urine, before being slaughtered and sold as a delicacy.[13] Regardless of the sex, the calf is taken away from its mother immediately after birth, so that all of her calf's milk can be harvested for human consumption.

Cows are social animals with particularly strong bonds between mother and calf. It has been shown that cows mourn the loss of close friends, just like we do. Surely we can relate and use our imagination to put ourselves in their place for a second? Mothers give birth and see their newborn being taken away crying. These cries can be heard for days. Imagine going through that emotional wrench, and then being hooked up to a milking machine several times a day, until you are artificially inseminated again, only for the cycle to continue. Round and round again until you are so broken, that you're only fit for the slaughterhouse.

Milking when done naturally is not painful. But in industrial dairy farms, it is a different story. A cow naturally produces around 8 liters (2.1 gallons) of milk per day for her calf. Cows in the dairy industry are bred and drugged to produce over double that - 5.2 gallons (20 liters) a day. That puts an incredible amount of strain on their body. To produce just one liter (0.26 gallons or 2 pints) of milk, a cow's body must pump half a ton of blood through her udder. Increasing her milk productivity means the cow suffers. One of the physical ways this manifests is mastitis, a condition where their udders become inflamed and painful.

So what about all those cows we see in the fields, grazing so peacefully? Most of these cows are either beef cattle before they are sent to CAFOs, or young dairy cows before their first calf. Commercial dairy cows live in cramped stalls where they are tied in place. They are unable to walk, turn around, or interact with other cows. Sometimes they are kept in cubicles. The floors tend to be concrete, which is slippery and stressful for the cow to move around on. Their urine and faeces are mechanically removed. They are milked by machines. Their tails are docked without anesthetics to allow for easy access to their udders. They are milked four to five times a day. This pattern is repeated for three to six years, or until the cow no longer produces enough milk. She is then sent to slaughter.

PIGS

A pig's natural lifespan is ten to fifteen years. In the industrial farming industry, they are slaughtered at six months old.[14] Breeding sows are slaughtered after three to four years.[15]

SOWS

Female pigs, or sows, are repeatedly inseminated to give birth. Their litters can be any number of piglets, up to twelve at a time. During their pregnancy and after birth, sows are kept in gestation crates so small that they can barely move or turn around. They eat, urinate, defecate, and give birth in the same tiny space, sometimes so tiny that the bars cut into their skin.

Mother pigs, just like humans and other animals, instinctively want to nurture and teach their young. In nature, sows would have the space, material and time to do so; they typically nurse their babies for 10–17 weeks. But in factory farms, the piglets are taken away from their mother after only three weeks.

Male piglets are castrated by scalpel or knife in the first three days of their life, without pain relief. They are suspended by their hind legs, and the testes are removed by pulling or cutting the spermatic cord. According to meat businesses like Smithfield Foods, this is necessary to "improve the smell and taste of the meat." That's because sexually mature boars (uncastrated pigs) release compounds like skatole and androstenone, which give the meat an unpleasant flavor.

Barrows (castrated pigs) can be raised beyond puberty without developing a strong boar flavor, they're also less aggressive, and develop more fatty deposits. So, good for business, but not for the pig. The American Veterinary Medical Association issued a review on the welfare implications of castration in 2013, stating that castration is traumatic for the piglets, who squeal throughout the procedure and lie trembling for days after it happens.[16]

With being kept in confined, unnatural and crowded conditions, pigs develop PTSD—just like humans do when faced with traumatic situations like war or physical trauma. This manifests as compulsive behaviors, one of which is biting their own tails. Instead of giving the pigs more room and better conditions, pork producers perform "tail docking" where they amputate the tail without anesthetic.

Another mutilation pigs go through is "ear notching." Factory farm workers cut notches out of the pigs' right ear to mark which litter they belong to, and cut into their left ear to mark the individual pig's number. Again, no anesthetic is provided.

MALE PIGS

Male pigs are genetically bred and medicated to reach their slaughter weight (250 pounds / 113 kilos) by the time they are just six months old. Due to their weight and lack of space to move, they develop arthritis and struggle to walk or stand. It is not uncommon for pigs to become stuck in their own waste, in dirty feedlots, until such a time as they are shipped to slaughter.

Transport to the slaughterhouse can take up to 28 hours. During this time, the pigs suffer severe overcrowding and extreme temperatures, with no food or water. By the time they arrive, they are exhausted and dehydrated. Many will suffer injuries along the way. Some die before they arrive.

A typical slaughterhouse kills 1,000 pigs an hour. The speed of the slaughter line means many are not properly stunned before their throat is slit. So they can see, hear and smell the pigs around them being killed and dipped into scalding water to remove their hair.[17]

In nature, pigs are extremely clean and social creatures. Scientifically, they have been shown to be just as intelligent as dogs,[18] if not more so. So why is it that dogs live in our homes and become our best friends, while pigs are bred for the sole purpose of becoming bacon? From the day they are born to the day they are killed, pigs, which are sweet, curious and intelligent, endure unimaginable torment and pain. Isn't it time to rethink our relationship with these clever gentle creatures?

CHICKENS

In their natural habitat, chickens will live up to ten years. Factory-farmed chickens live an average of forty-two days.

Ten thousand years ago, chickens were rare birds found in South Asia. They are now global, and are the most widespread domesticated animal in the world. You could therefore argue that chickens are one of the most successful animals on the planet. However, the ghastly trade-off is that they are also the most tortured animal in history.[19] Estimates by the World Economic Forum show that over 50 billion chickens are killed for food every year.[20] This figure does not include male chicks or unproductive hens killed in egg production.

Chickens raised for meat (broilers) and chickens raised for eggs (hens) begin their lives in giant incubators, alongside other chicks. They will never meet their parents. Within days of being born, they are placed beak-first into a machine that cuts off the tip of their beak with a hot blade or a laser. Chicken producers debeak birds to prevent them from pecking at each other, a result of cramped and stressful living conditions.[21]

BROILER CHICKENS

Over the last few decades, broilers have been genetically manipulated to drastically increase the amount of pectoral (breast) and thigh tissue, since these are the most profitable parts of the animal. Unfortunately, this means that these parts grow too fast and too big for their body, which cannot sustain this abnormal growth. They are bred and drugged to gain around 1.76 ounces (50 grams) in weight every day.[22] Their immune systems, organs and legs cannot keep up, resulting in painful bone deformations and congestive heart failure.

Some broiler chickens do not make it to the slaughterhouse. They die of thirst because they are physically unable to get to the water. Other causes of death include cancer, over-heating, and infectious diseases.[23]

Broiler chickens are given less than a square foot of space each. Ironically, they get more room in the oven than they ever got while they were alive. They are crammed, 20,000 to 30,000 to each closed broiler shed. These sheds are artificially lit, and computers control the temperature, feeding and watering. Both feed and water are medicated with drugs to control parasites or with antibiotics.

Chickens in the wild tend to live in small flocks of around thirty, with well-defined social hierarchies (this is where the term "pecking order" comes from). They enjoy scratching and pecking for food, taking dust baths, resting and playing together. None of this is possible in a broiler shed. They have no space to roam, they are stressed and tense. Units are only cleaned at the end of each cycle, so within two weeks the floor is covered in waste, and the ammonia fumes become so strong that they burn the birds' eyes. Observers have reported that chickens rub their eyes with their wings and squawk in pain.[24]

After six or seven weeks of these conditions, the broilers reach their kill weight. They are slammed into crates and taken to slaughter. Many sustain broken wings and legs from the rough handling. Many die from the extreme temperatures and stress of the journey.

Thanks to automation, slaughterhouses can kill over 8,000 birds an hour using the common method known as live-shackle slaughter. Workers strap the chickens into leg shackles on a moving rail. The birds hang upside down and move along to baths of electrified water, designed to stun them or immobilize them, before moving to a mechanical blade that cuts their throat. After they have bled out, they are plunged into boiling water to remove their feathers. Unfortunately, the speed of the assembly line means many chickens are aware of exactly what is happening to them. Some miss the throat cutting blade and are boiled alive.

EGG-LAYING HENS

For egg-laying hens, the conditions are even harder. The majority are kept in cages that are on average smaller than a sheet of paper (around 67 square inches / 432 square cm—that's just over 8x8 inches / 20x21 cm). For context, a hen needs 72 square inches to stand, and 303 square inches to spread her wings. These cages are piled up on top of each other, in sheds that hold tens of thousands of birds. Waste falls from the top cages to the lower ones, causing the same ammonia burn as for broilers.

In nature, chickens have a strong urge to nest. Mother hens carefully tend to their eggs, turning them every few hours and even clucking to them. In chicken sheds, they cannot build a nest for their eggs, the eggs just drop through the wires of the cage.

Left to their own devices, chickens lay around 10 eggs a year. In factory farms, they lay 300 a year. To get the hens to produce as many eggs as possible, chicken producers use methods like light manipulation (extended periods of artificial daylight are used to encourage laying) as well as forced moulting, a technique where hens are starved of food and water to force their body to produce more eggs.[25]

In these conditions, hens are unable to exercise. They sit in one position their entire life, with their feet pressing into the wires of the cage, and their wings rubbing against the sides. The constant egg laying leaches calcium from their body, so they develop osteoporosis and broken bones. This is a well-known phenomenon called cage-layer fatigue.

After one or two years, the hens' production decreases, and they are shipped to slaughter, most often to be turned into pet food or animal feed because their flesh is too bruised and battered for anything else.

Male chicks born to egg-laying breeder hens are useless to the industry (they cannot lay eggs, and are not bred to grow into heavy broilers for the meat industry), so they are either ground alive, or tossed into bags to suffocate. Four to six billion male chicks are killed this way each year.[26]

In 2003, there was a short spell of outrage in America when a lawsuit was filed against an egg ranch for killing 30,000 hens by dumping them, alive, into a wood-chipper.[27] No charges were brought, because as it happens, this is standard practice in the industry. The Humane Slaughter Act does not cover chickens.[28]

THE FANTASY FARM MYTH

"It is an indication of the extent to which people are now isolated from the animals they eat that children brought up on storybooks that lead them to think of a farm as a place where animals wander around freely in idyllic conditions might be able to live out their entire lives without ever being forced to revise this rosy image."

Peter Singer, 1975[29]

It has been nearly fifty years since Singer wrote his landmark book *Animal Liberation*, yet the fantasy farm myth persists. It is deeply rooted in the fairy-tale images from children's books that condition our young to accept the carnist storyline.

Throughout life, fast food companies, supermarkets and meat giants go to extraordinary lengths to promote this false narrative of the clean, friendly face of farming.

Cue the adverts that depict a farmer in a checked shirt and dungarees gently patting a cow's bottom as she walks through a wooden gate onto a lush green field or a flock of shiny-feathered chickens clucking and pecking in a large coop surrounded by trees.

In farm adverts, there is an absence of enclosures, crates, bars, and electric and barbed fences that confine real farmed animals. Let alone the truly horrific practices of the average factory farm.

I grew up on a small family-run fantasy farm. So profound was my cognitive dissonance that I could only recognize the abuse for what it is from a safe distance many years later. Even small family farms operate within a system of normalized violence. There is no such thing as cruelty-free farming or humane slaughter.

Farming is not a child-friendly story.

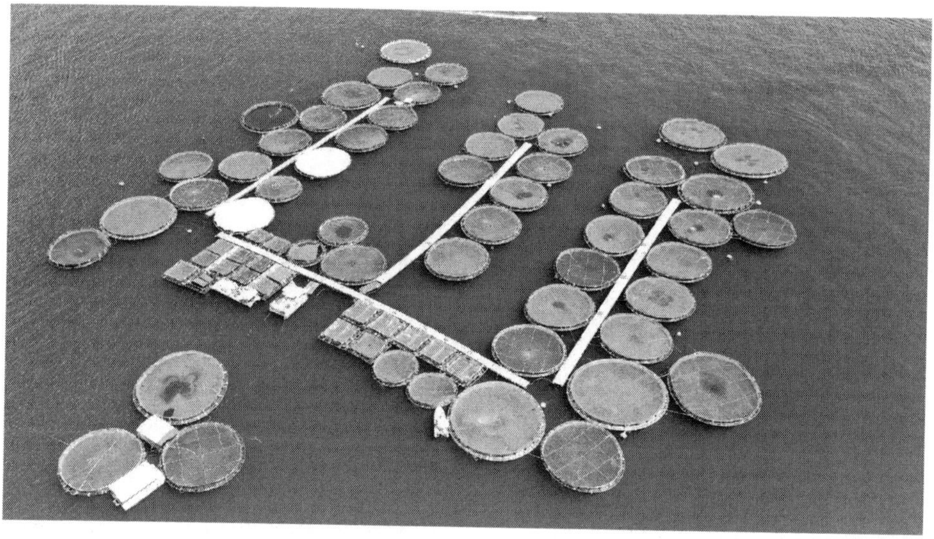

FISH: WATER FARMING

It is shocking for many to learn that fish are just another exploited farm animal. Half of all fish consumed globally come from aquafarms, and this industry is growing three times faster than land-based animal agriculture. This is perhaps a response to our almost exhausted natural fisheries. Aquafarms are like water-based concentrated animal feeding operations (CAFOs). Genetic engineering is used to ensure the fish grow faster and bigger than they would in the wild. In some countries, antibiotics are added to the water or fish feed. Residues of these drugs are present in the end product and on your plate.

Fish farmers cram as many fish as possible into the smallest space possible. Large farms, the size of four football fields, can contain over a million fish. These overcrowded conditions mean that fish cannot navigate properly and keep bumping into each other, causing sores and fin damage. Salmon, which are 30 inches (75 cm) long, are given space equivalent to a bathtub of water each.

Fish are continually sorted by size to ensure that the larger ones are moved to the appropriate size grouping. The process of "grading" involves netting or pumping fish out of their tanks, and dumping them onto grates of varied space gaps to divide them by size. Fish farmers sometimes starve the fish for 24 hours before doing this.

Parasite infestations and diseases are common in fish farms. As many as 40% of farmed fish are blind—this problem is not addressed because it does not cause a loss of profit. Sea lice eat at the fish, causing their scales to fall off which leave large sores. In ocean-based fish farms, sea lice often eat down to the bone.

Many species of farmed fish are carnivorous, so wild fish need to be caught to feed farmed fish. This is incredibly inefficient and unsustainable. It can take one pound of wild fish to produce one pound of farmed salmon or sea bass. Fish farmers sometimes give fish oil and fish meal to algae-eating fish to speed up their growth. They also add chemicals and antibiotics to help the fish survive the harsh conditions in aquafarms. This could be why levels of dioxin and PCB are up to seven times higher in farmed fish than in wild-caught fish.

Similarly to chickens, there are no regulations to ensure that fish are treated humanely. According to PETA, almost 40% of farmed fish die before it is time for slaughter. Those who survive are starved for up to ten days to reduce waste contamination of the water during transport. Common slaughter methods include leaving them to suffocate on ice or in the air, a process that can take more than ten minutes. Other methods include piercing their hearts or cutting off their gills, as well as immobilizing the fish with cold water before killing them with carbon dioxide.[30]

Wild-caught fish do not have to endure life on an aquafarm, but they still suffer fear and pain. It is estimated that one to three trillion fish are wild-caught every year. They are chased to the point of exhaustion by huge trawl nets. Once caught, they are crushed under the weight of other fish. It can take hours, sometimes days, for fish to be captured. During this process, many fish die or become injured. Once caught and landed, the fish are either left to suffocate, or die from processing (such as gutting, filleting, or freezing—all while still conscious).[31]

Cows, pigs, chickens and fish are not the only animals killed for meat. Ducks, rabbits, geese, turkeys, sheep, goats, mice, rats, pigeons, buffalo, horses, donkeys, mules, camels, as well as cats and dogs, are also tortured and killed daily for food.[32] And that's without mentioning the horrors they go through in product testing and medical research industries. That's another story and book in itself!

VOICE FOR THE VOICELESS

"Never, never be afraid to do what's right,
especially if the well-being of a person or animal is at stake.
Society's punishments are small compared to the wounds we inflict on our soul when we look the other way."
Martin Luther King Jr

If you have read through this section, thank you. It is not easy to examine and accept our involvement in this system and face the reality of today's food system. I too found it a struggle to research and write about billions of animals suffering unnecessarily. I feel that the meat industry depends on us wanting to turn the other way—it depends on us wanting to believe that what goes on in industrial animal farms is natural and even humane. Because the industry knows that if we saw how these animals are treated, most would not want to be part of it. We buy our meat nicely cut up, cleaned and plastic-wrapped in the supermarket, but there is nothing natural or humane about the way animals are bred, genetically modified, and intensively farmed to end up on our plates.

I have made every effort to give you this information in a straightforward and sober way. I was mindful to be factual, not emotive, to avoid shock tactics or gore. However, I would also urge you to be brave and watch the videos. There is nothing like seeing with your own eyes what these animals go through, to really cement your decision to go vegan.

Maybe grab a friend who is willing to go on this journey with you, or a vegan friend, and challenge yourself to look over the walls and fences of factory farms and slaughterhouses. Be open to letting the images change you. Allow yourself to feel that pain, to experience that rising indignation. Smash through those Ag-Gag laws and fluffy marketing to embrace the reality and your feelings. Because if it is unpleasant to watch, that only proves that you are a compassionate human and a budding *Rebel Vegan*.

Animal welfare is not only about animals. It's about us too. Because if we condone this type of treatment, what kind of message are we sending? Is it okay to treat other conscious beings this way? What kind of world are we accepting, if we accept this sort of everyday normalized violence? If we turn a blind eye to this, what else can we turn a blind eye to?

In a time in history when we are more and more polarized and when politics are getting more extreme, we should be careful about what we accept under the guise of "it's always been like this" or "they're 'only' animals." After all, this is how all oppression starts—by seeing certain beings as inferior to us, or ours to use and exploit. To stop the oppression, we must stop buying into an industry that knowingly tortures our fellow earthlings. This central driving force can empower us all to align our ethics of compassion and justice with a more sustainable and kinder way of living. **#voiceforthevoiceless**

Today and everyday - 200 million land animals are slaughtered in food production.

If we were killed at the same rate, the human race would become extinct in 2 and a half weeks.[33]

6

ENVIRONMENT

INCONVENIENT SCIENCE

"We must either let some eating habits go, or let the planet go. It is that straightforward, and that fraught."
Jonathan Safran Foer[1]

Do you remember "An Inconvenient Truth" (2006), that ground-breaking documentary by Vice President Al Gore? This was the first film that broke down the climate crisis, and it had a real impact on me. I made changes to my lifestyle on the strength of it and fancied myself as a radical eco-warrior. But I was still eating meat, in blissful ignorance of its devastating environmental impact. Thinking back, I can see that while that documentary was powerful and shone a light on the dangers of fossil fuels and some of our modern ways of life, but it also turned a blind eye to one of the biggest factors responsible for pollution and ecosystem collapse—the meat industry.

Perhaps Al didn't want to ruffle the feathers of his friends in Washington. As we have seen, the meat industry has persuasive power and strong links to policy-makers. That being said, Al Gore went vegan in 2012 and has since admitted, "It's absolutely correct that the growing meat intensity of diets across the world is one of the issues connected to this global crisis—not only because of the [carbon dioxide] involved, but also because of the water consumed in the process."[2]

Let's begin with a reality check. It is an uncomfortable reality based on inconvenient science; our current diet and food system is unsustainable. We cannot safeguard our environment for future generations while regularly eating meat. Animal agriculture is responsible for releasing powerful greenhouse gases into the atmosphere, burning down rainforests, and creating ocean dead zones, all of which are speeding up climate change towards a planet that is uninhabitable—not just for other animals, but also for humans.

It's now a classic, but when Cowspiracy hit our screens in 2014, it was radical and groundbreaking. Nobody had been talking about this, certainly not in the mainstream. Suddenly, the implications of animal agriculture for our environment were right in front of our faces, undeniable and frightening.

Being a true *Rebel Vegan* is about compassion and accepting that the future of our planet is our responsibility. This means going beyond energy saving light bulbs and recycling. We must make daily choices that protect the world we live in.

Climate scientists agree that eating plant-based is the most impactful and positive step we can all take to halt the climate crisis. And it is a step we cannot bypass. According to a report from the Intergovernmental Panel of Climate Change (IPCC), even if we do everything necessary to reduce emissions and halt climate change, we will not meet the Paris Climate Agreement's goals unless we dramatically reduce our reliance on animal products.

This is a sobering thought, and a catalyzing one. Each of us will have two or three meals today, so we can immediately take action in reversing climate change. We can do this simply by switching from meat to plants. The truth is we can all be *Rebel Vegans* and save the world one meal at a time.

GREENHOUSE GASES

The fact that animal agriculture is a disaster for the environment is not my opinion—it's not even an opinion—it's fact. Despite what certain strident climate deniers will have you believe, our modern lifestyles put incredible strain on our planet. Mother Nature has been whispering her pain for decades. She is now beginning to scream, and we need to listen before it's too late.

Let's begin with greenhouse gas emissions. The greenhouse gas effect is a natural occurrence whereby gases in the atmosphere trap heat from the sun and warm the planet. It is a good thing, because without it, our planet would be a freezing and uninhabitable place. The problem is our voracious burning of fossil fuels is causing the greenhouse gas effect to turn on us.

For almost a million years, the concentration of greenhouse gases has been around 200-280 parts per million (this means that for every million molecules of air, there were 200-280 molecules of greenhouse gases). In the last hundred years, this has jumped to 400 parts per million.[3] This has caused more heat to be trapped in the Earth's atmosphere and as a result global temperatures rise. In turn, this leads to the climate disasters we are seeing today, from soaring temperatures (for example, Canada hit a record

46.1 degrees Celsius / 115 *F in 2021[4]), to record ice melting (for example, Greenland ice sheets lost 8.5 billion tons in melted ice in one day in July 2021—enough to cover Florida in two inches of water[5]), to torrential rainfall, devastating floods and wildfires throughout the world.

Animals in feedlots are the primary source of methane (86 times more powerful than CO_2) and nitrous oxide emissions (310 times more powerful than CO_2). These greenhouse gases are a huge contributor to global warming.

Animal agriculture produces more greenhouse gas emissions than all the transportation sector (that's cars, trains and planes). Can it be true? The UN's Food and Agriculture Organization (FAO) says it is responsible for just 14.5% of greenhouse gas emissions, which makes it sound like animal agriculture is not the most urgent thing to tackle in the fight against climate change.

But a new report shows the FAO's calculations were flawed because they failed to include the negative impact of deforestation due to animal agriculture. With this being considered, animal agriculture is responsible for 87% of greenhouse gas emissions.[6]

Let that sink in for just a moment. Compare it to the 13% caused by other things. From that place, is it more important to buy an electric car, or switch to plant-based eating?

HOW CAFOS (LARGE FACTORY FARMS) POLLUTE THE AIR[7]

Warehouses where animals are kept:

The air pollution in these warehouses is potentially deadly to both animals and humans if the fans stop working. The fans simply blow this contaminated air (which contains ammonia, particulates, feathers and feces) out of the building into the environment.

Animal waste:

CAFO wastes are stored in structures that are neither treated nor aerated. This results in an off-gassing of pollutants when the waste is transported or sprayed onto farm fields.

Waste spreading:

Once or twice a year, the solid waste at the bottom of storage tanks is scraped out and spread onto fields, resulting in even worse air pollution.

Heavy air pollution:

Over 168 different gases are emitted from CAFO waste, including methane, hydrogen sulfide and ammonia.

LAND AND WATER

AN INEFFICIENT USE OF PRECIOUS RESOURCES

Animal agriculture gobbles up the lion's share of resources essential to our survival: land and water. Half of the world's habitable land is used for agriculture. Animal agriculture also accounts for 30% of all freshwater consumption.[8]

Using animals for food is one of the most energy-inefficient ways to eat. After all, the animal needs huge amounts of food and water to grow. In contrast, a plant just needs good quality soil and minimal water. Of the 19.7 million square miles (51 million square km) currently used for agriculture, 77% is used for livestock (this includes grazing land for animals and land used for animal feed production), while 23% is used for crops. Despite taking up such a huge percentage of agricultural land, only 18% of the world's calorie supply comes from meat and dairy.[9]

To put it another way, the land used for crops is four times smaller than the land used for livestock, and yet it supplies more calories for the global population. A sobering thought, but one that provides hope and solutions for the future, if we can listen and learn to change. Like the dilemma itself, the solution is right there on the plate.

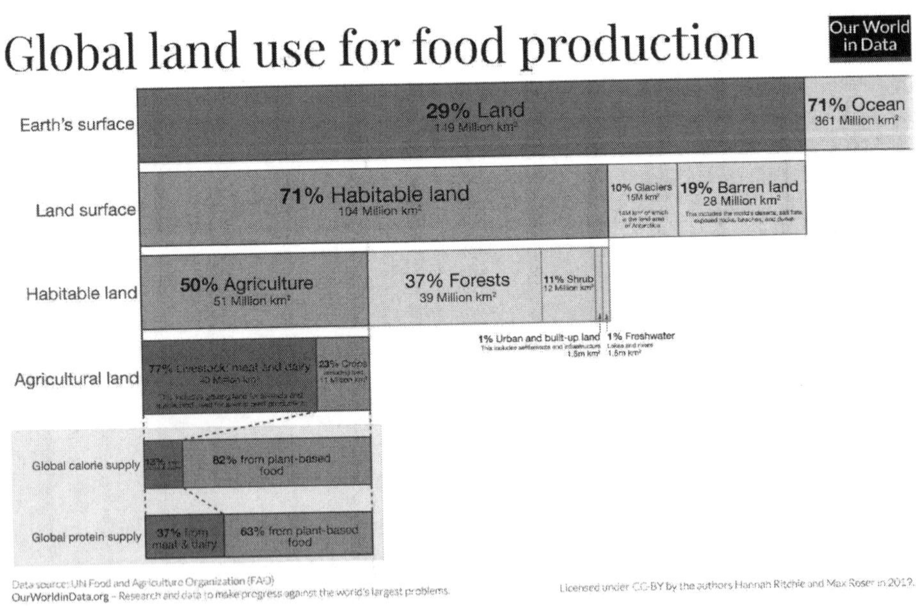

https://ourworldindata.org/global-land-for-agriculture

RAINFORESTS DESTRUCTION

We currently have a situation where rainforests are being cut or burnt down to make space for crops grown to feed farm animals to satisfy our taste for meat. The stats are shocking and get scarier by the day. The World Bank asserts that animal agriculture is responsible for nearly 90% of Amazon rainforest destruction[10], with more than 80,000 acres of tropical rainforest[11] and 135 animal, plant, and insect species lost[12] due to this destruction each day.[13] In the last 40 years, 1 billion hectares of rainforest have been destroyed. That's an area the size of Europe. We are losing a football field of forest every single second.[14]

Rainforests are much more than just trees or a trip-of-a-lifetime destination. They are a carbon-storage facility. They are an oxygen factory. They are an Ali Baba's cave of animal and plant species that have yet to be discovered and studied. They are home to indigenous tribes who have lived there for millennia.

Feedlots and grain production for cattle feed are the primary reason for deforestation, and there are two main reasons this must stop. Firstly, burning down trees releases carbon into the atmosphere. Secondly, fewer trees means the planet is less able to absorb carbon (including all that extra carbon we are pumping out because of our modern lifestyles).

Trees are carbon storers or sinks—they absorb CO_2 from the air and store it into their bark. When we burn them, we release all this back into the environment, compounding the global warming issue, and accelerating climate change.

Interestingly, during 2020, when the whole world ground to a halt for Covid, deforestation sped up. 12% more undisturbed tropical rainforests were razed down in 2020 compared to 2019.[15] For the first time ever, the Amazon rainforest emits more carbon dioxide than it absorbs. It used to store the carbon that drives climate change, now it is accelerating climate change.

Two reasons for this. The first is the fires deliberately set to clear land for beef and soy cause emissions. The second is hotter temperatures, and drafts mean the Amazon has become a source of CO_2 rather than a sink.[16] We may have passed the tipping point, or be very close to doing so.

Research from the World Resources Institute shows extreme weather events are on the rise everywhere, including within the rainforests themselves. Even the wetlands are burning. Combine global warming and deforestation, and you have the perfect storm of warmer, drier conditions, making forests even more vulnerable to disease and fire. Burning releases more carbon emissions, which speed up global warming. You can see how we have a vicious cycle on our hands. And the cycle is speeding up, unless we find a way to stop it. The most efficient way to do this is to stop supporting the industry responsible for deforestation.

OUR MOST PRECIOUS RESOURCE:

WATER—THE GIFT OF LIFE—MISUSED

Another inconvenient truth is we cannot survive without water. It's the basis of all life. Even if we colonize and build a community on the moon or Mars, they will need to import water. This is our most precious resource. Like oil before it, wars might well be fought over it in the future.

So consider that according to the Stockholm International Water Institute, we will run out of freshwater by 2050 if we continue to produce and eat animal products at the current rate.[17] Given that predictions are for meat consumption to increase, we can assume this date is a best-case scenario. So we are facing a situation where the freshwater reserves of the entire planet could be used up in under thirty years and in most of our lifetimes.

It sounds unthinkable that we could ever get to this state. But it makes more sense when you break it down and discover that it takes 4,000 gallons (15,000 liters) of water to produce 2 pounds (1 kilo) of beef.[18] Let me put that amount of water into context. It is enough drinking water for one person for 10,000 days (or just over 27 years) if that person drinks the recommended 3 pints (1.5 liters) a day. It took a moment for the significance of this to really sink in. Drinking water for a quarter of a century, or one kilo of beef. No wonder we are running out of clean water.

A question that pops up for me here is, shorter showers for life, or yummy Beyond Burgers?

But animal agriculture doesn't just use unprecedented amounts of freshwater, it also pollutes water—drinking water, rivers, streams and oceans.

WATER FOR MEAT[19]

2 pounds (1 kilo) beef - 4,072 gallons (15,415 liters) of water
2 pounds (1 kilo) goat - 2,315 gallons (8,763 liters) of water
2 pounds (1 kilo) pork - 1,582 gallons (5,988 liters) of water
2 pounds (1 kilo) chicken - 1,142 gallons (4,325 liters) of water
2.1 pints (1 liter) milk - 166 gallons (628 liters) of water

WATER FOR PLANTS[20]

2 pounds (1 kilo) pulses - 792 gallons (3,000 liters) of water
2 pounds (1 kilo) rice - 660 gallons (2,500 liters) of water
2 pounds (1 kilo) bread - 396 gallons (1,500 liters) of water
2.1 pints (1 liter) soy milk - 7 gallons (28 liters) of water
2.1 pints (1 liter) oat milk - 13 gallons (48 liters) of water

OCEAN DEAD ZONES

Across the world, approximately 70 billion animals are farmed for food every year, the majority of them in factory farms, and the numbers keep rising.[21] The waste these animals produce has to go somewhere. The USDA's Natural Resources Conservation Service encourages CAFO owners to "take voluntary actions to minimize potential air and water pollutants from storage facilities, confinement areas and land application areas."[22] This gives the polluters the responsibility to manage—or not—their own waste.

Again, we are expecting big business to police themselves and what we have learned is where there are bucks to be made from animals, corners will be cut and the voiceless suffer. If you think of it from their perspective, animal welfare is a barrier to their profits. Ultimately ensuring animal wellbeing 100% is prohibitively expensive and not a realistic option in the current system.

The latest figures show CAFOs produce 369 million tons of manure, which is thirteen times more than the entire US population. However, human waste is treated via sewer systems and is subject to strict laws to ensure it is processed properly. Animal waste, on the other hand, is stored in open ponds or pits (called lagoons, which make it sound almost pleasant and tropical), and is spread, untreated, onto fields. Let's remember that this is not old-style manure, like I was used to taking directly from the barn to spread over our fields. Those cows had munched on hay and grass all their lives. This is a mixture of animal excrement, antibiotic-resistant bacteria, hormones, bedding waste, antibiotic residues, cleaning and other chemicals, ammonia and even dead animals. It contains a high content of nitrogen and heavy metals, including copper, zinc and lead (due to these being added to animal feed).[23] The only thing between this toxic soup and the environment is a thin layer of clay, which can leak and allow the waste to seep into groundwater.

This untreated waste is also sprayed directly onto fields. The excess runoff ends up in streams and rivers, and eventually the ocean. Because of the chemicals and toxins, it causes an overgrowth of algae. These algae bloom and die off, depleting the oxygen in the water. The result is ocean dead zones—so called because there is no more oxygen left for other lifeforms, which means marine life either asphyxiates and dies, or leaves the area if it can.

Dead zones become oceanic deserts, empty of their usual biodiversity. The planet's largest ever ocean dead zone is located in the Gulf of Mexico and is larger than New Jersey[24], spanning an incredible 8,776 square miles (22,730 square kilometers). This area has been made completely uninhabitable due to agricultural runoff from the Mississippi floodplain, home to countless pig farms.

And it is likely to keep growing unless we make changes to the food system. The task-force responsible for reducing the dead zone to 1,900 square miles (4,920 square kilometers) has found that a reduction of 60% in waste runoff is required to achieve this goal by 2035.[25] As it stands, there are over 400 ocean dead zones around the globe.[26]

SPECIES EXTINCTION

I grew up surrounded by open countryside and watching nature documentaries that showed our planet teeming with wildlife. I took for granted this world would always be there, regenerating itself and working in harmony. Most of us still hold dear these images of the wild world populated by elephants, dolphins, whales, and lions. It's an image that's upheld by Disney movies and the National Geographic channel, but it is no longer a reality.

Today most big animals live on industrial farms. They both outweigh and outnumber other lifeforms on our planet. Altogether, domesticated animals weigh around 700 million tons, while humans weigh 300 million tons, and large wild animals weigh less than 100 million tons.[27]

We have created a gross imbalance. A groundbreaking report by the Intergovernmental Science-Policy Platform on Biodiversity and Ecosystem Services (IPBES) found that one million species are in danger of extinction, and human activity is the cause.[28]

"The health of ecosystems on which we and all other species depend on is deteriorating more rapidly than ever. We are eroding the foundations of our economies, livelihoods, food security, health, and quality of life worldwide."
Sir Robert Watson, Chair of IPBES[29]

Some species threatened with extinction have not even been discovered yet. Between 1999 and 2015, over 2,000 new species were found in the Amazon. In 2014 and 2015, 216 previously unknown plants, 93 fish, 32 amphibians, 20 mammals, 19 reptiles and one bird were uncovered,[30] showing how much diversity we are destroying for the sake of the standard Western diet[31]. And, as we saw earlier, we are losing a football field's worth of uncharted, unresearched, undisturbed, pristine rainforest every second.

The vicious cycle is speeding up
we are playing a dangerous game.

RESPECTING MOTHER EARTH

Is there something we can do?

Yes, there is. And there is still hope. If we can shift our diets, we can begin to turn things around. There is still a narrow window of time. And the time is now. A global food system based on a plant-based diet is a vital part of the remedy.

A new report by the international journal Science of the Total Environment explored over 300 different food system scenarios, all based around stopping deforestation. The standard Western diet[32] has the highest greenhouse gas emissions out of any dietary choice. In contrast, organic, plant-based food systems had negative greenhouse gas emissions, because the extra vegetation helps absorb carbon.[33]

Put simply, a meat-dominant diet releases unprecedented amounts of carbon into the atmosphere, whereas a plant-dominant diet absorbs that carbon out of the air. What's more, freeing up the land currently used for livestock would offer us opportunities to reforest and rewild areas that are currently barren, creating new habitats and breathing space for all species on earth. This space would drastically reduce the risk of future global pandemics (more on this in a moment). Finally, we would not have the millions of tons of toxic animal waste to dispose of, nor billions of animals to water, which would enable us to clean up our oceans and conserve freshwater supplies.

The result of a global shift towards plant-based living: a greener planet, one that we can pass on to future generations without shame or guilt.

At the current rate, animal agriculture will gobble up and pollute the world's land and freshwater reserves within thirty years. Within the next thirty years, the planet will be home to an extra two billion people. The diet we choose in the coming years will have a huge impact on the planet. The science is in and it's sobering. We need to urgently reassess our lifestyles and diets, as it is clear that any diet centered around meat and dairy will take a greater toll on the world's resources than a diet focused around vegetables, pulses, grains, nuts and seeds.[34]

I know that climate change is a complex and divisive topic. And I am not trying to suggest that animal agriculture is the only cause. Going more plant-based is not the only remedy required to solve all our ecological and climate problems, but no solution is complete without it.

There is no more time for indecision and hiding behind others. It is all of our collective and individual responsibility to protect and preserve our shared home.

Together, Rebel Vegans can save the planet.

B12
K
V
C
B6

7

HEALTH

BLUEPRINT FOR GLOBAL AND PERSONAL WELLBEING

"Let food be thy medicine, and medicine be thy food."

Hippocrates, the father of medicine[1]

For over a hundred years, meat and dairy have been held up as pinnacles of a healthy diet. This century of mass media marketing has made us believe that animal proteins are somehow integral to our survival, that it made us human and top of the food chain.

The truth is these foods threaten both our individual health and our global health. They give us cancer, heart disease, obesity and diabetes. Industrial farming creates the perfect conditions for antibiotic-resistant superbugs, not to mention zoonotic diseases such as MERS, SARS, vCJD (mad cow disease) and more recently, Covid.

Put succinctly, eating animals is slowly killing us.

GLOBAL HEALTH: THE MEAT INDUSTRY AND GLOBAL PANDEMICS

ZOONOTIC DISEASES AND THE NEXT PANDEMIC

Pandemics are neither accidents nor coincidences. Sixty percent of all infectious diseases in humans[2,] and 75% of all emerging infectious diseases are zoonotic.[3] Zoonotic means diseases that originate from animals, either wild or domesticated, and pass to humans.

Until recently, animals and humans lived more separately and had fewer interactions. There was a natural barrier between us, which to a certain degree protected us.[4] So-called disease reservoirs (also known as virus reservoirs, reservoirs of infection or natural reservoirs) were further away from us. A disease reservoir is the population of animals where an infectious pathogen (such as a virus) naturally lives and reproduces.[5]

The way we produce our food has eroded that barrier, and as a result, we are in closer proximity to pathogens, and at higher risk of virus epidemics.

According to the United Nations Environment Program (UNEP), a new infectious disease emerges in humans every four months.[6] While many of these diseases originate in wildlife (in so-called virus reservoirs), the bridge between wild animals and humans is livestock, and in particular intensively reared livestock.

WHY?

It makes more sense when you consider that farm animals are bred to be almost identical—there is no genetic diversity to provide resilience or resistance to infection. After all, livestock are grown for production characteristics (like being heavier than their normal counterparts), rather than for immune strength. What's more, these animals are kept in crowded, unsanitary, unnatural conditions that make it impossible for them to be healthy—indeed they are kept alive with drugs.

Zoonotic viruses are opportunistic. They tend to affect hosts already stressed by environmental conditions. The 70 billion factory-farmed animals in the food system today fit that bill perfectly. These vulnerable animals are a Petri dish for infections and live in close proximity to humans.

Our food systems are a disaster waiting to happen.

Zoonotic viruses are not new. Some scientists hypothesize that flu first became a human disease when the Chinese domesticated ducks around 4,000 years ago, and brought that animal disease reservoir into human communities for the first time.[7] Humans can also catch flu from pigs and horses.[8] The H1N1 influenza virus caused the 1918 Spanish flu, thought to have originated from a midwestern pig farm[9], and the mad cow disease epidemic that hit the United Kingdom in the early 1990s[10] was caused by feeding bone meal to herbivores—something that, worryingly, is still happening today.

Scientists have been warning for decades that global pandemics are a serious threat. And yet little has been done to prevent them from occurring.[11]

In the last few years, several zoonotic diseases have made the headlines, but they have all felt remote. SARS in 2003 remained in Asia, MERS in 2012 stayed in the Middle East. Ebola in 2014 was centered in Africa. It was easy for the West to largely ignore these epidemics, to attribute them to different conditions in faraway cultures. We don't ride camels, eat monkeys or handle bats in wet markets. Our meat comes plastic-wrapped, sanitized and safe. This had nothing to do with us. This could not happen to us. We were wrong.

Ignoring inconvenient science seems to be a running theme in this story. We have known for a while that the way we eat poses a dire threat to global health, but we have looked the other way and failed to address it.

After the SARS outbreak in 2003, an essay in the American Journal of Public Health accepted that "changing the way humans treat animals—most basically, ceasing to eat them or, at the very least, radically limiting the quantity of them eaten—is largely off the radar as a significant preventative measure."[12]

In other words, one of the most effective ways we could reduce the risk of future pandemics was basically ignored by governments and global health authorities. Instead of listening to science, they refused to challenge the status quo, and accepted defeat.

FACTORY FARMING AND PREVENTING PANDEMICS

To say that zoonotic viruses are just about wet markets and wild meat is to ignore a huge part of the equation. With the emergence of Covid-19, many have been quick to blame the Wuhan wet market and the trade of wild animals. Health authorities, including the head of the World Health Organization, have called for a clampdown on the sale of exotic animal meat, while remaining silent on the role of conventional food production.

The truth is that zoonotic viruses are an expanding threat, because we are increasingly encroaching on natural ecosystems, which serve as virus reservoirs. Prior to the industrial revolution, our contact with wild animals was limited, our settlements and agricultural endeavors were relatively small. These days, it's a whole other story, as we saw in the environment section.

We have taken once pristine land and transformed it, we have razed ecosystems to the ground to exploit them for crops, resource extraction, human settlements, but mostly for animal agriculture. This has provided pathogens with opportunities to spill over from wild animals to humans, often via farm animals.

At the same time, our conventional, large-scale, industrial farming practices have pushed small farmers into closer contact with wild animals. When large livestock firms lost market share in China, the government encouraged smallholders to breed and sell wild game. When local fishers in West Africa were pushed out of coastal waters by foreign trawlers in the 1970s, reliance on bush meat skyrocketed, leading to outbreaks of HIV and Ebola.

It is easy to point the finger at other people's taste for strange delicacies, while ignoring the West's reliance on pork, beef and chicken. There is a bigger issue at play here. Yes, contact with wild animals increases the risk of zoonotic diseases, but our industrial farming practices offer the perfect conditions for these viruses to spread. As these conditions increasingly intensify and multiply, we must now place responsibility where it ought to be—on the global, profit-driven, meat-centered food system.[13]

Although I know it may not feel like it, we had some degree of luck this time. At the time of writing, Covid has killed 6.5 million people worldwide.[14] But what would that number be if it was a more infectious and lethal virus?

SARS has a death rate of 15%[15], MERS has a death rate of 35%[16], while Ebola has a death rate of 50%.[17] Other recent viruses, such as the H5N1 and H7N9 avian flus that originated in Chinese poultry farms, killed over a third of people infected.[18] HIV was a death sentence for 15 years until a drug treatment was found. Covid-19 has a death rate of 1.4%.[19] Almost everyone survives it.

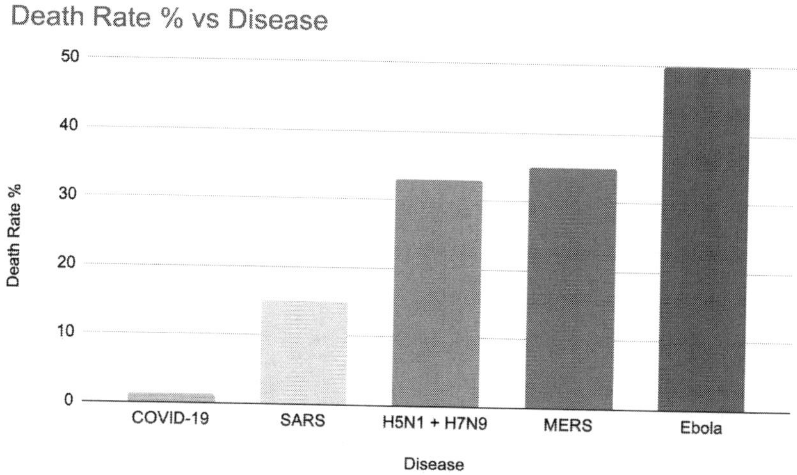

So, while it might not feel like a blessing, Mother Nature has been pretty kind to us on this occasion. We have been given an opportunity and life-saving lesson if we are humble enough to listen and learn. Covid-19 has shown us that a pandemic can very quickly become global, and that our food systems are in large part to blame. But it also demonstrated we can adapt and change our behaviors when faced with a global emergency.

The question is not whether we will have another pandemic, but when. If we continue to consume animals, it is only a matter of time before it happens again, and there's a strong risk the next virus will be more virulent, more lethal and more transmissible. What's more, we may not have any tools left to combat a pandemic.

Why? Because there is more to the problem than simply encroaching on natural ecosystems and closing the gap between virus reservoirs and humans. The drugs and methods used on industrial animal farms are also part of the problem.

ANTIBIOTIC RESISTANCE

Not only are these pandemics and zoonotic threats multiplying, but controlling them is becoming more complicated. Antibiotics are no longer as effective as they once were. The invention of penicillin (the first modern antibiotic) in 1928 changed world history, and provided us with the ability to prevent bacterial infections. But the effectiveness and easy access to antibiotics has led to their overuse, and as a result, some bacteria have built up resistance.

In its Antimicrobial Resistance Global Report, the World Health Organization states that antimicrobial resistance is a widespread "serious threat [that] is no longer a prediction for the future, it is happening right now in every region of the world and has the potential to affect anyone, of any age, in any country."[20]

Antibiotics have been over-used and exploited, mostly by commercial livestock farmers, both to prevent the spread of disease in dirty, overcrowded feedlots, and to increase animal size, meat production and profits.

Although the FDA banned using medically important antibiotics as growth promoters in 2017[21], the quantity of antibiotics sold for food-producing animals has increased.[22] In 2020, 160,000 tons of antibiotics were fed to farm animals. If the current trends continue, this number will grow to 200,000 tons by 2030.[23] In many countries, 80% of the total consumption of antibiotics is in the animal sector.[24] Consequently, we are seeing the rise of antibiotic-resistant superbugs.

Another vicious cycle has developed where our current food system creates the perfect conditions to support viruses that are putting us all under threat, while also weakening the tools we have to prevent pandemics and fight infectious disease.

It is a disaster waiting to happen.

Or rather, it is already happening. Some antibiotics given to farm animals, including penicillin and tetracycline, are the same as the ones used to treat humans. People who eat meat, dairy and poultry are exposed to both antibiotic-resistant bacteria and low doses of antibiotic residues in these animal products, which results in the drugs not working as effectively.[25] The CDC's report on Antibiotic Resistance Threats in the United States, published in 2019, revealed that more than 2.8 million antibiotic resistant infections happen every year in the US, and more than 35,000 people die as a result.[26]

"A lack of effective antibiotics is as serious a security threat as a sudden and deadly disease outbreak. Strong, sustained action across all sectors is vital if we are to turn back the tide of antimicrobial resistance and keep the world safe."

Dr. Tedros Adhanom Ghebreyesus,
Director-General of WHO, 2017[27]

The Covid-19 pandemic has shone a light on our global food systems—its dangers, failings and blind spots. This offers us a once-in-a-lifetime opportunity. Meat is kept artificially cheap, but how cheap is it if it causes millions of deaths and global lockdowns, as Covid is doing? We are being called to question our lifestyle choices and move towards a global food system that stops the spread of zoonotic diseases. One based on plants rather than animals.

Interestingly, a shift away from meat and towards plants is also an absolute must when it comes to our individual health.

"The world is heading towards a post-antibiotic era, in which many common infections will no longer have a cure and, once again, kill unabated.

No action today means no cure tomorrow.

At a time of multiple calamities in the world, we cannot allow the loss of essential medicines—essential cures for many millions of people—to become the next global crisis."

Dr Margaret Chan,
Director-General WHO[28]

COMPARISON BETWEEN NON-COMMUNICABLE DISEASES (CAUSED BY WESTERN DIET) AND COVID

Deaths from Covid 2019 to 2022: 6.57 million people.[29]

Deaths from noncommunicable diseases (lifestyle diseases): 41 million people each year. This equates to 71% of all deaths globally.

Top four causes of death:[30]

- **Cardiovascular disease**: 17.9 million deaths annually
- **Cancer**: 9.3 million deaths annually
- **Chronic respiratory diseases**: 4.1 million deaths annually
- **Diabetes**: 1.5 million deaths annually

ZOONOTIC DISEASE[31]

A zoonotic disease (also known as zoonosis) is a disease caused by an infectious agent (such as bacteria, fungi, virus or parasite) that has jumped from an animal to a human.

Examples of zoonotic diseases:

- Anthrax (grazing herbivores like cattle, sheep, goats, horses, camels and pigs)
- Bird flu (wild birds and domesticated birds like chickens)
- Bovine spongiform encephalopathy or mad cow disease, BSE (cattle)
- Covid-19 (suspected: bats, felines, raccoon dogs, minks)
- Cysticercosis (pigs and cattle)
- Ebola virus (monkeys, fruit bats, gorillas, chimpanzees)
- HIB (non-human primates)
- Leprosy (armadillos, monkeys, rabbits, mice)
- Lyme disease (deer, wolves, birds, dogs, rodents, rabbits)
- Q fever (livestock and other domestic animals)
- Rabies (dogs, bats, monkeys, raccoons, foxes, cattle, goats, sheep, horses, mongooses)
- Rift valley fever (livestock, buffaloes, camels)
- SARS (bats, civets)
- Smallpox (monkeys or horses)
- Swine influenza (pigs)
- Toxoplasmosis (cats, livestock, poultry)

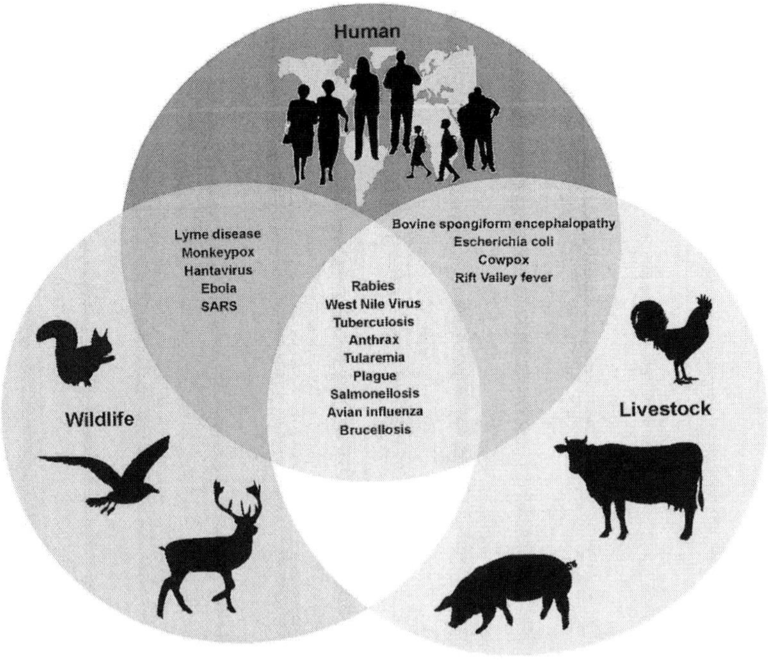

PERSONAL HEALTH

"So I am living without fats, without meat, without fish, but am feeling quite well this way. It always seems to me that man was not born to be a carnivore."

Albert Einstein in 1954 at age 75.[32]

THE MEAT INDUSTRY AND CHRONIC DISEASE

Even if we put to one side the ominous clouds of pandemics and superbugs gathering on our increasingly polluted horizon, we cannot escape the tangible reality that animal products are undeniably not good for us. Eating meat is associated with a higher risk of non-communicable or lifestyle diseases, like cancer, heart disease, diabetes, obesity and even Alzheimer's. While these are experienced individually, these are also, in a sense, global epidemics caused by our meat-centric diets.

Diet and disease are obviously linked. I always say that every time you eat, you are either feeding disease or fighting it. It may be cliché to say "food is medicine," but it is also a truism that could prolong your life. The key to your health is at the end of your fork! It's an incredibly powerful realization when you discover you hold the keys to your wellbeing and longevity.

In this section, I want to briefly demonstrate how meat, fish, and dairy impact our health. We have been fed a lie - that animal products are necessary for our wellbeing.

If we are serious about living a healthy life, then we need to debunk the lies, expose the marketing misinformation, and open up to the latest findings.

As we leave those long years of Covid restrictions behind, this is our opportunity to rethink and create our best lives.

CHRONIC INFLAMMATION - THE ROOT OF THE ISSUE

To understand the impact of the standard Western diet[33] on health, it is important to understand the process of inflammation in the body. There are two types of inflammation: acute and chronic. One is beneficial and helps the body heal. The other sets the scene for chronic disease.

Acute inflammation is short-lived and part of the body's tools for healing. It is designed to help you recover from injury or illness, by neutralizing a virus or reducing the movement in a sprained ankle. If you injure yourself or come into contact with toxins, your immune system jumps into action and releases cytokines (these are immune molecules that pass messages between cells) and white blood cells to deal with the issue. Once the problem has been dealt with, your immune system switches off its defenses, and the symptoms of acute inflammation disappear. The swelling subsides and all is well.

Chronic inflammation is acute inflammation that does not go away. Your immune system automatically launches an inflammatory response when it is faced with a threat. In other words, when it is faced with something that should not be in your body. It is supposed to flare up, deal with the problem, and go away. But when you are constantly exposed to toxins and pathogens, your immune system is on constant high alert.

The result is chronic inflammation. Your body's inflammatory response does not switch off and can begin to damage healthy cells, tissues and organs. Over time, this leads to DNA damage, cellular dysfunction and internal scarring. And this in turn leads to the development of several chronic diseases.

Chronic inflammation makes it harder for your immune system to do its job. It is a symptom of an immune system that no longer knows what to respond to. Think of your immune system as your body's special forces team. This team patrols your body, identifying threats and dealing with them. When chronic inflammation is present, these special forces never have a moment to switch off. Therefore, they are not as effective and eventually begin making mistakes that damage the body and make it more prone to disease.

Researchers from the National Institute of Health found that worldwide, three out of every five people die of diseases caused by chronic inflammation. These include cardiovascular disease, stroke, chronic respiratory disease, cancer, obesity and diabetes.[34] Chronic inflammation also makes it harder for your body to fight a virus.

It is not a coincidence that people already struggling with chronic inflammation or related diseases are more prone to getting Covid or dying of it. When it comes to keeping your immune system strong, avoiding foods that cause chronic inflammation is key.

Certain foods cause a temporary (or acute) inflammatory response. When these foods are eaten regularly, this temporary inflammation can become chronic. The standard Western diet[35] is to blame—high in inflammatory processed foods and low in anti-inflammatory whole foods.

Basically, we are eating foods laden with chemicals and not eating enough foods that contain immune-supporting nutrients. Meat and dairy play a big part here, because they contain residues of animal medicines and are known to trigger an immune response.

Another way eating meat increases the likelihood of chronic inflammation is that it impacts the composition of the gut's microbiome, which in turn affects how the immune system works. A high intake of red and processed meat can decrease the digestive system's mucosal layer, making it more permeable to bacteria and pathogens. The immune system reacts to these pathogens by launching an inflammatory response.[36]

When it comes to dairy, the problem lies in what else is present in milk. As mentioned earlier, dairy cows are made to provide twice the amount of milk they would naturally produce. Because of this, they contract something called mastitis. Mastitis is a painful inflammatory condition that affects the mammary glands. Healthy milk from healthy cows contains under 100,000 somatic cells per milliliter. Somatic cells are white blood cells, in other words: pus. A count of 200,000 somatic cells per milliliter indicates there is an infection.

The industry is legally allowed to sell milk that contains 750,000 somatic cells per milliliter.[37] Not only is this a gross admission that dairy cows are sick, it also means the milk you buy from the supermarket is likely to make you sick too. The immune system responds to these somatic cells in the same way as it would an invader, by increasing levels of inflammation.

I'm not saying meat and dairy are the only cause of chronic inflammation and illness. High sugar foods, artificial trans-fats from hydrogenated oils, refined carbohydrates, pesticide residues, pollutants, stress, smoking and excess alcohol can also trigger and maintain chronic inflammation. However, meat and dairy are a big part of the Western diet,[38] and studies show that people who eat this type of diet have a higher risk of chronic disease.

The problem is on our plate and so is the answer.

Plant-based diets help lower inflammation levels thanks to the antioxidants found in fruits and vegetables. A whole food plant-based diet contains sixty-four times more inflammation-busting antioxidants compared to the standard American diet.[39]

OBESITY

Obesity is defined as excessive body fat that causes a health risk. A body mass index (BMI) of over 25 is considered overweight, a BMI of over 30 is considered obese.

High BMI and elevated fasting blood sugar are the two most important health risk factors in the United States. Put simply, the number one cause of death in the USA is the Western diet.[40]

We have become our own worst enemies and our own biggest threat. Today more people die of excess sugar consumption than they do from war or terrorism. More people will die from over consumption than starvation. And the meat industry is involved in both extremes.

> *"For the first time in history, you are your worst enemies. Fewer people died in 2017 due to UN violence than due to obesity, car accidents and suicides.*
>
> *Statistically, you have a greater chance of killing yourself than any soldier or terrorist. Sugar is a greater danger than gunpowder. You are more likely to die of drinking too much cola than being blown up by Al-Qaeda."*
>
> **Yuval Noah Harari, Author of Sapiens**[41]

Obesity rates have tripled since 1975. The latest statistics from the World Health Organization show that almost two billion adults worldwide are overweight or obese.[42] In the United States, obesity rates went from 30.1% in 1999 to 42.4% in 2017.[43]

Chronic inflammation and obesity go hand in hand. That's because the accumulation of excessive fat stimulates the release of inflammatory chemicals, which predispose the body to be in a pro-inflammatory state. What's more, high levels of body fat reduce the production of adiponectin, a hormone that helps regulate glucose levels and break down fatty acids, thereby making obesity harder to overcome.[44]

Interestingly, meat-centric diets have also been touted as an answer to the obesity crisis. We had the Atkins' diet in the 90s, and the modern version, the keto diet. Centered around eating animal proteins and avoiding carbohydrates, this regime has grown in popularity in recent years. Yes, it can lead to temporary weight loss. But not as much long-term weight loss as going vegan.

In January 2021, the journal Nature Medicine published a study that compared the effects of an animal-based ketogenic diet versus a plant-based diet. The results were clear. Participants who ate a carbohydrate-rich, plant-based diet ate more food, but lost body fat and retained muscle. While those who followed a keto diet ate less food, but retained fat while losing muscle. The researchers attributed these results to the fact that plant foods contain more fiber.[45]

TYPE 2 DIABETES

Diabetes is another worldwide epidemic. In 2019, 473 million adults worldwide were diabetic[46] and this disease caused an estimated 1.5 million deaths.[47]

Type 2 diabetes is a condition where the pancreas does not produce enough insulin (a hormone that regulates blood sugar) or where the body cannot use the insulin effectively. As a result, blood sugar levels keep rising, and this leads to serious damage to many of the body's systems, particularly nerves and blood vessels. Being diabetic also increases the risk of heart attacks and strokes.[48]

You might be wondering what diabetes, a disease centered around blood sugar, has to do with meat. According to a review of studies published in The American Journal of Clinical Nutrition, eating red meat increases the risk of diabetes. Just one 3.5 ounces (99 gram) serving of meat increases a person's risk of type 2 diabetes by 19%.[49] One of the reasons for this is meat's high content of heme-iron.[50]

Type 2 diabetes also increases levels of chronic inflammation. High levels of glucose in the blood cause the formation of advanced glycation agents, which initiate oxidative stress—a condition where there are more free radicals in the body than there are antioxidant defenses.

In other words, there are more damaging molecules circulating in your body than there are molecules that can defend your body against the damage. This causes a further increase in inflammation that makes it harder for your cells to respond to insulin. It's a vicious cycle.

The solution for more and more diabetics is to switch to a plant-based diet, one that includes plenty of vegetables, plant proteins like beans, nuts, seeds, whole grains and fruit. A 74-week study, published in the American Journal of Clinical Nutrition, found that a plant-based diet controlled blood sugar three times more effectively than a traditional type 2 diabetes diet that limited calories and carbohydrates.[51] The reason for this is that plants contain plenty of fiber, which adds bulk to meals without increasing blood sugar levels, helps keep you fuller for longer, and provides nutrients for healthy gut flora.

Even more exciting, scientists have found that a vegan diet can reverse type 2 diabetes. In another study, diabetes patients following a personalized whole food plant-based diet protocol were able to come off medication after 20 weeks.[52]

CARDIOVASCULAR DISEASE AND CHOLESTEROL:
Strokes, Heart Attacks, Heart Disease, and Heart Failure

Cardiovascular disease is an umbrella term that covers disorders of the heart and blood vessels—high blood pressure (hypertension), heart attacks (coronary heart disease), and strokes (cerebrovascular disease). Cholesterol is the risk factor in all these disorders because it causes plaque deposits that narrow blood vessels, while also increasing levels of inflammation.

A study published by the United States' National Institutes of Health found that eating meat triples the amount of the chemicals related to heart disease. Gut bacteria from something called trimethylamine N-oxide (TMAO) as a byproduct of digesting meat. Research shows that TMAO enhances the formation of cholesterol deposits on blood vessel walls. It also impedes normal clotting responses, increasing the risk of heart attacks and strokes.

But the study also found that levels of TMAO were reversible. When participants switched to plant proteins for a month, their TMAO levels decreased significantly.[53]

Cardiovascular disease is a lifestyle disease. It is caused by an excessive intake of saturated fat and cholesterol. These fatty substances build up in blood vessels as plaque, impeding blood flow. The biggest sources of saturated fat and cholesterol in the Western diet[54] are dairy and meat. Incidentally, plant-based diets are very low in saturated fat and dietary cholesterol. It is incredible to think that even though this is accepted scientifically and common knowledge in the medical community, the United States dietary guidelines continue to promote meat products and a daily intake of three cups of dairy.

A review published in the Journal of the American Medical Association analyzed six studies and found that for every 0.01 ounces (300 milligrams) of dietary cholesterol consumed per day, the risk of cardiovascular disease increased by 17%, while the risk of all-cause mortality increased by 18%.[55]

To give you an idea of what that means in terms of food, an egg contains around 0.007 ounces (212 milligrams) of cholesterol, 3.5 ounces (99 grams) of shrimp contains 0.0068 ounces (194 milligrams) of cholesterol, and 3.5 ounces (99 grams) of ground beef contains around 0.003 ounces (90 milligrams) of cholesterol.[56]

Heart disease is the top cause of death globally. In the United States, a person dies of cardiovascular disease every thirty-six seconds. Heart disease causes one in every four deaths.[57] And it is an absolutely preventable illness.

If we made healthier lifestyle choices, we could prevent most cases. In 2017, researchers reviewed forty-nine studies comparing plant-based diets with omnivorous diets. Their findings? Plant-based diets lowered total cholesterol levels by 15-30%.[58]

A study published by the Journal of the American Heart Association followed over 12,000 adults for a period of twenty-five years and analyzed their dietary data. It found that the more plant foods were consumed and the fewer animal products were consumed, the lower the risk of cardiovascular disease. In fact, plant-based diets reduced the risk of heart disease by 16% and the risk of cardiovascular death by 32%.[59] The same study found something else that is relevant here—eating fish and low-fat dairy (both generally considered to be superfoods and essential for good health) did not provide any benefits for cardiovascular health.

We have the solution at our fingertips, and we've known about it for years. We need to harness the healing power of plants.

CANCER

There is no easy way to talk about Cancer. I feel like it haunts most of our families in the developed nations. This is an epidemic that has touched all of our lives. Worldwide, an estimated 19.3 million new cancer cases, and almost 10 million cancer deaths happened in 2020. The global cancer burden is expected to almost double to 28.4 million by 2040.[60]

I remember when the World Health Organization ruffled feathers in 2015 when they published their Meat and Cancer report. The report examined over 800 peer-reviewed studies and found a correlation between the consumption of red meat (beef, pork, veal, lamb, mutton, horse, goat) and processed meat (all meats that have been transformed through salting, curing, fermenting, smoking, and other processes to enhance flavor and shelf life, such as hot dogs, sausages, corned beef, beef jerky, canned meat, and meat sauces) and the incidence of colorectal cancers.

On the strength of the data, the International Agency for Research on Cancer classified red meat as a Group 2A Carcinogen (probably carcinogenic to humans) and processed meat as a Group 1A Carcinogen (carcinogenic to humans).[61] To put this into perspective, tobacco is a Group 1A carcinogen, and nobody is in doubt of its effects.

The report found that every 1.7 ounces (50 gram) portion of processed meat increases the risk of colorectal cancer by 18% and that every 3.5 ounces (100 gram) portion of red meat increases the risk of colorectal cancer by 17%.[62]

Though groundbreaking, this report caused a quick uproar before being relegated to the mountain of information governments choose to ignore when it comes to their health policies and nutritional guidelines.

While the WHO's report could show a correlation between meat-eating and cancer, it fell short of demonstrating causation—the way meat causes cells to mutate remained unclear. However, this has changed in June 2021.

A new study published in the journal Cancer Discovery has identified specific patterns of DNA damage triggered by meat-centric diets. This damage, called alkylation, was significantly associated with processed and unprocessed red meat. The specific compounds involved are nitroso compounds (which are made from heme-iron and are plentiful in red meat), and nitrates (often found in processed meat). Patients with the highest levels of alkylation damage had a 47% greater risk of colorectal cancer deaths, compared with patients with lower levels of damage.[63]

Another link between meat and cancer was explained in a study by the Proceedings of the National Academy of Sciences of the United States of America. Researchers discovered that the human immune system attacks a sugar in red meat called Neu5Gc, causing chronic inflammation that can eventually trigger cancer. According to the lead author of the study, "red meat is great, if you want to live to 45."[64]

There's more. A new study of over 300,000 women found that a diet high in meat, dairy and processed sugar increases the risk of breast cancer by 12%. The research, carried out by the World Health Organization, the Imperial College in London, and the Catalan Institute of Oncology, concluded that the reason for the spike in cancer risk was these foods' inflammatory properties.[65]

Again, the answer is all around us and always has been—a plant-based diet.

A review of studies published in the journal Clinical Reviews in Food and Nutrition found that a vegan diet can reduce the risk of cancer by at least 15%. The researchers concluded that the benefits are due to the fact that plant foods are high in fiber, antioxidants, and vitamins that support the immune system and protect against cell mutations.[66]

Another study, this time published in the Journal of Unexplored Medical Data, found that a plant-based diet can protect against the fifteen leading causes of death, including many cancers and chronic diseases, such as diabetes, heart disease and obesity.[67] It goes on to conclude that adopting a vegan diet centered around whole, natural foods is "a simple and cost-effective intervention that can be used alone to prevent disease or adjunct with conventional treatment when the disease is already present."

Profoundly simple and life-changing knowledge. All we need to do is start putting it into practice.

DEMENTIA AND ALZHEIMER'S

Our cognitive health is a choice we make with every bite we take.

Research shows that the saturated fats found in meat, dairy, processed foods, and fast foods increases the risk of cognitive decline. This is because these foods increase chronic inflammation, and inflammation causes the build-up of plaques that lead to cognitive impairment.

Today, there are over 40 million people suffering from Alzheimer's, a condition characterized by amyloid plaques in the brain that impact mood, memory, and motor skills. People with Alzheimer's struggle to reason, experience personality changes, suffer a gradual decline in memory, and develop problems speaking and moving. It devastates families as they lose the final years of their elderly loved ones into the fog of dementia.

By 2050, it is estimated Alzheimer's will affect 150 million people. That means that as many of you, my readers, get older, you will likely either suffer from it or know a friend or loved one who has it. If you live to 85 or older, your chances of getting it are one in two.[68]

Pretty grim stuff. But there is increasing and exciting evidence showing that dementia is not an inevitable part of getting older. It can be prevented with the right lifestyle choices, particularly what we choose to put on our plate.

A study published in the journal Innovation in Aging examined the association between a plant-based diet and dementia risk in over 12,000 people. It found that vegetarians had a lower risk of dementia compared to people eating an omnivorous diet.[69] That's because a plant-based diet, rich in antioxidants and healthy fats, helps protect brain health. In fact, research shows that a diet based around plants can reduce the risk of Alzheimer's by more than 50%.[70]

In parts of the world where people eat a predominantly plant-based diet, for example, the Greek island of Ikaria (one of the world's Blue Zones, renowned for its inhabitants commonly reaching their 100th birthday), people live on average eight to ten years longer than Americans with almost no cases of dementia. In Ikaria, you have less than a 10% chance of getting Alzheimer's.[71]

BUT FISH IS HEALTHY, ISN'T IT?

Many people stop eating meat, but keep eating fish, believing it is one of the healthiest sources of protein and brain-friendly fats. We need essential fatty acids for our brain, as well as our cell membranes and nervous system. They are also important for regulating blood pressure, the immune system and inflammation. They're called "essential" because the body does not make them itself, and we must obtain them from food.

There are three Omega-3 fatty acids: alpha-linolenic acid (ALA), which is found in plants such as flaxseed, which the body converts into eicosapentaenoic acid (EPA) and docosahexaenoic (DHA). Fish obtain their ALA Omega-3 from algae and then convert it to EPA and DHA. This conversion can be difficult for the human body, which is why some people insist that oily fish is essential to obtain enough Omega-3. But this is incorrect.

Research from Cochrane finds that EPA and DHA from oily fish or fish oil supplements have little or no effect on heart health.[72] ALA from plant foods, on the other hand, did slightly reduce the risk of cardiovascular illness. A review of studies published in the British Journal of Nutrition found that ALA from plant foods helps reduce the risk of heart disease.[73] In other words, plant-based Omega-3 is better for you. Just like protein, it is more efficient to get Omega-3 straight from the source (plants) instead of the middle man (animals).

As we learn more about fish and fish oils, things go from bad to worse. It turns out they could do more harm than good.

The first issue comes from methyl-mercury, an environmental pollutant found in fish. A study in Eastern Finland found that men who ate the most fish had the highest levels of mercury, and an increased risk of cardiovascular death.[74]

Our oceans are polluted, not just by mercury, but also by polychlorinated biphenyls and dioxins, which are known neurotoxins. These pollutants accumulate in fish, and this cancels out any potential benefits from their Omega-3.

Pollutants aside, shellfish like mussels and oysters accumulate bacteria and viruses from their environment. One of these viruses is norovirus, which is one of the most common causes of food poisoning. Another is hepatitis E, which spreads via a fecal-oral route. Livestock, such as pigs, can act as reservoirs of hepatitis E. High levels of the virus have been detected in wastewater and manure from industrial pig farms. Animal waste enters waterways, it can then accumulate in shellfish, and end up on your plate.

Farmed fish is no better. The farms are overcrowded, the fish are stressed, unhealthy, and pumped with antibiotics, anti-parasite treatments, disinfectants, and feed additives. What's more, farmed fish usually contain less Omega-3 because they are fed a diet rich in Omega-6, as well as fishmeal and fish oils. You read that right—wild fish are caught to feed farmed fish (and livestock). Almost 90% of some species of fish have been depleted, all this because of the myth of brain-healthy fish.[75]

The solution? Eating plant foods that are naturally rich in ALA Omega-3, such as walnuts, flaxseeds and chia seeds, or taking an algal-based vegan Omega-3 supplement that provides EPA and DHA without the pollutants or viruses.

BUT DAIRY IS HEALTHY, ISN'T IT?

In a word, no. Let me tell you why.

Dairy products are one of the top sources of saturated fat and cholesterol-raising fat in the American diet.[76]

Dairy contains IGF-1 (insulin-like growth factor 1), which has been associated with an increased risk of cancer, diabetes, and chronic inflammation.[77]

Dairy can increase the risk of breast cancer by up to 80%.[78]
Dairy can increase the risk of prostate cancer by up to 65%.[79]

"Cows' milk protein may be the single most significant chemical carcinogen to which humans are exposed."

T Colin Campbell,
Professor of Nutritional Biochemistry at Cornell University[80]

We are told dairy is a superfood, that we need it for our bones, that it "does the body good". But the truth is it makes us sick. A recent study by the International Journal of Epidemiology studied 53,000 women over eight years and found that those who drank 2-3 glasses of milk (the current USDA recommended amount) had a 70-80% increased risk of breast cancer. Women who replaced cow's milk with soy milk were 32% less likely to have breast cancer.[81] Another study involving over 1 million participants noted that a high intake of dairy products was associated with a 65% increased risk of prostate cancer. Men following a plant-based diet had a 36% lower risk.[82]

Milk is good for your bones. I heard my mother say it a hundred times. It seeps into your thinking and becomes an unquestioned belief. Now my sisters are feeding their children cow's milk. In North America, we drink large glasses of milk every day under the assumption that it will keep our bones strong. But here's an interesting question—why do women who drink milk have a higher risk of brittle bones?

American women are the biggest consumers of dairy, and yet they have one of the highest rates of osteoporosis in the world. A study by the US National Dairy Council compared postmenopausal women who drank three 8 ounces (240 milliliters) glasses of skimmed milk a day for two years with women who drank no milk. The women who drank dairy lost bone at twice the rate of women who didn't.[83]

We need calcium. But we do not need dairy. There is nothing in dairy that we cannot get from plants. You can get calcium from leafy greens (like Swiss chard, broccoli and kale), as well as winter squash, almonds, and tofu. And calcium in certain plant foods is more bio-available than calcium in dairy.

According to the Harvard School of Public Health, dairy products have a calcium bioavailability of around 30%. This means that if a cup of milk contains 300 milligrams of calcium, the body will only absorb around 100 milligrams of calcium. On the other hand, calcium from bok choi (a leafy green similar to Swiss chard) has a bioavailability of 50%.

One cup of bok choi contains 160 milligrams of calcium, or 80 milligrams of bioavailable calcium, which makes a cup of bok choi comparable to a cup of milk in terms of calcium content. However, leafy greens also contain fiber and antioxidants that support health, whereas a cup of milk contains saturated fat that promotes disease.[84]

THE BLUE ZONES: ANOTHER WAY IS POSSIBLE

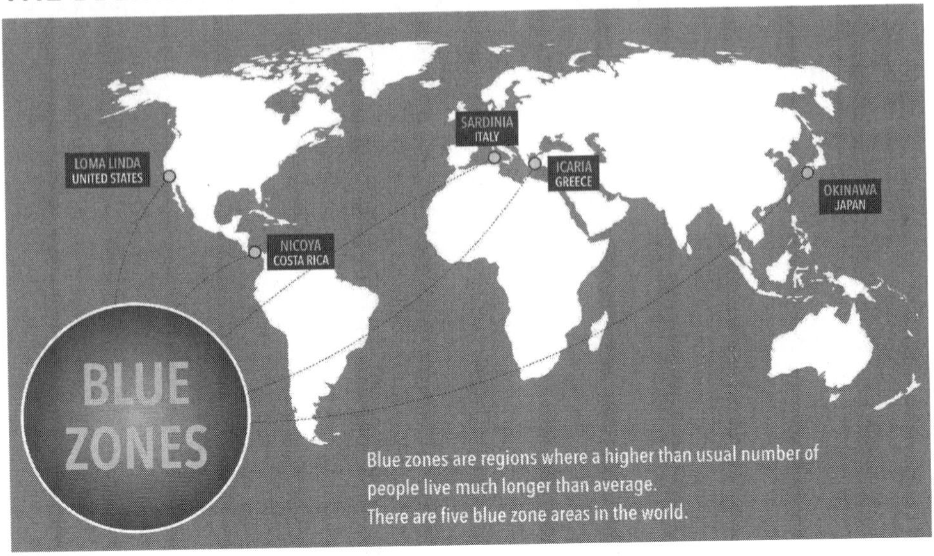

The Blue Zones are five remote regions in Europe, Latin America, Asia, and the United States, which stand out for having the highest number of centenarians in the world. While each region has its own unique diet, they have one thing in common—they're very light on meat and heavy on plants.

Dan Buettner, explorer and founder of the Blue Zones, examined and inventoried each region's diets to identify the pillars of their longevity. He found that their diet consists almost entirely of minimally processed plant food, foods like whole grains, greens, nuts, tubers and beans. People there eat meat on average five times a month.

What that means in practice is that one meal every week contains meat—everything else is plant-based. They drink mostly water, herbal tea, coffee, and some wine. They drink little or no cow's milk, and fizzy drinks hardly ever feature. As a result, inhabitants of the Blue Zones live longer, healthier, happier lives than people living elsewhere.

Unfortunately, as globalization spreads, even these areas are falling prey to the scourge of the Western diet.[85] Now, the gap between life spans in the Blue Zones and the rest of the world is gradually closing.[86] The arrival of processed foods, animal products and fast foods has pushed up the rate of chronic disease, even in the Blue Zones.[87] While this is bad news, it does at least show us the link between meat and disease and offers us a clear path towards a healthier way of life.

*"And there you have it:
The vast majority of the calories eaten in the traditional diets in the blue zones come from plant-based whole foods. Grains, greens, nuts, and beans are the four pillars of every longevity diet on Earth."*
Dan Buettner, founder of the Blue Zones[88]

When it comes to driving forces for veganism, health is often at the forefront. It was for me. Covid has only placed a spotlight on a bigger problem that has so far remained hidden and rarely talked about. But it has highlighted something else—that when needed, the whole world can mobilize against a disease.

Something we do almost without thinking—eating meat—is leading to the health crises we face today. And the way we produce meat and dairy opens the door to pandemics like Covid. If we don't adapt, we will likely see further global pandemics. And next time we might end up with something more virulent and deadly.

The Western diet[89] is also in great part to blame for the obesity, cancer, and heart disease epidemics that kill millions of people every year. But both pandemics and chronic diseases are preventable: a plant-based diet is the solution we have been waiting for. By coming on this journey, you are part of the solution!

"We have just been doing some calculations looking at the question of how much could we reduce mortality by shifting towards a healthy, more plant-based diet, not necessarily totally vegan, and our estimates are that about one-third of deaths could be prevented."
Dr Walter Willett, Professor of epidemiology and nutrition at Harvard Medical School, 2018[90]

8

SOCIAL INJUSTICE

THE IMPACT OF MEAT ON COMMUNITIES

"Injustice anywhere is a threat to justice everywhere."
Martin Luther King Jr

While researching this book while in isolation during the long lockdowns, several shocking reports came out exposing the terrible conditions of slaughterhouses in both the US and Europe. Finally we were seeing behind the tall walls of slaughterhouses and "meat packing" factories and I knew I had to investigate further and include it here as one of the driving forces that make veganism such an urgent and essential movement.

How our modern food system impacts society is an overlooked topic and is usually brushed under the carpet. It's not on any school syllabuses and the meat industry works hard to keep us in the dark.

It's time to bring these important civil liberties issues into the light.

So, what does animal agriculture have to do with social issues?

A lot, as it happens.

Today's industrial meat industry doesn't just harm your personal health, animals, and the environment—it also causes huge suffering to humans within the system.

FEEDING FAMINE

If modern industrial food production can feed the world, why are people going hungry? Why is famine still happening?

Animal foods are not an energy-efficient way of eating. A report by Compassion in World Farming found that for every 100 calories of human-edible crops fed to livestock, we get only 17-30 calories of animal protein. It is not just a wasteful use of grain crops, but also the resources (land, water, energy) used to grow them.[1] For every 2 pounds (1 kilo) of animal protein, livestock is fed almost 12 pounds (6 kilos) of plant protein.

Famine is a growing problem. We find ourselves in the ridiculous situation where poorer developing countries need to export their harvests to rich countries instead of feeding their starving population. Many post-colonial or emerging nations need to grow these "cash crops" to pay off crippling debts at the expense of providing basic nourishment for the indigenous people.

We are part of this system that's taking the food out of their hands.

According to a recent analysis by the United Nations' World Food Program, 41 million people are currently teetering on the edge of famine, compared to 27 million people two years ago. This is not an unsolvable problem. A report by Cornell University found that the United States alone could feed 800 million people with grain that livestock eat.[2]

Clearly, the industrial animal industry is not feeding the world; quite the opposite in fact. But solutions are at our fingertips.

Industrial farms do not produce most of the world's food. There are more than 570 million farms in the world, and 90% of these are run by individuals or families. These small farms produce 80% of the world's food. According to the United Nations' FAO, investment in smallholder production is the most urgent and promising method for combating world hunger while minimizing the ecological impact of industrial agriculture.[3]

But even more relevant here is the fact that animal proteins are an inefficient use of resources; plants are fed to the animals instead of feeding people. The best way forward is directness. Let's cut out the middle-man and go straight to plant power!

DRIVING INEQUALITY

According to population forecasts, the world will be home to almost 10 billion people by 2050. Food production would have to increase by 50% to accommodate this. But, as we saw in the environment section, that would be a disaster for the planet. If food production increases along with the current trends, we would require a landmass twice the size of India. This would spell the end for many of the world's remaining forests and wild areas, releasing the carbon stored there, and accelerating climate collapse.

Climate change is a social issue as well as an ecological one. In 2020, 55 million people were forced to move from their countries because of extreme weather conditions.[4] The majority of these people find themselves in an even more precarious position. Uprooted from their home, they struggle to settle in countries where they are met with hostility and where they face financial hardship.

While climate change is now having an impact on developed countries, the countries that have so far fared the worst are low to middle-income countries. Natural disasters in Asia, Africa, Latin America and the Caribbean have cost over $108 billion in economic losses. The food production loss in these countries equates to 6.9 trillion calories per year (that's the annual calorie intake for 7 million adults).[5]

LOCAL SLAVERY: JOBS AND COMMUNITIES

According to an economic impact study commissioned by the North American Meat Institute, the meat and poultry industry creates 5.4 million jobs in the United States, with an estimated 527,019 jobs in production and packing, importing, sales, packaging and distribution.[6][7] But the kind of jobs we are talking about here are not jobs anyone would want, given the choice.

I've never heard anyone ever say that working in a meat-packing plant or slaughterhouse was their dream job. Who in their right mind would want to spend 10–12 hours a day killing animals, chopping carcasses, or cleaning blood, guts and shit off the kill floor, for minimum wage. This kind of work attracts people who have little choice in the matter.

In the United States, it is estimated that almost 40% of factory farm workers are illegal immigrants. These workers are vulnerable to exploitation. They are more likely to accept low wages and hazardous working conditions, and they are less likely to unionize. The meat industry capitalizes on their situation to abuse their rights. Human Rights Watch describes slaughterhouse work in the United States as a human rights crime.[8]

According to the worker advocacy group Project Protect Food System Workers, many factory farm workers operate dangerous equipment without proper training, making them more vulnerable to injuries and deaths. Like the recent death of a dairy worker who drowned in a manure pit containing the waste of more than 3,000 animals, while operating a manure vacuum truck.[9] He is not the first to suffocate in a waste pit. Many workers who have entered waste pits or "lagoons" to perform maintenance tasks have been asphyxiated by the hydrogen sulfide gas emitted by liquid manure. Unconscious, they quickly drown. Often, these incidents involve more than one person as co-workers attempt to rescue one another.[10]

Factory farmworkers are exposed to hazardous materials, such as particulate matter (from dry fecal matter, feed, animal hair and skin cells, feathers, fungi, dry soil and bacterial endotoxins[11]), ammonia and hydrogen sulfide gases. These are bad enough individually, and when combined, they cause serious health complications. As a result of inhaling this cocktail of chemicals, workers suffer from chronic respiratory disorders, asthma, cardiovascular disorders and premature death.[12]

Nothing slows production. One poultry farmer working for Tyson Foods (the largest meat producer in the US) reported that it is not uncommon for slaughterhouse workers to urinate on the production line or defecate in their pants—they are expected to keep working.[13] This fact is also reported by Oxfam America. Workers are often required to wear diapers because they are not allowed breaks.[14]

Imagine having to hoist live birds and lock them into shackles on a fast-moving line that takes them to the electric stun bath and then the mechanical blade. Workers have to shackle 35 birds a minute. The birds fight back. Once locked in place, the birds empty their bowels. Despite protective coverings, feces from flapping birds get into the workers' eyes, nose, mouth, and ears.[15]

Imagine having to spend your working life among animals that it is your job to abuse—whether that's by debeaking, tail docking, castrating, pushing or prodding them towards the stun gun, or disembowelling them.

Slaughterhouse workers are seven times more likely to suffer repetitive strain injuries than people in other types of work. In the United States, an average of two amputations every week involves slaughterhouse workers. Every month at least one Tyson Foods employee loses a finger or a limb.[16]

For her book Slaughterhouse, Gail Eisnitz, chief investigator for the Humane Farming Association, interviewed slaughterhouse workers equivalent to over two million hours of experience. Without exception, they told her they had beaten, strangled, boiled or dismembered animals alive.

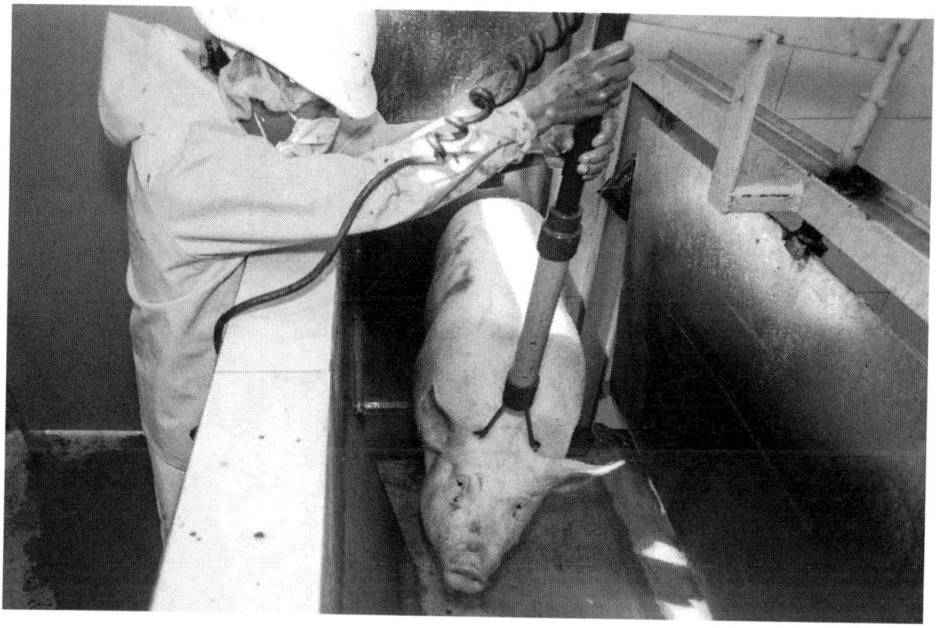

Because of the speed at which employees are required to work, pigs and cattle are routinely skinned while they are still conscious, kicking and shrieking. This isn't just cruel to the animals, but dangerous for the workers too. Cows weigh several thousand pounds and can kick out and debilitate anyone near them.[17]

Much of this is caused by the speed of the production line. Instead of slowing things down, the US government has given the go-ahead to new rules that eliminate production line speed limits at pig slaughterhouses. The USDA said maximum line speeds were an "unnecessary regulatory obstacle to industry innovation." It is unclear how this will help reduce the high number of injuries suffered by meat plant workers.[18] Clearly, what is being protected is profit, not people.

There is often a lot of kickback against factory farmworkers. Footage from undercover animal rights activists that show workers abusing animals makes people, understandably, angry. But these workers are victims of the industry as much as the animals are. They too are being exploited and abused by a system that puts profits over people, animals and the planet.

Working in the meat industry is fraught with physical dangers, but the damage goes deeper. It leads to psychological damage and crime. Several studies show that factory farm workers consistently experience lower physical and psychological wellbeing, as well as an increased risk of negative coping strategies, such as abusing drugs and alcohol.[19]

It isn't surprising.

These employees are hired to kill animals that are largely gentle creatures. Carrying out their job requires workers to disconnect from what they are doing and from the sentient being in front of them. This causes emotional dissonance and leads to domestic violence, social withdrawal, anxiety, drug abuse, and Perpetrator-Induced Traumatic Syndrome, a form of PTSD. This is reflected in crime statistics. A study by criminologist Amy Fitzgerald states that "slaughterhouse employment increases total arrest rates, arrests for violent crimes, arrests for rape, and arrests for other sex offenses in comparison with other industries."[20]

Humans are not predators.
We are not designed to kill.

Animal cruelty is an indicator of a deep mental disturbance.

Robert K. Ressler, who developed profiles of serial killers for the Federal Bureau of Investigation (FBI), states that "murderers very often start out by killing or torturing animals." Studies show that violent or aggressive criminals are more likely to have abused animals as children.

According to a police study in Australia, most sexual homicide offenders have a history of animal cruelty. The school shootings that have been happening more and more frequently in the United States have a common theme—in most cases, the violence started with cruelty to animals.[21]

We've seen how this impacts workers in this industry, but what about us? Doesn't eating meat require us to somehow accept the cruelty that goes on behind closed doors? By accepting these unspoken beliefs, what is that doing to our psyche? We too, like the kill-floor workers, have to switch off the part of our natural, caring, compassionate nature, in order to keep consuming meat and dairy.

IMPACT ON THE COMMUNITY

Living near a slaughterhouse or large factory farm is a nightmare. Here are just some of the problems that nearby communities must endure.

The first is air pollution. CAFOs release large amounts of particulates (especially in dry seasons or dry regions where manure turns to dust), ammonia, hydrogen sulfide, methane and nitrous oxide, among others. These chemicals cause respiratory conditions, some of them are neurotoxic. Hydrogen sulfide poisoning can cause irreversible brain damage.

What's more, studies have found high levels of antibiotics and antibiotic-resistant genes in air samples downwind from feedlots.[22] Huge amounts of animal waste are disposed of by either spraying onto fields or in the air. Facilities can do this without a permit despite the reality of leaks, spills, and runoff.[23]

The second issue is drinking water quality. Phosphorus and nitrogen can leach into drinking water reservoirs, causing a potentially fatal blood disorder called blue baby syndrome.[24] Aside from the serious health implications, just imagine the smell for a moment. Then imagine living beside it for a lifetime!

And thirdly, higher rates of crime. A large statistical analysis by the University of Windsor and Michigan State University found that counties where slaughterhouses are located have four times the national average of violent arrest, and significantly higher rates of alcoholism, domestic abuse, and suicide.[25]

In some states, CAFOs are located in poor and African American communities. For example, in North Carolina, there are seven times more swine CAFOs in areas with the highest percentage of non-Caucasian residents compared with areas with the lowest percentage of non-Caucasian residents. People in these communities cannot afford to move. The proximity of these CAFOs leads to social, economic and health burdens to already disadvantaged communities.[26]

COVID AND THE ANIMAL INDUSTRY: Hotspots and Breakouts

Far from helping to fight the spread of Covid, the meat industry has been capitalizing on this epidemic whilst putting its workforce in danger.

In May 2020, reports found that at least twenty meatpacking workers in the US had died of coronavirus, and over 5,000 had become infected. A wave of meatpacking facility closures swept across the country, most of them operated by the largest food manufacturers in America. As a response, Tyson Foods (the world's second-largest meat processor) took out paid adverts in major newspapers to warn that these closures would lead to a limited supply of their product.

Ever mindful to protect big business, the president of the United States, Donald Trump at the time, used the Defense Production Act to mandate meat processing plants remain open during the pandemic.[27] This move basically elevated meat production to an "essential service" and protected the industry from being liable if their employees catch Covid.[28]

Where there is political will, there is a way. This potential could have been used to shift towards sustainable infrastructure that supports our health and protects the planet. Instead, it was used to prop up an industry that does the opposite.

And so it was that meat packing staff found themselves on the frontline, working in factories that offered no social distancing or ventilation systems to keep them safe. A worker at Koch, another one of America's largest meat processors, alleges the company withholds the details of workers who catch Covid and forces staff to wear the same surgical mask over two or three shifts.[29]

According to Michael Osterhold, an infectious disease epidemiologist, deep cleans and surgical masks are not enough to stop the spread of the virus in meatpacking factories.[30] So while lockdowns have kept us all isolated, Covid hotspots like these stayed open. This is yet another example of the industry's blatant disregard for its workers, and the world at large.

While the meat industry waxes lyrical about its contribution to feeding the world, the truth is that it gobbles up resources that could otherwise be shared with people who need them the most. While it speaks of job opportunities and wealth creation, it creates dead-end, poorly paid jobs and an environment riddled with violence, crime, and pollution.

This is an industry that has as little care for people as it does for animals and the planet. The only way we can stop the cycle is to stop feeding into it.

"Hogs get stressed out pretty easy. If you prod them too much, they have heart attacks. If you get a hog in the chute that's had the shit prodded out of him and has a heart attack or refuses to move, you take a meat hook and hook it into his bunghole. You try to do this by clipping the hipbone. Then you drag him backwards. You're dragging these hogs alive, and a lot of times the meat hook rips out of the bunghole. I've seen hams—thighs—completely ripped open. I've also seen intestines come out. If the hog collapses near the front of the chute, you shove the meat hook into his cheek and drag him forward."

Quote from slaughterhouse worker.

"If all the grain currently fed to livestock in the United States were consumed directly by people, the number of people who could be fed would be nearly 800 million."

David Pimentel, Professor of ecology at Cornell University's College of Agriculture and Life Sciences[31]

"Meat is an inefficient source of nutrition. Chicken is the most efficient form of meat, but still requires 9 calories of energy to produce 1 calorie of meat and 0.2oz (5g) of protein to produce 0.035oz (1g) of protein. Pork is less efficient, requiring 10 calories of feed to produce 1 calorie of meat. If the world adopted an entirely plant-based diet, current agriculture could easily produce enough food to feed the growing population[32]."

We are currently living with the consequences of the standard Western diet[33] and its reliance on animal products: a world of pandemics, chronic disease, climate collapse, and suffering for humans and the creatures we consume.

Although the truth is confronting, all the crises we face today have solutions that we can be a part of.

We can vote for change three times a day.

The remedy is a more conscious, compassionate lifestyle and diet.

9

LIFE ON THE SPECTRUM

A VEGAN ADVENTURE

"It's important to see carnism and veganism on a spectrum."
Dr Melanie Joy, author of
***Why We Eat Pigs, Love Dogs, and Wear Cows*[1]**

Throughout life, we grapple with a range of nuances within most beliefs, viewpoints, or conditions, whether we were mindful of it or not. We are all somewhere on a number of spectrums, for example, mental health, politics and sexuality—all of us fall somewhere between two extremes. Our position on a spectrum is not fixed, but fluid. Take mental health—depending on circumstances, we might feel depressed, but eventually, we can move out of that and into stability, motivation, and enthusiasm.

I believe we should treat our diets similarly, on a spectrum between carnism (and I'll get into this term in a moment), and veganism. As we gain more knowledge and confidence, we are empowered to move along this spectrum, towards a diet that supports a kinder, healthier, more sustainable world. Here we can reach a place where we are more aligned with our core values.

I always say that veganism, like life, is about the journey and not the destination. I celebrate my unique journey and hope to empower others along the spectrum to a place of compassion and alignment. It is a beautiful feeling of confidence and contentment knowing your lifestyle aligns with your ethics and worldview. I have come a long way from my farming life and I would be honored to share this peace with you and inspire real change.

Now that you have identified your unique mix of driving forces, you can jump into the driving seat and start making changes. Moving along the diet spectrum you will find your sweet spot, and your optimum destination. This is where it can seem tricky or overwhelming. Many people balk at labeling themselves vegan, anxious not to be associated with a seemingly extreme or ascetic movement with its fair share of in-fighting and division.

But I have good news. You don't have to shout your veganism from the rooftops. There isn't a secret handshake or a badge you have to wear. You can make this trip uniquely your own. Find your own way and know where to stop when it feels right. You don't even have to go 100% vegan before you start making a difference. Every step along the path towards veganism is a step in the right direction for you, then animals, and the planet.

In fact, I would argue that 100% vegan does not necessarily mean 100% ethical. After all, with the largest global food retailers jumping onto the vegan bandwagon, you could still be contributing to an industry that profits from animal exploitation. The best-known fast-food outlets now have vegan options. While I support increased choice, veganism is about more than just choosing something because it has a vegan label. Veganism is about asking yourself, "how compassionate, sustainable and kind is my choice?"

It is important to forge your own path and set your own speed and course, rather than simply attaching a label. For example, one of my friends is vegan, but she will eat eggs when she house-sits for friends who keep a couple of hens as pets. The hens are happy, loved, cared for, and their eggs are a byproduct of that, rather than industrial farming, and as such they fit her view of conscious, sustainable eating.

Even some of my strictest vegan friends admit they have moments of weakness. You can be a good vegan and have that slice of your grandmother's shortbread at Christmas. There is no right or wrong. It isn't about being the vegan police, but about YOUR transition towards veganism, and being compassionate and tolerant about other people's choices.

As you move along the dietary spectrum, from carnism towards veganism, make the changes from a place of calm and acceptance. Think of this as a great adventure. There can be many steps between those two points. The important thing is not to get to the other side as quickly as possible, but rather to move in that direction, taking the time to integrate changes into your life for the long haul.

Ultimately, you are already on this journey! By diving into the why's behind veganism, you have already stepped towards a more compassionate lifestyle. Trying out this lifestyle is an exciting opportunity to focus and rethink your daily choices in a new way, not a route to personal perfection.

"The perfect is the enemy of the good."
Voltaire

We must accept that "vegan perfection" is unattainable. To be truly and completely ethical would entail living outside of our current economic and social system. As tempting as life in a wooden cabin in the forest may seem, 99.99% of us cannot escape like this—we have to operate in a world where most of our choices have some negative repercussions. Our smartphones, our energy systems, our cars, our shopping malls, our food delivery services all involve some form of exploitation, some form of environmental damage. To accept this is to free yourself from unrealistic expectations. You alone cannot save the world. But your choices do have repercussions. As we saw in the last chapter, the meat industry is responsible for damage on many levels. It is therefore one of the most pressing areas for change. And it's a change that is relatively straightforward to put into practice, especially if you focus on the journey rather than the destination.

You have the power to change the world one meal at a time!

Ta-Da!

Going vegan is easy. After all, it can be stripped back to a simple one-step formula. Here it is: stop buying or using products made from animals. What it boils down to is just saying NO animal products "wherever possible and practical." The original definition from over 75 years ago provides us with the big takeaway, the perfect strategy to protect the planet's future, stop harming animals, and improve our emotional and physical wellbeing. In the next chapter, you will find practical tips and tricks to inspire and empower you to start creating your plant-based life.

But first, let's explore the dietary spectrum.

SPECIESISM: ITS A THING.

The assumption of human superiority alongside the belief that animal species are inferior, leading to the exploitation of animals. Speciesist thinking considers that animals are just a means to human ends.[2]

Carnism: The invisible belief system that conditions us to eat certain animals. The term carnism was coined in 2001 by Melanie Joy, a social psychologist and author of Why We Love Dogs, Eat Pigs and Wear Cows. Central to this ideology is the acceptance that meat-eating is natural, normal, and necessary. Carnism classifies certain species of animals as food and accepts practices towards those animals that would be regarded as unacceptable if applied to other species (which is why people can get very emotional about dog-eating festivals while ignoring the same atrocities carried out on pigs and cows).[3]

These are the common rationalizations people use to defend their choice to eat meat...[4]

Natural: Eating meat is written in our biology, we naturally crave meat, our species evolved to eat meat.

Normal: Eating meat is what most people in civilized society do and expect.

Necessary: Eating meat is essential for survival. People need to consume it to be healthy and strong.

It is interesting to note that the three N's of this justification system have also been used to rationalize slavery and sexism. For example, opponents of women's suffrage often appealed to the "necessity" of denying women the vote to prevent "irreparable damage" to the nation, the "natural superiority" of male intelligence, and the "normalcy" of men-only voting as "designed by our forefathers." When scrutinized and challenged, the 3N's ideology collapses, hence the importance of the vegan movement.[5]

THE SPECTRUM—FROM CARNISM TO VEGANISM

Carnism is the opposite of veganism. It is currently the dominant belief system in our culture that influences our dietary choices. It is woven through the fabric of society. We've internalized this ideology and the conflict it creates to such a degree that we can ignore the cruelty needed to sustain our expectation for meat and dairy.

If annual meat consumption doubles from 250 million tons to 500 million tons, as is predicted by the FAO, the system will collapse[6], and so will the world as we know it. We are already on the brink. To avoid this, we all have a part to play. We have to make a conscious choice to move away from animal products and towards plants; away from cruelty, pollution and exploitation, and towards foods that are kind to animals, the planet, and people.

But between carnism and veganism, we have options, room to explore and find our way. One of my favorite expressions is "all those who wander are not lost." We are all wandering somewhere on the spectrum whether we know it or not. There are many variations of diets and many ways of eating.

To achieve the changes needed to sustain our world's population and health, we all need to move towards a plant-based life. In an ideal world, we would all be vegan. I am also a vegan realist: I accept the world can't go vegan overnight (but I will keep trying!). So I think it is time to get real and recognize that we can all still make a dramatic difference to our world by reducing our consumption of animal products. At every step of the dietary spectrum, there is scope for you to have a positive impact.

Take a look at the spectrum below—where are you now, and where do you want to be?

A Rebel Vegan is aware of the impact of food, knows they have the power to create positive change, and wants to make sustainable, compassionate choices.

CARNISM TO VEGANISM SPECTRUM

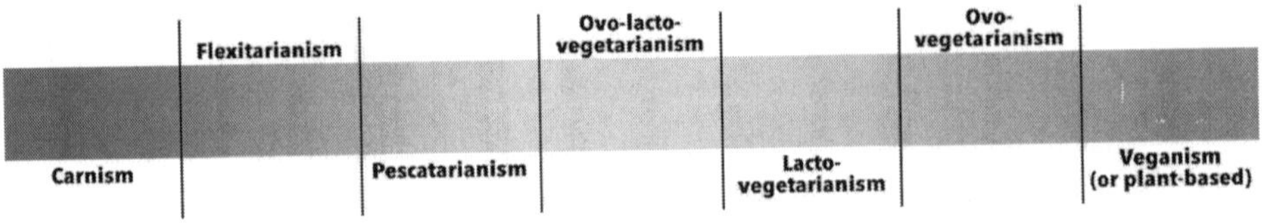

- **Carnism:** The dominant diet that's been developing since the agrarian revolution. A carnist diet includes meat, fish, eggs and dairy. These items are consumed daily, often several times a day. The standard Western diet[7] is a carnist diet.

- **Flexitarianism:** A flexitarian diet focuses on a higher intake of plant foods while reducing meat. Animal products are viewed as a side dish rather than the main event. The Blue Zones diets are flexitarian. Although they include a small amount of meat, fish and dairy, they are heavily dependent on whole foods like vegetables, pulses, grains, nuts, and seeds.

- **Pescetarianism:** A pescetarian diet combines fish and seafood with plant-foods such as vegetables, beans, fruits, and grains. Pescetarianism can also sometimes include eggs and dairy.

- **Ovo-lacto-vegetarianism:** The most common form of vegetarianism. Meat and fish do not feature in this diet, but eggs and dairy do.

- **Lacto-vegetarianism:** Lacto-vegetarians consume dairy, but no eggs, meat or fish.

- **Ovo-vegetarianism:** Ovo-vegetarians consume eggs, but no meat, fish or dairy products.

- **Veganism (also known as plant-based):** Vegans do not consume any meat, fish, dairy, eggs, honey, or other products derived from animals. They try to avoid any products that may have involved animal exploitation or abuse.

WE ARE ALL IN THIS TOGETHER

For me, veganism and plant-based are interchangeable. However, within the vegan movement there's some discussion and debate about safeguarding the term vegan. Some vegans consider the term plant-based too open and more about the diet or health over the wider lifestyle or ethical concerns. I want to foster unity and focus on our shared values. I think these are semantics, as ultimately we're all trying to move towards a more compassionate life. We're all in this together.

Wherever you are between carnism and veganism, you can have a positive impact on the environment and your health. Once you begin moving towards veganism, you'll find that you naturally keep going. The benefits you will experience will make it easy to carry on. That sense of wellbeing and the confidence that your core values and lifestyle are aligned is profound. But you must begin with the acceptance that your pace may differ from other people, and that's okay. The more compassion you can show yourself on this journey, the easier it will be to transition towards being fully vegan.

I hope the information in this book is transformational, but I am not here to preach or guilt-trip anyone. Your path is unique and doesn't have to arrive at 100% veganism to make a difference. In fact, you can begin making a difference wherever you are on this spectrum by infusing the principles of veganism into each aspect of your life—compassion, sustainability, and ethics. That means if you choose to move towards veganism by going flexitarian, pescatarian or vegetarian, you do so while sourcing products that are as ethical, sustainable and humane as possible, for example by ditching the big suppliers and choosing to shop from local, independent businesses.

Do not be so rigid that you give up. I can't tell you how many people have tried veganism for a few weeks, only to throw in the towel because it was "too hard" or they were "so hungry" or got "bored of eating the same meal over and over again." This can happen when you switch to veganism too quickly, without proper planning, or if you blindly follow somebody else's protocol instead of sitting down to work out how to make this new lifestyle work for your body and your circumstances.

The trick to make changes stick is to have a clear plan of action, take it slow, and accept it is a journey with twists and turns. It might take you a few attempts to find the right vegan cheese, vegan burger, or plant milk alternative. It might take a few months before you have enough plant-based dishes in your repertoire. There may be moments when you revert to something familiar because you're in a rush, stressed or socializing. This is okay. It is better to allow yourself the space to make mistakes and keep going, rather than aiming for perfection and giving up. Don't forget that you're not just changing your diet, but rethinking your traditions, upbringing, and belief system!

MY VEGAN ORIGIN STORY:

OPPOSITE ENDS OF THE SPECTRUM

Like most of you, I was raised a meat-eater. In fact, I was raised on a farm and at the opposite end of the diet spectrum to where I find myself today. As a child, I kept my head down and accepted the world around me as the natural order and how things are done. So it's been my personal pilgrimage along the spectrum to find my happy place of contentment and alignment as an out and proud vegan.

I first embraced the plant-based lifestyle at a monastery hidden in a lush jungle in north Vietnam. My first weeks as a vegan were easy, as I was within the safety of the monastery walls and the monks made all my meals. They showed me the importance of balance and simplicity in food. I began to appreciate the serenity felt when you don't have dead beings in your system. I was dipping my toe into a whole food plant-based diet before I had even heard of the concept.

I felt so revitalized that I decided to maintain the diet after leaving the monastery. However, establishing myself as a vegan while living my life on the road was tricky. I had my favorite haunts dotted around Asia, but they were used to serving me Bò lac (shaking beef) or Gà den (grilled chicken), or even Tiết canh (blood pudding). I needed a total rethink, and this was a daunting prospect.

While touring the world, I had built up a loyal network of connections with quirky locally-run restaurants whose owners had become friends. They knew all my favorite dishes and liked to indulge me as a loyal patron. I remember walking into a small town I'd not been to in over a year, and wondering if anyone would remember me.

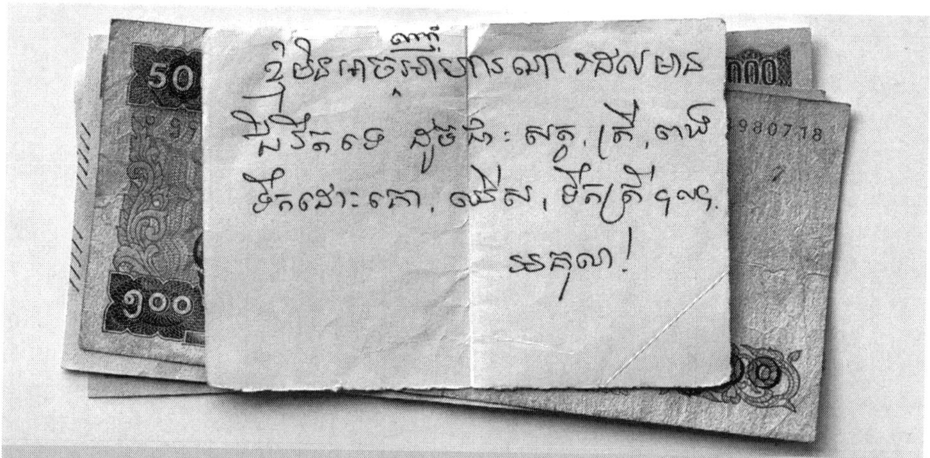

I needn't have worried. I hadn't walked ten feet along the ramshackle main road before screams of excitement sounded, and I was grabbed off the street by old friends and thrust into the best seat in their restaurant. They disappeared into the kitchen without a word, and soon proudly presented me with my favorite curry and a freshly opened coconut. The curry contained their best meat, as a gesture of friendship, and I needed to figure out how to respect our connection while still honoring my new values.

The concept of veganism was alien to many. There is no word for vegan or plant-based in many Asian languages, and lots of people laughed at what they thought of as a crazy diet. They told me I was skinny and needed to fatten up. Old friends would offer to kill a chicken just for me!

I wrote cards in each local language to show the foods I couldn't eat and photocopied them to hand out to friends, waiters, and restaurant owners. Often I would go into the kitchen and explain, or get behind the counters and help adapt my favorite dishes. This always sparked a wider conversation about vegan philosophy and the driving forces for my dramatic shift in lifestyle. When done right—when it remained a conversation rather than an opportunity for one-upmanship—these conversations were inspiring, fascinating, and a unique opportunity to laugh and bond with my old friends.

I learned that many of the so-called "classic dishes" were Westernized versions, with meat added to appeal to travelers. Originally, meat wasn't in every meal. Their intricate and world-famous flavors were developed with plants alone.

Becoming vegan never restricted me. On the contrary, it opened up my world. My connections grew stronger. My friends in all those little cafes around the world grew to respect my choices and even started to veganize their menus to appeal to a new class of traveler. I think our open conversations also helped some to rethink their increasingly meat-centric diets.

These days, when I return, they still jump up, excited to feed me their latest vegan creation. We are on the map!

"You are not the vegan police."
REBEL VEGAN

COMPASSION TO OTHER VEGANS:

The optimum diet, when it comes to health, animal welfare, and the environment, is a fully plant-based diet. Having said that, any movement towards this ideal is a positive that should be supported and celebrated. Unfortunately, I have all too often seen vegans judge and condemn anyone who isn't 100% vegan. We are *Rebel Vegans*, not the vegan police. Veganism should be a judgment-free zone. We must welcome and encourage all who are making their way to veganism wherever they are on the spectrum.

One of the saddest things for me is the conflict and arguing I see happening among vegans. We are all on the dietary spectrum, and we need to support each other, not criticize or break into cliquey groups. Our voices are louder when we stand together and our message is stronger as a united movement.

While we're busy fighting among ourselves, we're going against the core principle of veganism: compassion. Being a *Rebel Vegan* is also about creating a welcoming and safe space for others to join us. And that won't happen if we criticize and judge ourselves or others for being "not vegan enough."

"Live by your rules, be confident in your choices, and kind towards other people's choices."

Everything—even you—can be veganized. Even with that in mind, it is important that you allow yourself to move through the spectrum with grace and at your own pace. Perhaps you will be determined to throw all animal products out of the window and never buy them again. Or you will be more measured and slow in your approach, taking it week by week and slowly phasing out your usual meals with plant-based alternatives. It does not matter. Wherever you are, I celebrate that you are here. What matters is that you are on your way. In my book, that makes you a *Rebel Vegan* and you have a seat at my table.

However you choose to navigate this, you must set an example. Veganism is not about being perfect, it is about being compassionate. That means extending your compassion to include all earthlings, including fellow humans still involved in carnism.

Put it this way: judging or shaming somebody's actions never results in positive change. It just puts people's backs up and keeps people polarized. You inspire positive change with your energy when you stand in your authentic truth with tolerance and understanding.

That does not mean you condone the act of eating meat, it means you understand that the person doing so is currently enmeshed in a pervasive ideology. Let's embrace and celebrate everyone's efforts to create a better world, one meal at a time.

MOVING ALONG THE DIETARY SPECTRUM

You are a Rebel Vegan, informed and motivated to create your best life. Remember that like life, veganism is about the journey.

Enjoy.

There is no rulebook—no one way— to do vegan. With the strategies in the next two chapters, you can begin to create your unique plant-based lifestyle. I always say veganism is a journey, not a destination - so let's enjoy the ride!

How committed or chilled you are, and wherever you find your sweet spot on the dietary spectrum, is entirely your choice to make. Only you know your goals, only you can align your ethics, and only you can find the best way to navigate this brave new world. Don't be afraid of others judging you—just do you.

Yes, you will face challenges. You may experience friends and family questioning your choices, you may stumble and make mistakes, you may move at a different pace than others. Wherever you are on the spectrum, and wherever you're going, you do not need to label yourself, just align your newly awakened beliefs and motivations with your everyday life.

I believe the path to veganism is like a homecoming—to return to your original compassionate self.

You become who you were always meant to be.
Welcome home.

2
4
1
3

10

REBEL VEGAN STARTER KIT

CREATING YOUR OWN PLANT-BASED LIFE

"The best way to make a difference in the world is to start by making a difference in your own life."
Julia Louis-Dreyfus

Treat this chapter as your starter kit to establishing and maintaining your plant-based life. In this chapter, I want to confirm your motivations with a concise summary of the benefits of going vegan, and give you a blueprint for starting your vegan journey.

No matter how far along you are on the diet spectrum, as you move towards being more plant-based, you are improving your health, saving animals, and helping fight climate change. It's not about perfection, the focus is better placed on living your best life and doing the right thing. When you believe in something, it is so much easier to make the changes you need to align with that mission.

BENEFITS FOR EARTHLINGS:

1. YOU SPARE THE LIVES OF MANY ANIMALS:

Maybe this one is obvious, but with 70 billion land animals being bred, farmed, and slaughtered each year, your choice to leave them off your plate is the first step to ending animal suffering. Not to mention the millions of animals you'll spare from being made homeless due to deforestation. You also help prevent species extinction by eliminating the need for livestock and feed crops.

2. YOU STAND UP FOR HUMAN RIGHTS:

Most factory farm workers are exploited and underpaid. They are denied breaks and have to work in unimaginable conditions doing jobs that damage the body and soul. By going vegan, you stop contributing to this industry and stand up for human rights.

3. YOU HELP FIGHT WORLD HUNGER:

According to the United Nations World Food Program, 690 million people go to bed hungry every night.[1] The more people transition to a plant-based diet, the more farmland could be used to grow grains and vegetables to feed the world, rather than feed farm animals for the meat industry.

4. YOU STAND UP AGAINST TORTURE AND FOR A KINDER WORLD:

There is nothing kind about what happens in factory farms. Not eating meat means you no longer contribute to an industry that depends on the torture and slaughter of sentient beings.

"You must be the change you want to see in the world."
Mahatma Gandhi

BENEFITS FOR THE WORLD:

5. CONSERVING WATER:

It takes 1,000 gallons (3,785 liters) of water to produce 1 gallon (3.7 liters) of milk. It takes 4 million gallons (15 million liters) of water to produce a ton of beef. On the other hand, it takes 85,000 gallons (321,760 liters) of water to produce a ton of vegetables. By going vegan, you can save 219,000 gallons (829,000 liters) of water every year.

Animal agriculture is notoriously polluting to freshwater reserves as well as the oceans due to the toxic run-off and leaks from CAFO waste pits. When you go vegan, you are also helping to keep our water clean.

6. PROTECTING THE SOIL:

Animal agriculture depletes fertile soils. Not only because of the high level of chemicals in waste sprayed onto fields, but also due to deforestation. On the other hand, growing a large variety of plants and trees can reverse these effects, helping to remineralize and renourish the soil.

7. REDUCING CARBON EMISSIONS:

According to Nobel Prize-winning physicist and president of the American Association for the Advancement of Science, Steven Chu, "If cattle and dairy were a country, they would have more greenhouse gas emissions than the entire EU 28."[2] According to Cornell University, producing animal protein takes eight times more fossil fuel energy than producing plants.[3]

When you follow a vegan diet, you produce the equivalent of 50% less carbon dioxide and 1/11th of the oil compared to a meat-eater.[4]

8. LAND USE

It takes 1/6th of an acre to feed one person for one year on a vegan diet. It takes 3 times more land to feed a vegetarian. It takes 18 times more land to feed a meat eater.[5]

1.5 acres of land can produce 37,000 pounds (16,783 kilos) of plant-based food, or just 375 pounds (124 kilos) of beef. [6]

"You cannot escape the responsibility of tomorrow by evading it today."
Abraham Lincoln

BENEFITS FOR YOUR HEALTH:

"If you desire to make a difference in the world, you must be different from the world."
Elaine S. Dalton

9. YOU WILL LOSE WEIGHT:

The standard Western diet[7] is implicated in the global obesity epidemic. By switching to a vegan diet, you avoid sources of saturated fat and toxins that contribute to weight gain, thereby helping you reach your ideal weight.

10. YOU WILL LIVE LONGER AND FEEL HEALTHIER:

A vegan diet is richer in nutrients that help protect against disease. But you don't even have to go 100% plant-based to experience these benefits. Studies show that even flexitarians live longer, healthier lives.[8]

11. YOU WILL PROTECT YOURSELF FROM CHRONIC DISEASES:

The standard Western diet[9] increases your risk of metabolic syndrome. This syndrome is characterized by the so-called "deadly quartet"—abdominal obesity, high blood sugar, high cholesterol and high blood pressure.[10] If you follow a plant-based diet, you reduce your risk of metabolic syndrome.

12. YOU WILL EXPERIENCE A HAPPIER, MORE PEACEFUL MOOD:

The standard Western diet[11] is associated with a higher risk of mood disorders. On the other hand, a plant-based diet significantly improves depression, anxiety and productivity.[12] And there's a lot to be said for the peace-of-mind that comes from knowing that you are taking action to help the world.

A PERSON WHO EATS A VEGAN DIET SAVES, PER DAY:[13]

- 1,100 gallons (4,163 liters) of water.
- 45 pounds (23 kilos) of grain.
- 30 square feet (9.1 square meters) of forested land.
- 20 pounds (10 kilos) of CO_2.
- One animal's life.

THE FIRST STEP: PLANNING

MOVING ALONG THE DIET SPECTRUM

"If You Fail to Plan, You Are Planning to Fail."
Benjamin Franklin

So now you are motivated, the question is...how to begin? As much as going vegan is relatively straight-forward, it is also challenging. Firstly, because it can be difficult to change your behaviors when the behaviors of those around you remain the same. You might be the first vegan in your family or friend group, which means you will have to make an effort to stand your ground (see chapter 12 - Empowerment for vegan comebacks). Secondly, going vegan can be challenging because you are breaking the habit of a lifetime.

Habits run deep. Most of us grew up eating meat and dairy and not giving it a second thought. Our reflexes, taste buds, and habitual patterns will work against us making these positive changes. But with creativity and courage, we can challenge these ingrained beliefs and traditions.

We do this by creating new traditions and new habits that are kinder and more sustainable. Finding and strengthening your personal why—that mix of powerful driving forces that turned you towards this path in the first place—will help you face these challenges and any bumps in the road.

But motivation will only take you so far. Failure to plan is planning to fail. So the first step on your journey along the diet spectrum is to plan ahead! My favorite way to do this is to journal about it, but you can also just follow along or find a method that resonates with you.

As you turn the page, you will find my step-by-step pathway to veganism to inspire your Rebel Vegan journey.

PATHWAY TO VEGANISM

1. GET SUPER CLEAR ON YOUR WHY:

You've read the driving forces. You had your own motivations beforehand. What are your reasons for going vegan? It might be your health, or that you no longer want to contribute to a cruel and polluting industry, it could be that you cannot stand the thought of what is happening to our planet because of our food choices. A clear why will help you stay strong and stick to your choices when the going gets tough.

2. VISUALIZE THE BENEFITS:

How will you feel as you make these changes? What are you going to achieve? What are the benefits you will experience as you transition to a plant-based way of life? A clear vision of the positive outcomes of your choice will help cement your decision and support your goals.

3. BE AWARE OF YOUR CHALLENGES:

Write about (or think about) the obstacles that could get in your way and how you will navigate them. For example, if your go-to coffee shop doesn't have vegan options, are there cafes nearby that do? Or if you tend to get hungry mid-morning and reach for a shop-bought muffin, can you prepare vegan snacks in advance so you don't get caught out? If and when people question your choices, how will you respond? Where might you be prepared to compromise, and where are you not prepared to compromise (for example: if your mum has made a fish stew, versus if your friends try to drag you to a kebab shop after a night out).

4. PLAN FOR CHANGES:

Make a plan and stick to it. I like to take it one week at a time. What changes will you make in the first, second, third, and fourth week? Start small. Do it step by step and build from there. For example, it might feel overwhelming to go completely vegan from week 1. But you could decide that the first week will focus on finding plant-based alternatives to your usual dairy foods, and the second week will have two or three plant-based days. Or you might start by sampling vegan "meats" to find the ones that you enjoy.

5. READY, SET, VEGANIZE:

We are in an exciting time, vegan-wise. There is literally a vegan option for everything now: milk, yogurt, butter, mince meat, chicken, burgers, cheese, fish. Any dish you enjoy can be made vegan. Get online and start looking for vegan versions of your favorite foods.

Remember this is not a race! It's about building in lasting change, so go at your own pace, and just do your best. Before you know it, you'll have transitioned to a way of eating that supports your health, animal welfare, and the planet.

We have covered the practicalities, so now let's learn some tips and tricks to start putting your new lifestyle into action.

For a more detailed approach to Nutrition and how to live a vegan lifestyle please see book two in the *Rebel Vegan* range—*REBEL VEGAN LIFE: A Plant-Based Nutrition & Beginner's Guide.*

"If you can visualize it,
you can veganize it."
REBEL VEGAN

EGO

11

THE HOW

LET'S GET PRACTICAL

Q: What's the hardest thing about being vegan?
A: Waking up to milk the almonds.

Wherever you are, I want to support you to follow your unique path towards your sweet spot on the spectrum.

Our food choices are emotional, irrational, and wrapped up in our childhoods and culture. As a *Rebel Vegan*, you need to be prepared to challenge old beliefs and change your lifestyle. Although this journey is challenging at times, it will ultimately bring much joy, make a positive impact on the planet, on the animals, and on your health, with every single bite. In the last chapter, I shared my strategy to plan your plant-based life. In this chapter, I'm going to share a few tips and tricks to help you on the journey:

1. **Be prepared and motivated:** Use this book as your springboard and reference to start a healthier and more sustainable life. Think of it as a bible to return to and renew your inspiration. Use the resources section in the Appendix to find further information, inspiration, recipes, and support groups.

2. **Go at your own pace and go your own way:** There is no one way to do this. Don't compare yourself to others or feel pressured to conform to someone else's idea of what you should be doing. Celebrate your accomplishments, no matter how small.

3. **Be open-minded and push yourself outside—or to the limits of—your comfort zone:** A negative attitude will guarantee failure. View this as an incredible opportunity to explore new foods, tastes, restaurants, and cultures. Keep it fun! It's an adventure that also saves the planet!

4. **Don't judge or become the vegan police:** It's hard not to become zealous with your newfound health and wisdom and want to shout it from the rooftops. But if you want to make the change and keep your friends while you're at it, you have to realize that not everybody is at the same point in their life, and not everybody has the same value system. And that is okay. As a *Rebel Vegan*, you inspire and lead by example.

5. **Be prepared to be questioned and challenged:** When it comes to something so ingrained and sensitive as food, everyone thinks they are an expert and will come at you with unsolicited advice that may require a lot of gritted teeth, filtering, and magnanimity. No one cared when I ate meat. Now I'm vegan, everyone has an opinion on my health! Try to stay strong and positive, and be a bigger person. They can't argue with how great you look!

6. **Find your tribe for community and support:** You are not alone on this journey, so reach out to others for mutual support and connection. This is also part of the adventure. I look back and it astonishes me that something I initially found so isolating has now come full circle and created a new community I cherish. One of the top reasons many people give up or fall back into old habits is isolation.[1] See this as a great opportunity to open up your world and connect with others in the plant-based community. (See our Facebook groups in resources.)

7. **Make starchy vegetables and whole grains the foundation of your diet:** Despite popular myth, even the most hipster of vegans can't survive on kale salad alone! You need to eat enough healthy calories to satisfy your appetite (a pound of spinach has only 92 calories), otherwise you will fall back into old habits. This means putting starchy vegetables, whole grains, and plant protein at the center of your plate: potatoes, sweet potatoes, pumpkins, carrots, rice, quinoa, buckwheat, oats, beans, lentils, and soy products. I knew I could happily be a full time vegan when I tasted plant-based burger options and made sweet potato lasagna!

8. **Pack your kitchen with tasty vegan staples:** This way you'll always have something healthy to whip up and snack on. Some of the things I always have on hand are hummus, trail mix, granola, peanut butter (to spread on oat crackers, sourdough, or to have with an apple), canned beans (that way you can quickly add protein to your salads or blend up a quick bean dip), dried herbs and spices (so you can sauté vegetables into a delicious stir fry you can serve with noodles, or make a quick curry or stew), several types of grains (I always have rice, dried noodles and pasta in my cupboards), nuts and seeds (the easiest snack in the world! Roast them and keep them in an airtight jar ready to grab when you're feeling hungry), frozen fruit (I put frozen blueberries in my muesli and use them to make smoothies), plant-based milk (for those mourning flat whites and afternoon cups of tea). The staples you choose will depend on your unique tastes and requirements, but ensuring you have a well stocked vegan pantry will guarantee your success as a *Rebel Vegan*.

9. **Make a simple pasta dish more nutritious:** Dried pasta is usually vegan, while fresh pasta is commonly made with eggs. There are also some amazing lentil and chickpea pastas out there to try! To make your pasta dishes more filling and nutritious, switch to a bean or high quality, whole grain pasta made with ancient grains (for example buckwheat, brown rice or spelt). Add more protein with tempeh, tofu, beans, chickpeas, or hummus. Add some healthy fats with avocado, seeds, or nuts. You can also add creaminess with oat, almond, or soy cream. Add antioxidant-packed veggies like broccoli, purple cabbage, mushrooms, or spinach. This meal is much more nutritionally dense and will keep you full longer, versus a stand-alone bowl of pasta.

10. **Smoothies:** If you don't want to blend on a daily basis, you can blend or cold press your favorite berries, greens, and fruits, then freeze in zip-lock bags, ready to go. To ensure your smoothies keep you full until lunch, turn them into smoothie bowls topped with granola, nuts, seeds, and coconut shreds. Or you can add a source of protein to the smoothies, such as chia seeds, hemp seeds, nut butter, or plant protein powder.

11. **Have food on standby:** This way you don't have to succumb to take-aways. Freeze some home-cooked or store-bought vegan meals for those lazy or stressful days.

12. **Time to tool up:** You don't want your new diet to be time-consuming or take over your life. I recommend a pressure cooker. It will slash cooking time, preserve food nutrient value, and has multiple cooking functions. A decent blender is also a good idea (for smoothies, but also vegan mayo, cheesecakes, energy balls, soups, etc).

13. **Be ready to feel lighter and stay regular:** Your diet is about to get healthier with more nutrients and fiber. Meat products contain negligible amounts of vitamins and no fiber whatsoever. Fiber is what keeps your bowel movements regular. This is essential, as it is one of the ways your body gets rid of toxins. Eating enough plant fiber helps prevent (and even reverse) colon and bowel cancers.[2] What's more, fibre keeps you fuller, so expect to experience better appetite control and healthy weight loss.

14. **Veganize your favorite dishes:** There are incredible replacement options available, and hundreds, if not thousands, of vegan cookbooks out there. Enjoy the journey, find new flavors, and have fun experimenting. There is a plant-based version of everything, whatever your preferences. This change is not restrictive, but opens up your world.

15. **Plan ahead:** Don't rely on pre-made or junk foods. Oreos and French fries are technically vegan, I know, but they won't deliver the health benefits that whole foods do. Make a plan so you can make (and freeze) home-cooked meals and have healthy vegan snacks on standby. Learn a few simple go-to recipes. Stock your fridge with your favorites, like vegan pizza or burgers, for those weak moments. Explore and find your new signature dish. Mine was jackfruit curry!

16. **Support local restaurants and become a vegan social butterfly:** Post-Covid, we lost a lot of restaurants, but new vegan ones are opening up everywhere. Let's support and champion them! (See the resource list in the Appendix and download the HappyCow app!)

17. **Don't forget supplements:** The only essential nutrient missing from a vegan diet is B12. Find a good quality, food-grown supplement to ensure you get enough. Some people also choose to top up on iron and Omega-3 as well. In addition, a wide-spectrum multi-vitamin will help you keep your nutrient levels topped up.

18. **Don't sweat the small stuff:** Try to keep focused on the bigger picture and your goal of transitioning to a more plant-based life. Don't get too lost in sourcing only organic, reading every label, or knowing everything, because this can become stressful and make anyone give up. The moment any diet stops being fun is the moment you begin to think it might not be worth it. By becoming aware and more plant-based, you are already making a bold move to improve your life and the world around you. Be kind to yourself!

19. **Give yourself time to adjust as your knowledge and willpower grow:** Your thoughts and taste buds evolve as your horizons and options expand. Taste is acquired, and soon you will start to crave all things plant-based. Many people find one thing hard to give up, like cheese. If you need to fall back on that while you transition and find a vegan alternative, that's okay. You are a *Rebel Vegan*, walking your own path, still creating a better life and making a positive impact.

20. **Don't let perfection get in the way of progress:** You will, by mistake or design, eat animal products again. When accidents happen, try to forgive, learn, and move on!

21. **Don't get disheartened:** There will be bumps in the road, but stay focused on your new life. Veganism is a journey, not a destination. Enjoy the ride!

Q & A: PROBLEM SOLVING

Q: Why does vegan cheese taste bad?
A: It hasn't been tested on mice.

WILL I EVER STOP CRAVING MEAT?

I never miss meat anymore. I always say our taste buds are fickle with short term memory. Basically they will crave what they are most used to. Switching to a plant-based diet is very similar to moving to a far flung country after growing up on your mother's traditional cooking. You have to give yourself time to acclimatize and discover new flavors.

Another thing to remember is that most packaged foods are hyper-sweet, mega-salty, or over-flavored thanks to all the artificial additives, and this causes our taste buds to become desensitized and overwhelmed. But you can retrain your tastebuds to appreciate and crave new foods simply by eating new foods. With every bite, your tastebuds learn to savor something else.

Give yourself time, and it will happen - usually over a few weeks or months. I missed old fashioned cheese for a year, and now I turn my nose up at it. Time and commitment will open up your world.

CAN MY PETS BE VEGAN?

Cats are carnivores, natural predators, and the opposite of vegans. Their physiology demands they eat meat. There are stories of cat lovers creating carefully fortified vegan cat foods and raising healthy cats. However, it is okay to accept your cat's nature and feed it with meat products. I am not the vegan police, and you are still a *Rebel Vegan* and a good person. On the other hand, dogs are omnivores like humans, which means they can thrive on a plant-based diet. There are many healthy vegan dog food options out there. Actually, the oldest living dog, Brambles, was a *Rebel Vegan* and lived 27 years![3]

Dogs need protein, but protein is not exclusively found in meat. Protein is made from amino acids, which are found in plant foods. The only reason there are amino acids in meat is because animals (cows, chickens, etc.) eat plants. Meat-based dog foods also contain antibiotic and medication residues, so much so that it is considered "unfit for human consumption."

Our pets are part of the family, let's feed them like we love them.

DO I NEED TO GET RID OF MY LEATHER SHOES AND BELTS?

How far you want to go with your veganism is a personal choice. If animal welfare is one of your driving factors, you probably won't want to buy any more leather products. What you do with the items you bought in the past is up to you. The leather I already had in my pre-vegan closet, I consider vintage and have held on to. However, knowing the violent system that produced these items, I find I don't want to wear them anymore.

The good news is that you don't have to buy leather shoes and belts anymore. There are great faux leather and faux fur options now. Let's support those brands.

DO I NEED TO BUY ORGANIC FOODS?

Small-scale organic produce is better for the environment and contains more nutrients than produce grown conventionally. However, it is important that you do whatever feels right and is within your budget.

You have already made brave choices that will have a huge impact on your health and the environment. I suggest you do not take on the world all at once! If you choose to go organic, I suggest finding a local vegetable box scheme and independent suppliers. The main thing to remember if you aren't buying organic is to thoroughly wash your fresh produce to remove pesticide residues. You can find vegetable wash in most health food stores, or make your own using baking soda, lemon juice and water.

ISN'T SOY BAD FOR YOUR HEALTH?

Is soy good or bad? There has been a lot of conflicting information about soy. Much of this controversy revolves around a supposed link between soy and higher levels of the hormone estrogen. Scare-stories about soy-cause man-boobs are guaranteed to send many men running to the meat aisle, but these links have been fully refuted and debunked.

Firstly, soy does not have an adverse effect on men. Quite the opposite: soy products can even prevent cancer. A review of 47 studies and reports found that neither soy nor soy products affect testosterone levels in men.[4] Another analysis of 14 studies showed that eating soy reduced the risk of prostate cancer by 26%.[5]

Soy is a legume (like chickpeas, peanuts, and pinto beans). It is packed with plant protein, fiber, and vitamins (including calcium). According to the Physicians Committee for Responsible Medicine, soy products offer many benefits, such as reducing the risk of breast cancer and chronic inflammation, and improving bone and heart health.[6]

Of course, discernment is necessary. Health benefits come from consuming whole soy foods, such as tofu, tempeh, soy milk, and soy miso, rather than processed soy products. The more processed a food, the less nutritious it is likely to be.

WHAT'S WRONG WITH EATING HONEY?

Honey is produced by bees for bees. When we harvest honey for our consumption, we are putting the bees' health in danger. According to the Vegan Society, honey production is exploitative.[7]

Bees will visit up to 1,500 flowers to fill their "honey stomach," a separate stomach containing enzymes that break down the nectar into honey. This is deposited in the hive, where "house bees" complete the honey making process. In her lifetime (about a month), each bee will produce a twelfth of a teaspoon of honey. This honey is essential to the hive's wellbeing, providing energy and micronutrients.

In commercial beekeeping, all the honey is taken away and replaced with sugar or glucose syrup , which lacks nutrients and impacts the bee's health. To remedy this, the hives are sometimes doused in antibiotics. Just like in animal farming, conventional beekeepers selectively breed honey bees to increase their productivity. This creates genetically narrow populations of bees that are more prone to diseases. These diseases spread to other pollinators, like native bumblebees. Antibiotics are used to keep parasites at bay. If hives develop parasitic infections, they are often burned with the bees inside.[8]

Another common practice is for hives to be culled post-harvest to keep costs down, and for the queen bee's wings to be clipped to stop her leaving the hive and creating a new colony (since this would decrease productivity and profit).[9]

Honey bees are highly intelligent creatures with complex social systems. What's more, their survival is essential to our survival on earth (over a third of our food depends on pollinators like bees). At the end of the day, we need them more than they need us!

The good news is there are some fantastic honey alternatives out there, whether you want to cook with it, add it to your tea, or drizzle it onto sourdough toast. Maple syrup, rice syrup, molasses, agave syrup, date syrup, not to mention some wonderful vegan honeys!

I am so vegan, I don't even call my boyfriend Honey!

ECO

12

EMPOWERMENT

COMEBACKS FOR CONFRONTING SKEPTICISM

"People eat meat and think they will become as strong as an ox, forgetting that the ox eats grass."
Pino Caruso[1]

Sometimes you need to rebel, to fight for what's right. So get ready to ruffle feathers just by living authentically as the best version of you—a healthy, confident advocate for compassionate living.

I find it endlessly fascinating that being vegan can cause such consternation and conflict. A vegan arriving at a dinner party can create tension before they even say a word. I believe it has to do with the unspoken belief system we all grow up with that eating meat is normal, natural, some kind of "right."

A vegan's very existence challenges this assumption, and it can be uncomfortable and confronting to some. This kind of moral schizophrenia allows people to love their pets, but eat meat anyway—to say they care for animals while supporting industries that make no secret of their mistreatment of animals.

This is part of a wider problem. We are forced, in today's world, to shut down or tune out our natural human compassion in order to live within a system that produces such pain and injustice. A child would never want an animal to be in pain. As we grow up, we absorb an ideology that makes it normal, whether we think animals were put on this earth purely for us to use at will, or whether we believe in the "survival of the fittest" model, where humans are at the top of the food chain, so must consume animals lest they take over the world.

Just by turning up somewhere, vegans shine a light on this cognitive dissonance, this moral schizophrenia. You are a rebel, so get ready to cause a stir!

Even as the most discreet vegan who doesn't use the V-word, you still must be prepared to be challenged on your personal and philosophical choices. It can involve a lot of forced smiling and magnanimity to have to continuously explain yourself—to come out again and again. Even if you are determined not to say a word about your diet, someone will bring it up. This chapter is about equipping you with the tools and information to answer anything that's thrown at you, and answer with compassion, understanding, and strength.

I have experienced many responses to my veganism. Very often, whoever I'm speaking to is quick to tell me that they don't eat much meat anyway. This points to a fear of judgment, as well as an understanding that meat-eating is not all that good for anyone. If you are faced with this response, celebrate it. Tell the person that it's wonderful they don't eat much meat, because if everyone reduced their reliance on meat, we would already be heading in the right direction on many pressing issues. You might just inspire someone to make brave choices and continue further on their plant-based journey.

But a lot of the time, the response isn't quite as neutral. I've had people telling me that my muscles will waste away due to lack of protein, that there's no way I'll get enough nutrients, crazy claims that veganism is just as bad for the planet, and what about plants, don't they have feelings too? (See below!)

BEFORE EMPOWERMENT: UNDERSTANDING

"You can, you should,
and if you are brave enough to start, you will."
Stephen King

Before we get into debunking some of the misinformation and skepticism you may face, let's explore where this conflict and push-back comes from. I love to watch and understand the dynamics at play, like being a vegan anthropologist!

I believe at the core of this conflict is the assumption or sense that eating meat is some kind of basic human right that vegans are trying to take away. "They're taking our meat" is almost as divisive as "they're taking our jobs" or "they're taking our guns." Meat has become a symbol of resistance against "wokeness" and progressive thinking. Veganism is regarded as another snowflake fad, peddled by a bunch of new-age hippies who have no respect for tradition and freedoms.

Eating meat has become aligned with a kind of toxic conservative alpha-masculinity. Donald Trump famously loves junk food and well-done steak with ketchup. Men's rights advocate Jordan Peterson is known for his beef and salt diet. There's even a subset of cryptocurrency enthusiasts who call themselves bitcoin carnivores. Remember Gatis Lagzdins? Many vegans know him as that guy who turns up at vegan festivals and eats raw meat (stunts have included a squirrel and a pig's head) as a way of raising awareness of the dangers of malnutrition from going vegan.[2] Before turning his attention to people trying to live a more compassionate life, Lagzdin was best known for promoting racist ideology and right-wing conspiracies on his YouTube channel.[3] Social justice warriors are routinely called "soy boy", "cuck", and "beta" in alt-right circles, terms designed to mock their perceived lack of masculinity. This is echoed by a study entitled "It ain't easy eating greens: Evidence bias towards vegetarians and vegans from both source and target", which found that respondents with a right-wing background and holding rigid gender values see vegans as alarmingly subversive and deserving of mockery.[4]

Full disclosure: I wasn't always vegan. For most of my life, I had my head in the sand with regards to diet. In my meat-eating days, I didn't (want to) understand what motivated people to go meatless, and I also poked fun at vegans. I didn't question my behavior at the time. It's only now, looking back, that I see my derision was caused by discomfort. Just by being present, vegans shone a light on choices I subconsciously knew to be toxic. And so I would have a little dig, I would get a little defensive. I am not proud of this. Maybe you have done the same? It's okay. No judgment here. These are natural reactions when faced with an uncomfortable truth.

REBEL VEGAN RETORTS

It's time to embrace your choices and celebrate being a *Rebel Vegan* who takes new paths, challenges the status quo, and embraces a new way to live. As a *Rebel Vegan*, you will ruffle some feathers before you even open your mouth.

To arm you for every conflict and avoid getting caught out, here are some common arguments you may face, and how you can respond. I have had it all thrown at me, and wish I knew then what I know now. I would have had the information to fire back (with compassion, of course)!

THE FOUNDING FALSEHOOD: HUMANS ARE CARNIVORES.

Actually, humans are omnivores, meaning we can eat both plants and meat. However, from an anatomical perspective, we are herbivorous. Humans have short, soft fingernails and small canine teeth. You wouldn't want us hunting and ripping apart flesh in the wild. In contrast, carnivores all have sharp claws and large canine teeth capable of tearing flesh. Like other herbivores and omnivores' teeth, humans' back molars are flat (ideal for grinding fibrous plant foods).

Carnivorous animals swallow their food whole, relying on extremely acidic stomach juices to break down flesh and kill the dangerous bacteria in it, which would otherwise sicken or kill them. Our stomach acids are much weaker in comparison, because strong acids aren't needed to digest chewed fruits and vegetables.

Animals who hunt and eat other animals have short intestinal tracts that allow meat to pass through quickly, before it can rot and cause disease. Our intestinal tracts are much longer than those of carnivores. Longer intestines allow the body more time to break down fiber and absorb nutrients from plant-based foods, but they also make it dangerous for humans to eat a lot of meat. The bacteria in meat have extra time to multiply during the long trip through our gut, increasing the risk of food poisoning and increasing the risk of developing colon cancer.

The biological reality is that we are part of the great apes family. We just need to look at our nearest cousins on earth (like gorillas, orangutans, and chimpanzees): they all eat a plant-based diet.[5]

IT IS NATURAL FOR US TO EAT MEAT BECAUSE HUMANS ARE AT THE TOP OF THE FOOD CHAIN.

In today's industrialized world, we are far removed from any natural food chain or ecosystem. And when we were still in any natural world order or food chain, we were far from the top!

There is a statistical way to work out a species' trophic level—that means its level or rank in a food chain. In 2013, French researchers used food supply data from the UN Food and Agricultural Organization to calculate humans' trophic level. The scale goes from 1 to 5, with 1 being the score of a primary producer (like plants and trees) and 5 being a pure apex predator (animals that only eat meat and have few or no predators of their own, like tigers, sharks, crocodiles, or boa constrictors). They found that humans score 2.21. We are roughly equal to an anchovy or a pig.

Their findings confirm common sense. We are omnivores, we eat a mix of plants and animals, as opposed to top-level predators that only consume meat. Obviously, in modern society, we don't need to worry about a predator eating us or our family. But to truly be at the "top of the food chain" in scientific terms, you have to strictly consume the meat of animals that are predators themselves.[6]

We don't hunt and kill animals with our natural abilities. In fact, most of us would balk at the idea of killing an animal with our bare hands or our teeth. We buy our meat nicely packaged in supermarkets. And there is nothing natural about the way we have bred, genetically modified, and intensively farmed animals we consign to be food in our culture.

THE DESPERATE PLEA: PLANTS HAVE FEELINGS TOO.

This seems desperate and hardly worth your time, but it's surprising how much it comes up! Is pulling a carrot from the soil the same as slaughtering a baby calf?

Let's begin with the science—plants do not have a brain, a central nervous system or pain receptors. So, from a scientific point of view, plants do not have the capacity to feel pain.

The confusion comes from the fact that plants are alive. We can watch them grow from a seed into something incredible—but they do this on a cellular level. They react, rather than respond, to their surroundings. Think of it as a doorbell. A doorbell buzzes because it has been pressed, not because it is consciously aware of a finger pressing it.

Animals, on the other hand, respond and react. Anyone who has interacted with a pet knows this. The difference between plants and animals involves sentience. Animals are sentient beings—they have interests, preferences, desires, they use language. It may not be the same language as humans, but that is irrelevant.

From an ethical perspective, we cannot look at the life of a plant in the same way we look at the life of an animal. If I intentionally step on a flower in your garden, you might be mildly annoyed. But if I intentionally kicked your pet, I hope your upset would be quite different!

Bold declarations, such as "vegans murder plants", are thrown out to get a reaction and trigger an argument. Don't rise to the bait. If you feel so inclined, then you could gently remind your antagonist that plants don't feel pain, unlike animals—which is where they should focus their concerns and compassion.

VEGANS DON'T GET ENOUGH PROTEIN.

"Where do you get your protein?" is probably the most common question vegans need to rebut. We're brainwashed from childhood to associate meat with muscles. We're taught that meat and eggs are protein rich, and that's all there is to it. Here you can respond that all the protein from meat-centric diets comes from plants. Cows are only the middleman, and not a very efficient one at that.

The largest study comparing the nutrient intake of meat eaters to plant eaters found that the average person on a plant-based diet doesn't just get enough protein, but 70% more than they need. Ironically, even die-hard meat-eaters get more than half of their protein from plants![7]

Ultimately, you can get more than enough high quality protein on a fully plant-based diet. A peanut butter sandwich or a cup of cooked lentils has the same amount of protein as 3 ounces (90 grams) of beef or 3 eggs![8]

And let's face it—many of the world's largest and strongest animals eat plant-based diets. I've yet to hear anyone ask a horse where it gets its protein. What do the largest and strongest land animals all have in common? The elephant, rhino, and hippopotamus are all vegans and build their massive muscles entirely from plants. And then there is that old expression; strong as an ox—who also happens to be vegan!

MILK BUILDS STRONG BONES.

Q. How do you keep milk fresh?
A. Leave it in the cow.

Humans are the only mammals on the planet that drink the milk of another species. No other animal does this. In evolutionary terms, drinking cow's milk is extremely recent. Humans began domesticating cattle around 10,000 years ago. Before then, only children would drink milk (and it was their mother's milk, not another animal's). When they stopped breastfeeding, they stopped making the digestive enzyme responsible for breaking down and absorbing lactose (the sugar in milk). We have not evolved to drink milk beyond childhood—most of us are lactose intolerant.

The confusion comes because aggressive marketing pushes milk as a healthy drink, while ignoring the mountain of cautionary science. The truth is that the saturated fat, hormones and growth factors in milk are linked to many illnesses, including heart disease, certain cancers, diabetes and obesity. Dairy products also increase the risk of acne, which, while not life-threatening, is emotionally distressing.[9]

With regards to milk being good for bones, studies show that in populations with the highest intake of dairy, like the US, rates of osteoporosis are still incredibly high. This points to the fact that milk does not automatically lead to stronger bones. Calcium does, and you can find calcium elsewhere (see next point).

Basically, we are not baby cows and need milk made for humans. The good news is there are tons of fantastic vegan alternatives to explore, from oat and soy to almond and hazelnut, and even some made from peas and potatoes!

YOU NEED TO EAT DAIRY TO GET ENOUGH CALCIUM.

Calcium comes from the earth. The plants pull it from the soil, cows eat the vegetation, and the calcium passes into their milk. Just like cows get their calcium from plants, we can get calcium directly and more effectively from plants as well. Broccoli, leafy greens, soy, beans, almonds, sesame seeds, amaranth (an ancient grain), berries and figs are all good sources.

What's more, fortified plant milk has a calcium content that is about the same or higher than cow's milk. A glass of whole cow's milk has about 300 milligrams of calcium per cup of milk (around 240 ml). Almond milk contains 451 mg calcium per cup; oat milk contains 350 mg calcium per cup; soy milk contains 450 mg calcium per cup; hemp milk contains 283 mg calcium per cup.[10] So as you can see, you don't need cow's milk to get enough calcium.

IF THE WORLD WENT VEGAN, WE WOULD BE OVERRUN BY ANIMALS!

Another common argument thrown our way is the belief that if we didn't kill all these animals, they would somehow multiply and take over the world. And it's a tricky one to answer and understand.

The main thing here is that the animal farming industry works on a supply and demand basis. You buy meat, and that signals that there is a demand for more of this product. The farming industry is profit driven and would not breed animals if they could not sell them, as this doesn't make economic sense.

We need to be realistic and accept that the world's population will not go vegan overnight, so we will never be faced with a situation where we have 70 billion animals let out to roam free. It will be gradual: as we make more sustainable and vegan choices, meat demand will decline, which means fewer animals being bred for consumption. The populations will adjust—as vegans grow in numbers, the number of farm animals will slowly decline.

IF WE DIDN'T BREED THESE ANIMALS, THEY WOULD GO EXTINCT.

Several things here. The first is that the animals on factory farms would not exist in the wild anyway—they have been genetically manipulated and selectively bred. They are not natural animals. For example, dairy cows are bred to produce ten times more milk than their natural counterparts, and broiler chickens are bred to develop enormous breasts and thighs. They would not survive outside factory farms, so they would need human care. Thankfully, there are many animal sanctuaries, as well as people who dedicate time and money to caring for rescued farm animals.

What's more, with less livestock, we would be able to re-wild and regrow areas razed to make room for CAFOs and feed crops, thereby creating natural habitats for other animal species to flourish.

If you truly care about animal extinction, consider that we are currently in the midst of the largest mass species extinction,[11] and that one of the main drivers for this is animal agriculture. Going vegan is one of the best things you can do to protect the world's biodiversity.

BUT I LOVE THE TASTE OF ANIMAL PRODUCTS!

One of the main justifications for not going more plant-based. Many people profess to love the taste of steaks, chicken, and cheesy pizza. I guess I told myself this as well. But most people don't go vegan just because they don't enjoy the taste of meat.

The important questions to consider are: Do you value taste over life? Are your tastebuds and preferences of more importance than the lives of other sentient beings?

I hope you agree that sensory pleasure is not enough to morally justify any action. Just because it tastes good, that does not justify the torture, nor does it justify the destruction of the Amazon rainforest. What makes it okay is speciesism, the notion that some animals are there to be exploited by humans. This type of reasoning could be applied to any animal—cats, dogs, dolphins, pandas, or elephants. When this justification is used to keep killing some animals, you have to accept it for all animals, including those you love. If this is uncomfortable, perhaps the taste of meat isn't worth it after all.

EATING ANIMALS IS PART OF OUR CULTURE AND TRADITION.

Yes, we have eaten animals for eons. It is ingrained in our culture and tradition. But does it make it morally justifiable?

Why not apply this logic to a human situation to see if it stands up. Not long ago, it was part of culture and tradition to not allow women the right to vote. Only last century, it was cultural and traditional to keep slaves. In some cultures, it is tradition to carry out female genital mutilation. But would we consider these things morally acceptable, just because they are traditional or part of a culture?

Let's apply this logic to animals most of us in the Western world love. China's Yulin dog meat festival takes place every year. It lasts ten days, during which over 10,000 cats and dogs are killed and eaten.[12] Dog eating is a tradition in China, but does that make it okay? What about the Faroe Islands annual whale slaughter, considered an example of traditional aboriginal whaling, where around 800 long-finned pilot whales and some dolphins are killed?[13] It is tradition, but does that justify it?

So the question that follows naturally is, if tradition does not morally justify the slaughter of animals we love (dogs, cats, dolphins, etc.), then how does it morally justify our killing of cows, pigs, and chickens?

The answer is simple.
It doesn't.

WHY AREN'T VEGANS FOCUSING ON HUMAN RIGHTS INSTEAD?

With so many human rights issues, why are vegans so bothered about animals? Shouldn't they focus on human problems instead? This is a common criticism thrown at vegans.

Firstly, being vegan does not preclude you from being passionate about other issues facing our world. You can be vegan and a humanitarian activist. The two aren't mutually exclusive. Also, ranking injustices and arguing about which one should be solved first doesn't get us anywhere. Should it be homelessness? Should it be the war in Syria? Should it be worker exploitation? Should it be childhood poverty? Should it be famine? While we're debating what to focus on, nothing changes.

You can be vegan and fight for all sorts of other causes. Just because you choose to eat plants doesn't mean you ignore all the other problems going on in the world.

What's more, industrial animal farming is not just an animal welfare issue. It is a human rights issue because the majority of people working in the industry are exploited, poorly paid, and work in atrocious conditions that destroy their physical and mental health. It's a global human rights issue because the grain fed to livestock could feed the millions of people currently going hungry. Human rights are an intrinsic part of going vegan.

BUT ISN'T ORGANIC OR ETHICALLY SOURCED MEAT OKAY?

You must have heard something like the following: "I really care about animal welfare, so I only buy humane and free range products, so the animals have lived a good life and felt no pain."

Labels like Red Tractor Approved, RSPCA Approved, Humanely Slaughtered, High-Welfare, and Free-range don't mean much. They don't represent any improvement for the animals. Taking a hen out of a cage and putting it into an overcrowded barn doesn't actually improve its welfare. These labels are simply there to ease the consumer's conscience. Animals are still being exploited, are still suffering, are still scared, and are still slaughtered on a factory line with little consideration for whether or not they want to die.

Humane slaughter is an oxymoron. It is not possible. Being humane means having and showing compassion and benevolence. Can you compassionately, benevolently, humanely take the life of an animal that does not want to die? The only way to humanely slaughter animals is...to not slaughter them. The only happy animals are those who get to live out their lives in freedom—not confined to cages and airless sheds, not standing in their own feces, not castrated, tagged, mutilated and pumped full of medications.

Yes, improving the treatment of these animals is better than not doing anything. But the impact these measures can have is tiny, because at the end of the day, the animal still has to suffer and die. There is no right way to do the wrong thing.

Let's take free-range as an example. It is simply a marketing ploy. We believe free-range means that the hens that produce the eggs live a happy, fulfilled life. This is a lie. These hens are still debeaked, the male chicks are still killed at birth, the sheds are still so overcrowded that most of these free range hens will not experience sunlight or the outside world, and they will still be sent to slaughter once they are no longer laying enough eggs.[14] Legal requirements for free range eggs are nine hens per square meter, one drinker per ten birds, and ten centimeters of feeder space.[15] How spacious and airy does that sound to you?

Animals don't want to be free-range, they want to be free. Free to live their life without human-inflicted suffering. The thing is, no matter how "good" animals' lives have been, the moment we exploit them for something that is not ours, the moment we take them to the slaughterhouse, we are abusing them. There is no way to morally justify this when we can obtain all the nutrients we need from plants.

VEGANS ARE MALNOURISHED.

This is another common "concern" we may receive from friends and family. If it's not about protein, then it's about B12 and Omega-3. The first question that comes up for me when asked about this is: do you ask everyone about their protein/B12/Omega-3? Given the high occurrence of chronic disease due to the standard Western diet,[16] it would make more sense to target people who eat meat and junk foods with your concern.

Actually, vegan diets are perfectly adequate on all levels. This is not an opinion, but a fact supported by the Canadian Dietetics Association, Dietitians of Canada, the British Dietetic Association[17] and the American Dietetic Association.[18]

According to these recognized and respected institutions, "Well planned vegan and other types of vegetarian diets are appropriate for all stages of the life cycle, including during pregnancy, lactation, infancy, childhood and adolescence." They go on to say that plant-based diets offer "a number of nutritional benefits, including lower levels of saturated fats, cholesterol, and animal protein, as well as higher levels of carbohydrates, fiber, magnesium, potassium, folate, and antioxidants such as vitamins C and E and phytochemicals."[19]

If a plant-based diet was such a problem for nourishment, then why are so many elite athletes changing to plant-based rather than the high meat/high protein diets of days gone by? And when we are talking about elite athletes, we mean it—these are the ultramarathon runners, world-class athletes and body-builders who employ the top nutritionists to squeeze out every last ounce of energy to improve their game.

VEGANS DON'T GET ENOUGH VITAMIN B12

Yes, it is difficult to get on a vegan diet, but vegans are not alone in being at risk of vitamin B12 deficiency. Some people lack the intrinsic factor (a protein made by the cells of the digestive tract) necessary to absorb B12. People with anemia or who take proton pump inhibitors (for stomach acid) also struggle to absorb B12.[20]

According to the National Institute of Health, up to 40% of the Western population has low or marginal vitamin B12 status.[21] This could be because the B12 naturally present in animal foods is difficult to absorb. For this reason, the Institute of Medicine advises the intake of foods (cereals, plant milks, etc.) that have been fortified with B12. Another option is to take a high-quality B12 supplement.

As for Omega-3, as we explored in the Health section of the Driving Forces chapter, fish get their Omega-3 from algae, and vegans can too. There are plenty of algae-based Omega-3 options. You can also obtain this nutrient from plant foods such as walnuts, hemp seeds, flax seeds, chia seeds, edamame beans, and kidney beans.

Aside from B12, there is no nutrient that you cannot obtain from plants. By eating a wide variety of plant foods, you will give your body everything it needs to thrive and live a long, healthy life.

KNOW THYSELF: QUIET CONFIDENCE

There is a quiet confidence that comes with living your best life in line with your values. But you still need to be ready to be confronted by people who have an opinion about your dietary choices. Be ready to stand your ground. But do so with kindness, grace and tolerance. The best way to respond to skepticism is simply to state your truth, accepting that the person in front of you may disagree.

I believe that the best thing you can do is lead by example. Compassion is at the core of veganism, so remember to be understanding to people who are at a different point on the diet spectrum.

THIS IS HOW *REBEL VEGANS* CAN SUPPORT THE MOVEMENT AND HELP SAVE THE WORLD. NOT BY FIGHTING OR ARGUING, BUT BY BEING OPEN, AUTHENTIC, COMPASSIONATE, AND FABULOUS!

13

FINAL THOUGHTS

VIVA LA REVOLUTION

"If they don't give you a seat at the table, bring a folding chair."

Shirley Chisholm, First Black congresswoman (1968) and presidential nominee (1972)

There comes a time when we need to take an honest look at life. That is what you've done by reading this book—you've confronted the truth behind our traditional diet. It can be an uncomfortable truth but one we ignore at our peril.

We all grew up within the dominant belief system, where eating meat is promoted as natural, and part of who we are, but it is killing us. As we have seen in the driving forces chapters, eating meat is detrimental for your own wellbeing as well as that of society, animals, and the planet.

Today's industrialized meat industry is unimaginably cruel to animals, undeniably destructive to our planet, and shockingly exploitative of its workforce. It has gifted us pandemic after pandemic and is in part responsible for the chronic diseases that plague our world. The mounting evidence is unequivocal, undeniable, and requires us all to act. We all have a role in creating this brave new world and it needs us to take our heads out of the sand.

We have a tiny window of opportunity left to us if we want to turn things around. However, no solution is complete without us moving further along the spectrum towards a plant-based diet. No amount of shorter showers or solar panels will save our world if we keep alone if the industry grows, as predicted. By coming on this journey, you are part of the solution.

As I travel the world, spreading the good word, I realize that vegan values are all our values. We're more alike than different. We all care about animals, justice, the environment, and our health. We all want the same things. And we are in this together.

You are a *Rebel Vegan*, and you are part of the solution. Wherever you are on the dietary spectrum, as you move towards a more plant-based life, you are sending a strong message: the world is changing, and you are changing with it.

This book was always about celebrating what's great about food, and not about restricting yourself. Returning to my true state of compassion and alignment has been the most rewarding adventure of my life. Veganism is the ultimate destination of one of life's greatest journeys.

Thank you for joining the rebellion, making this brave choice, being a force for good and on the right side of history. It takes determination and strength of character to stand in the face of the dominant belief system and challenge a lifetime of conditioning. But, together, *Rebel Vegans* will soldier on, keep flying the flag until the rest of the world catches up.

We are starting a revolution,

one meal at a time!

14

APPENDICES

APPENDIX 1 - LABELS EXPLAINED

Crate-free (pork)

This claim is not defined by the USDA. It indicates the animal was not housed in a gestation crate (used to confine sows during pregnancy) or a farrowing crate (used to confine sows from just before birth until the piglets are weaned). Some producers use the claim to signify no gestation crates only, while still using farrowing crates. This also does not tell the buyer anything about how the pigs were treated.

Ethically raised / Responsibly raised / Thoughtfully raised

None of these claims are defined by the USDA, and there is no third-party certification program to check these claims. The only thing the producer must do is explain what they mean by the claim that animals were "thoughtfully" raised. If you see this on a label, consider it a marketing tactic with no relevance to animal welfare.

Halal

The US Humane Methods of Slaughter Act exempts animals killed for religious purposes from the requirement that they be stunned (to make them insensitive to pain), before shackling, hoisting and cutting. This means Halal products come from animals slaughtered without being stunned. In other words, animals are fully conscious of what is happening to them.

Kosher

As with Halal products, kosher meats and poultry are typically produced from animals that have not been made insensitive to pain prior to slaughter.

Natural

This claim can be used on eggs and dairy, but the USDA definition only applies to meat and poultry. The claim "natural" can be used on products that have been minimally processed and are free from artificial ingredients or added colors. An explanation must accompany the claim for the use of the term. Unless stated, "natural" does not mean that no antibiotics or hormones were given to the animal. The claim has no relevance to how the animals were raised.

Naturally raised

This claim indicates the product has come from animals that have not been given antibiotics or hormones, and were fed a vegetarian diet. However, this does not require any improvement to living conditions, such as access to pasture or range.

No added hormones / No hormones administered

The US government prohibits the use of hormones for poultry, veal, eggs, bison and pork. A claim of "No added hormones" should come with a statement to say the administration of hormones is prohibited by federal regulation. This has no relevance to how animals are raised and slaughtered. It should be considered purely a marketing ploy.

Omega-3-enriched

This just means that Omega-3 (in the form of flaxseed, algae or fish oil) was added to feed given to the hens that produced those eggs. This claim bears no relevance to animal welfare.

United Egg Producers (UEP) certified

This certification program was developed by and for the egg industry, and is therefore not independent. The standards allow hens to be crowded in tiny cages for their entire lives, beak trimming without pain-relief, and no access to pasture, fresh air or sunlight.

USDA Process Verified

The USDA offers this "Process Verified Program" seal as a marketing tool to producers. Producers can submit their own standards for consideration, and the USDA audits to verify that the company is following the standards they set themselves. This means terms like "humanely handled" and "animal care" vary widely between producers, but are all eligible to receive the USDA Process Verified certificate. Many of these products come from factory-farmed animals, where animal welfare is not a priority.

Vegetarian fed

Putting aside the fact it's worrying that cattle should be fed anything other than plants, being herbivores, this claim only means that the animal feed used is free from animal-derived by-products. It has no relevance to how the animal was raised or slaughtered.

APPENDIX 2 - MEAT MOTIVATORS IN ADVERTISING

ALPHA MALE COMPLEX

Desire: Strength, muscles, masculinity.

Fear: Being a weakling, being called a "beta" man (as opposed to alpha).

Ah, that old, reassuring status quo of the man as a big beefy meathead who slaps down a carcass on the table for his cavewoman concubine to cook. Never mind if that's not really how it went down, men still want to feel like men - preferably alpha, big and strong. And you can't get big and strong on beans, can you? (vegan athletes prove differently, but let's ignore that for now). More meat equals more muscle! Somewhere in the back of our mind, we still believe if we eat three chickens a day and egg smoothies, we'll get big like Arnie or Stallone.

GOOD MOTHER COMPLEX

Desire: To give your baby everything they need.

Fear: Not doing right by your baby.

Mothers just want the best for their children. And so here come those soothing, pastel-shaded adverts that, in a soft voice, tell us baby formula contains everything your baby needs for health. The dairy industry knows we want to be good parents, and capitalizes on it. Unfortunately, baby formula is not the best for your baby, however many images of reassuring motherhood are plastered on our screens. Cow's milk is for baby cows. Not for baby humans.

HEALTHY AGING (FOR WOMEN)

Desire: Staying youthful and agile as long as possible.

Fear: Bones turning to dust post-menopause.

The myth that milk protects us from osteoporosis is still spread as if rooted in solid science. This does not explain why in countries with the highest intake of dairy, like the USA, rates of osteoporosis remain incredibly high. If dairy really protected against brittle bones, how is it that while dairy consumption has increased year after year (going from 32.1 pounds (14.5 kilos) of cheese consumed per year per person in 2000 to 40.4 pounds (18.33 kilos) of cheese per year per person in 2019), osteoporosis rates have also gone up? (from 33.6 million people in 2002 to 47.5 million people in 2020)

Something is not quite aligning.[1]

TRADITION AND BELONGING

Desire: To belong.

Fear: The loss of familiar, secure traditions.

Meat is part of our lives, and the industry won't let us forget it. Whether it's the comfort of a bacon sandwich in the morning, the joy of a sizzling summer barbecue, the quintessential greasy kebab after a night out, the celebratory roast turkey at Christmas or Thanksgiving, rare are the seasonal adverts that don't feature some type of animal product. This keeps meat firmly in our culture, even though our health and that of the planet is calling for us to release these old habits and forge new ones.

APPENDIX 3 - WHAT DO FACTORY-FARMED ANIMALS EAT?

Animal feed includes the rendered remains of animals. This means things like meat and bone meal, poultry by-product meal, dried animal blood, feather meal, hydrolysed leather meal, eggshell meal, hydrolysed whole poultry, hydrolysed hair, unborn calf carcasses, animal digest, bone marrow, and animal plasma.

Rendering is an industrial process in which animal carcasses, body parts and waste are ground up, heated, and further processed to produce various products, including animal feed.

Here is a short sample of some of the ingredients used in animal feed:

1. **Ingredients from slaughtered food-producing animals:** Around a third of the weight of an animal is not used directly for human consumption. Fat trim, viscera, blood, bones, feathers and hide is collected and processed by the rendering industry.
2. **Ingredients from animals that have died other than by slaughter:** This includes animals that were too ill to reach the slaughterhouse, as well as roadkill, euthanized companion animals (cats and dogs) and other euthanized animals.
3. **4-D animals (dead, dying, diseased or disabled):** 4-D animals are sold to salvagers for use as animal feed.
4. **Animal waste:** Animal waste such as dried cow manure, dried poultry waste, dried poultry litter and dried swine waste. The issue is that poultry litter can contain poultry feed that has spilled onto the litter. Poultry feed contains bovine meat. So we still have a situation where cows can be given feed that contains cow remains. This is what originally gave rise to mad cow disease (BSE).
5. **Dairy products:** Skimmed milk, buttermilk, chocolate milk, whey products, cheese rinds and dried milk protein also make it into animal feed.
6. **Polyethylene:** Plastic pellets are used to replace roughage in feedlot rations for finishing slaughter cattle. It is used at 0.5 pounds (0.23 kilos) per head for six days.
7. **Hazardous waste:** For example, zinc oxide from emission control dust from electric arc furnaces (which is listed as hazardous waste) is authorized to be used as a nutritional feed supplement for animals.
8. **Other additives:** such as artificial sweeteners, colour additives and extracts (used to give chicken skin and eggs a yellow colour) and formaldehyde (used to keep feed free from salmonella for 21 days).

And all this doesn't even take into consideration the amount of drugs and hormones pumped into the animals to keep them the right size and growing at an accelerated rate to maximize profits. Nor have we touched on the vast volume of antibiotics required to keep them alive long enough to even reach slaughter. The potential for antibiotic resistance to grow is enormous as a ludicrous 80%[2] of all antibiotics in the world are used in animal agriculture, not for treating humans.

Locked up, crammed in, abused, and fed a diet a million miles from their natural one. Is there any part of these animals' lives that is not traumatized by the industrial farming industry?

APPENDIX 4 - COMMON PATHOGENS IN MEAT & DAIRY

SALMONELLA:

The salmonella bacteria are present in the digestive tract. Salmonella food poisoning is caused by eating foods contaminated by feces. According to a study published in the journal Clinical Microbiology and Infection, the main sources of salmonella infections in humans are meat products, and in particular poultry meat.[1]

This is not surprising given the conditions in which the animals are kept, and because the speed of slaughter lines does not allow enough time for the animals to be properly eviscerated. As a result, much of the meat is contaminated with salmonella.

Salmonella causes 93.8 million illnesses and 155,000 deaths worldwide every year. [reference: S.E. Majowicz, J. Musto, E. Scallan, F.J. Angulo, M. Kirk, S.J. O'Brien, et al. The global burden of nontyphoidal Salmonella gastroenteritis, Clin Infect Dis, 50 (2010), pp. 882-889).

CAMPYLOBACTER:

One of four key global causes of diarrheal diseases worldwide, and the most common bacterial cause of human gastroenteritis. According to the World Health Organization, 1 in 10 people fall ill with campylobacter every year, causing a loss of 33 million healthy life years.[2]

In the UK, 80% of campylobacter infections are due to contaminated poultry.[3] In the USA, it causes an estimated 1.5 million illnesses every year.[4]

Campylobacter is found in the guts and feces of warm-blooded animals. Here again, contamination happens because animals live in their own waste for months and because industrial slaughterhouses and meat packing plants do not allow for proper food safety protocols.[5]

STAPHYLOCOCCUS AUREUS:

This pathogen is one of the major food-borne pathogens in the world. Staphylococcus aureus bacteria is found naturally on the skin, hair and mucosal lining of humans and animals. It is generally a commensal part of the microbiome (commensal means there is a mutually beneficial relationship between host and bacteria), however it can also become an opportunistic pathogen and is a common cause of skin infections, pneumonia and food poisoning.[6]

Staphylococcus aureus can adapt to its environment and quickly become resistant to drugs. One example is MRSA (methicillin-resistant S. aureus), which is now a worldwide problem and was listed by the World Health Organization as one of the 12 families of bacteria that pose the greatest threat to human health.[7]

MRSA strains have been found in pigs, cattle and poultry, as well as raw meat.

A study published in the journal Clinical Infectious Diseases found that 47% of all meat and poultry samples in the USA were contaminated with staphylococcus aureus, and half of those were resistant to three classes of antibiotics. [reference: The Translational Genomics Research Institute. (2011, April 15). US meat and poultry is widely contaminated with drug-resistant Staph bacteria, study finds. ScienceDaily.[8]

Drug resistant salmonella, drug-resistant campylobacter, and drug-resistant staphylococcus are all listed on the CDC's Antibiotic Resistance Threats in the United States, 2019 report.[9]

E. COLI:

E. Coli bacteria is found in the stomach, intestines and feces of warm-blooded animals. Shiva toxin-producing E. Coli (STEC) causes severe foodborne disease, and the primary cause of STEC outbreaks are ground meat products, raw milk, and fecal contamination of vegetables.[10]

During the slaughtering and butchering process, E. Coli gets on the surface of the meat or can become incorporated into meat products, like minced beef. This again is due to fast-moving slaughter lines. Some strains of E. Coli can cause diarrhea, bloody diarrhea, vomiting, stomach pain, cramps, as well as kidney failure.

STEC infection was the third most reported zoonosis in humans between 2015 and 2019, according to the European Centre for Disease Prevention and Control.[11]

VOLUME 2

THE PATH TO COMPASSION: HOW TO ALIGN WITH YOUR VALUES

INTRODUCTION

REBEL'S HOMECOMING

"In a time of universal deceit - telling the truth is a revolutionary act."
George Orwell[1]

Welcome home, fellow rebels.

Although veganism has recently become a buzzword and is breaking through into the mainstream consciousness, we are still the outsiders fighting for truth and compassion within a cruel and powerful system. Simply by being here, on page one, you are part of the solution and welcomed into our movement to create a kinder, refined future.

This book is all about celebrating, demystifying, and uncomplicating veganism to inspire and liberate the rebel in us all. Inside are the keys to help you find your way with a complete plant-based nutritional guide and a flexible 4-step program to reduce or exclude animal products in an easy and lasting way. I also share all my secrets and stories for an ethically aligned and sustainable life. We are all rebels here.

However, this is not a typical how-to guide, because you are not just another vegan. We all have our own unique relationship with food and must forge our own path to a more sustainable and healthy life. I see it as a homecoming to our original, authentic, caring selves. We all must find the compassion and truth inside us, and this book is a safe space to explore these different paths and find your way home. To be aligned with your values and build your best life.

Your journey towards a more sustainable, healthier lifestyle does not have to be difficult, nor should it include guilt trips or restrictions. I am not the vegan police. I promise never to preach, shame, or condescend. I will walk with you through this journey, offering inspiration and practical tips every step of the way.

This fully revised second edition of *REBEL VEGAN LIFE: A Plant-Based Nutrition Guide* is updated to reflect our rapidly shifting times, and includes the latest research and a whole new chapter on how our diet choices can help save ourselves and the planet from ecological collapse. It is crucial to be armed with the facts, to be open to change, and to be on the right side of history. We are rebels with a cause!

The *REBEL VEGAN LIFE* ethos is about expanding your horizons and revealing new possibilities, not restricting them. Many people feel put off from adopting a vegan lifestyle because of the judgment or infighting that is unfortunately part of any movement. I appreciate that this may lead to some turning away or feeling skeptical. My aim is to arouse and arm the inner rebel in everyone by opening up the vegan space. We are in this together, sharing our planet and its resources. Everyone is welcome at my table.

We cannot ignore that our diet and our health are linked. Eating meat and dairy leads to a greater likelihood of obesity, coronary heart disease, high blood pressure, cancer, and the development of zoonotic diseases.[2] And it's important to remember that humans are not carnivores by nature, but rather omnivores. We evolved, survived, and thrived on a primarily plant-based diet. Our diet is a choice. Our taste buds are habitual. It is an empowering and profound realization that changing our diets can bring so many benefits to ourselves and the world around us.

I am both a rebel and a realist. So I am proposing a new way to go vegan. To make lasting change, we need to stay connected—to each other and to our shared values of compassion and justice. If we can support each other and embrace a life in line with these essential ethics, we can find our way home and solve many issues facing our world today.

So *Rebel Vegan Life* is a safe space for everyone—one where even mindful meat-eaters are welcome to pull a seat up and learn what all the fuss is about. Anyone open to exploring vegan values can find something that resonates or motivates them to make positive changes. So let's join the compassionate revolution.

If you are going to rebel, do it with purpose.

*"The inside of my fridge used to look like a morgue.
Now it is a garden, full of color and life."*
REBEL VEGAN

THE REBEL VEGAN PHILOSOPHY

The Vegan Society's official definition of "vegan" is:

"... a philosophy and way of living which seeks to exclude - as far as is possible and practicable - all form of exploitation of, and cruelty to, animals for food, clothing, or any other purpose; and by extension, promotes the development and use of animal-free alternatives for the benefit of animals, humans, and the environment."

For many, this definition might seem intimidating–it's a lot to take on at once. This is why you meet so many naysayers, ex-vegans, and ex-vegetarians. Veganism has been portrayed as an extreme diet, but take a closer look at the definition and you'll see that it accounts for individual circumstances and offers some flexibility.

And put succinctly, veganism is simply a cruelty-free philosophy and way of living. This should not be hijacked by the media and made into an ascetic cult or joke. If you tell yourself that starting tomorrow you will never have cake, cookies, fast food, you will likely cave in rather quickly. The same happens with veganism. I have known vegans who seemed to have had a sudden enlightenment and went from carnism to veganism overnight. But not everyone can nor should. We all have our own paths, even when we share the same goals and ultimate destination.

I recognize that there is not one single way to go vegan. I see veganism as a way to navigate through life, trying to do the best for you and the world. You might go fully vegan, or you might start as a flexitarian. There is a dietary spectrum when it comes to cruelty-free eating, and we are all on it.

THE MAD COWBOY:

OPRAH'S DAIRY FARMER TURNED VEGAN ACTIVIST

I vividly remember the controversial story that first appeared on the Oprah show about twenty-five years ago. The dormant baby vegan in me was glued to the TV set. It stopped me in my tracks because I knew his story could be my story. The gentle farmer at the center of the storm could have been one of my uncles working the family farm.

Oprah's 'mad cowboy' was often portrayed as "radical" or "extreme", and yet everything he said was calm and rational. It struck a chord with me because he challenged everything I held true at the time, yet also made a lot of sense.

Howard Lyman was a fourth-generation dairy farmer and owned one of the biggest cattle farms in the Midwest. He hit the headlines in 1996 when he challenged America's powerful meat industry on Oprah's show "Dangerous Foods: Could It Happen Here?", where he discussed the possibility of mad cow disease happening in the US, and famously getting Oprah to utter the words "That just stops me cold: I'll never eat another burger."

Oprah was subsequently sued by the Texas cattle industry for $10 million in damages. Although she was eventually victorious, it took two years of litigation whereby she had to relocate her entire show to Texas and to this day seldom speaks on the subject. The actual show has never aired again and can't be found on Youtube. It did make a star of Dr. Phil who was actually Oprah's junior trial lawyer. For most people it highlighted just how sensitive the farming industry is about protecting it's image and position.

Overweight and suffering from sky-high blood pressure, Howard went vegetarian in 1990 and experienced a complete turnaround in his health. A year later, he went vegan and turned his entire life and livelihood upside down. He transformed his factory farm into a wildlife sanctuary, and has been advocating for veganism, organic farming, and animal rights ever since. At 83, Howard is still active in the vegan movement and inspires each new generation.

"I realized my livelihood was built on sand. Everything I'd believed in my entire life was at risk because there I was with a business built on killing animals."
HOWARD LYMAN

I was much too naive to completely understand what Howard was saying, or to challenge my own inbuilt cognitive dissonance to see past my own conditioning. But I also felt he was a trailblazer and truth-speaker. He seemed so solid, just like my uncles, and yet he challenged the status quo and my upbringing. He was the first REBEL VEGAN in my life–someone who made me question the system and want to find out the truth.[1]

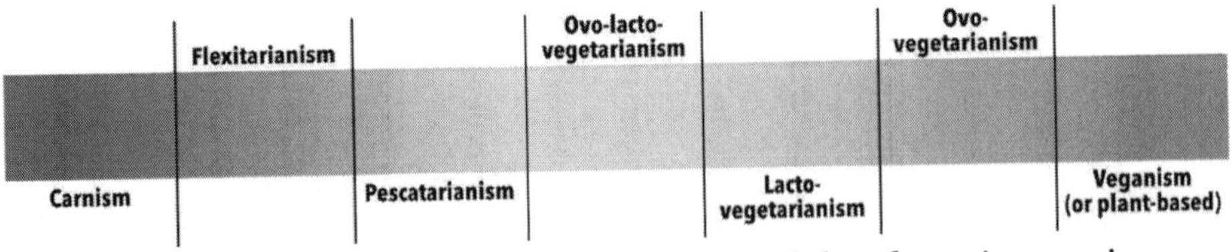

While the optimum place for yourself, others, and the planet is veganism, it is true that every step is just that–a step in the right direction. You can work your way along the spectrum at your own speed, using it as a guide for progression, rather than restrictive rules.

The *REBEL VEGAN LIFE* series aims to inform and empower readers to make their own decisions about where they fit on the spectrum and what shifts they would like to make in their lives towards a more compassionate way of being.

As your confidence grows, you will gradually move further along the spectrum. I am a realist, and I know that we won't change the current food system and turn the world vegan overnight. This is a long-haul process and transformation of the dominant culture. But we can all be part of this cultural shift and the momentum that this movement is building. By taking this journey—joining this rebellion—you are recognizing and directing the power you have in making a positive difference in the world on a daily basis.

Ask most vegans what they regret and the answer is unequivocal: Not doing it sooner. This lifestyle is a means to emanate dignity, celebrate compassion, promote justice, and live authentically in alignment with your core values. It should not be radical to uphold these principles and live a cruelty-free life. I vow to seek out the truth, debunk the myths, and uncomplicate the real issues in this heated debate, so that you feel fully empowered and inspired to build your best *Rebel Vegan* life.

I believe veganism is the future. After everything we've lived through, and with all the challenges we face globally, it is time for a compassionate revolution. And going vegan is an integral part of that. It may not solve all the problems facing the world, but no solution is complete without it. I know that future generations will remember *Rebel Vegans* as trailblazers, heralding the changes needed to build a brave new world.

And while this is an urgent and important undertaking, it can also be fun. It is a quest to find fresh ways to do things. It is a dare to experiment with new recipes and an excuse to taste unfamiliar flavors. It is the joy you feel when you know you are doing the right thing, and the sense of contentment when your ethics are aligned with your actions. And there is a sense of belonging to a bigger cause and community who are fighting on the right side of history.

Welcome to a revolution.

This book is your roadmap for this brave new world.

"Through my books and story, I hope to make veganism accessible and fun for everyone. To me, veganism is for everyone to share and pass on.

It belongs to anyone with compassion and a sense of justice. It's like this book—everybody who finds their way here will take away something different and create their unique plant-based journey.

Welcome to the table, fellow rebels."

15

A COMPASSIONATE REVOLUTION

Becoming an Agent For Change

"I do not see any reason why animals should be slaughtered to serve as human diet when there are so many substitutes. After all, man can live without meat. Compassion is the radicalism of our time."

The Dalai Lama.[1]

What is the core of veganism? There is a lot to it, and we will touch on that soon. But for now, let's keep it simple. Let's start with what veganism is not.

Veganism is not cruel, avoidant, carnistic, nor violent. The modern vegan movement is not some ascetic cult or extreme belief system. It is a philosophy based on kindness and justice for the planet, our fellow earthlings, and ourselves. I believe vegan values are all our shared values. However, veganism is not perfect or some badge of honor that gives free rein to criticize others—whether vegan or not. Veganism doesn't foster callousness nor hostility—quite the opposite, actually. At the core of veganism is compassion. It is an antidote and a reaction to the injustice, lies, and brutality of today's meat industry. Because of this unchecked and corrupted food system, our compassionate revolution has never been so critical, timely, and urgently needed to help solve many issues facing humanity.

Today's industrial global meat industry doesn't consider or protect values like compassion, respect, or truth. As one of history's most powerful industries, it has money as its driving force—profit over welfare and revenue over compassion.

Worryingly, the meat industry's power extends beyond the beings caged in its factories. The industry hurts the animals, the environment, and you without so much as a moment's thought. They have instilled in our society a system of normalized violence based on death, disease, and destruction, and they have called it progress. It is time to rebel, but we need to use an opposite force. Our secret weapons are compassion and justice. My motto is: Knowledge is power. And power should be used with compassion.

WHY A REVOLUTION?

History shows us that the people who end up changing the world - the revolutionaries - are always nuts, until they are right, and then they are geniuses.

John Eliot[2]

Animal agriculture is the leading cause of species extinction, ocean dead zones, water pollution, and habitat destruction. Livestock and their byproducts account for at least 32,000-million tons of carbon dioxide (CO_2) per year, or 51% of worldwide greenhouse gas emissions. Even without fossil fuels, we will exceed our 565-gigatons CO_2 limit by 2030 - just by raising animals. In addition, 1,100 land activists have been killed in the last twenty years. And this statistic accounts only for the brave people taking a stand in Brazil. And to top it all off, 82% of starving children live in countries where food is fed to livestock instead of to their people, and then the animals are shipped off and eaten by wealthier western countries, leaving the children to starve.[3]

How has humankind let this happen? How have we turned a blind eye to all the suffering and damage? Our food production systems are wreaking havoc on our world, and for what? Profit. Endless greed has allowed the creation and uncontrolled growth of industries that spread pain and suffering and cause waves of extinction around the globe. They don't care about feeding us. If they did, they would take the 135-billion pounds of food fed to cows every day and give some of it to humans who, by the way, only need 21-billion pounds of food per day worldwide.[4] It's time to challenge the systems that have built up around us. What we eat has never mattered more.

It can be hard to grasp how our diets can cause all this harm and destruction. Let's take a closer look at how things have gone wrong.

ANIMAL WELFARE

"We are all animals of this planet. We are all creatures. And non-human animals experience pain sensations just like we do."
Joaquin Phoenix

We are brought up to believe that the consumption of meat and dairy is natural, even necessary, to our wellbeing. The image of life on the farm is romanticized until there is no death, gore, or truth left to it in the slightest. You only have to look at children's picture books full of smiling farm animals to appreciate how disconnected we are from reality. I know this moral conflict and cognitive dissonance more than most, having grown up on a dairy farm in eastern Canada.

My family loved our animals. My father and his ancestors poured their all into ensuring their care and wellbeing. I grew up seeing the calves as my companions. Our cows were free to graze the fields during the day and slept in warm, comfortable beds of hay in the large wooden barn at night. Our farm was closer to the romanticized image than an industrial farm is, or could ever be. But, my journey from one end of the diet spectrum to the other has given me perspective. It is only from this distance that I can understand the suffering even in this idealized setting.

Looking back, I can see the pain and torment the animals endured. Even though my family meant well, the practices used at the time still resulted in traumatizing memories of calves crying all night , and the neighbor casually ripping chickens' heads off with his bare hands every time one escaped from their battery cages. I realize now how this was normalized. I was desensitized to the abuse surrounding me.

If my family's humble farm caused harm to the animals they took pride in raising, the harm and terror the animals are experiencing in today's factory farms—where they are seen as product units on an assembly line instead of sentient beings—is unimaginable. If you want to do a deeper dive and gain a true understanding of what is happening on these farms, refer to chapter five of the first book in my series: *REBEL VEGAN A Radical Take in Veganism For a Brave New World*. And for those brave truth seekers, I recommend watching "Earthlings" narrated by Joachin Phoenix (see our Resources section).

But why should we care about animal welfare? We can't bear to see a dog being kicked, yet eat and wear other animals without a thought.

THIS IS WHY.

Most of us are fully disconnected as to where our food comes from. We brand our meat 'pork' or 'beef', but cringe at the thought of eating 'pig flesh' or 'ground cow'? Have you noticed how the animal agriculture industry shows images of smiling baby animals behind white picket fences at the feet of loving farmers, but never the reality of the horrors of the factory farms? Did you know that many western governments have even introduced legislation to make it illegal for their citizens—us—to take pictures or videos inside farms, where the result of doing so is being placed on the terrorist registry! So damning and alarming is the reality of modern farming methods that they need to build these walls and keep us disconnected.

AND THIS IS WHY.

Animals are conscious, intelligent beings with complex social and emotional needs that cannot be met in a factory farm setting. We know that animals feel pain in the same way that we do; we know they experience emotions just like we do. Studies detailed in National Geographic by evolutionary biologist and author, Marc Bekoff, and postdoctoral fellow at the Natural History Museum of Los Angeles, Bree Putman, tell us that:

> *"Mammals share the same nervous system, neurochemicals, perceptions, and emotions, all of which are integrated into the experience of pain... Reptiles, amphibians, and fish have the neuroanatomy necessary to perceive pain and have been shown to avoid painful stimuli."*[5]

If we really tune into ourselves, we see that we naturally balk at inflicting physical or mental pain onto another creature. More importantly, we know deep down that we don't like the way meat gets on our plate—so much so that we can't even bear to think about it. This is why I believe vegans are often shunned and ridiculed. Just by our very presence, we can create an unease or tension in some. I believe our choice to act in line with our shared values brings up feelings of cognitive dissonance in those who have chosen to turn away from their innate instincts and cling to the status quo of the dominant carnist system. That violent ideology that has hoodwinked us all into believing that the Standard Western[6] is healthy and natural. My question to those who feel this unease or dissonance, but choose to ignore it and settle for what is on their plate, is this:

If we have to avoid thinking about something to do it, shouldn't that be evidence enough that something is wrong? If you can't bear to view the horrors of what happens inside factory farms, is it right to consume their products and expect nourishment or peace of mind? If any of this disturbs you, it is likely time to nourish the soul and be in alignment with your core values.

HOW SPECIESISM AND CARNISM ARE UNDERPINNING OUR TREATMENT OF ANIMALS[7]

We only have to compare the value we give to a puppy over a piglet to understand the concept of speciesism. One will lead an indulged life at the heart of our family. The other is considered a product for profit and will be fattened up and slaughtered at six months old, having spent it's brief life in a small pen. Yet there is nothing intrinsic that morally separates the dog and the pig. Scientific studies show that pigs are highly complex animals that can solve puzzles and are actually smarter than dogs. Our society has created these misguided moral distinctions, and this is speciesism.

Speciesism is a form of oppression like racism, and is the bias or practice of treating one species as morally more important than other species. I believe our future ancestors will look back at the way we treated and consumed other animals with horror. It is a dark mark on humanity and does not belong in our world. It is a symptom of a society completely disconnected from one simple truth: we are all connected and essential—all of us earthlings, sharing this planet, invested in our survival.

"One day the absurdity of the almost universal human belief in the slavery of other animals will be palpable. We shall then have discovered our souls and become worthier of sharing this planet with them."

Martin Luther King, Jr.

In her groundbreaking book *Why We Love Dogs, Eat Pigs, and Wear Cows: An Introduction to Carnism*, Dr. Melanie Joy first introduced the concept of carnism - the hidden belief system that enables us to support the use and consumption of animal products.

It is based on the assumption that humans have dominion over other animals by divine authority—in other words, animals are merely there to serve humans. Dr. Joy compared carnism to patriarchy, stating that both are dominant ideologies rarely challenged because they are so ubiquitous and yet unspoken.

"We don't see meat-eating as we do vegetarianism, as a choice, based on assumptions about animals, our world and ourselves. Rather, we see it as a given, the 'natural' thing to do, the way things have always been and the way things will always be. We eat animals without thinking about what we are doing and why, because the belief system that underlies this behavior is invisible. This invisible belief system is what I call carnism."

Dr. Melanie Joy[8]

If you have picked up this book, you may already appreciate or empathize that our treatment of other species is somehow intrinsically wrong. You have recognized that there is a disconnect—what I call moral schizophrenia. Maybe you recognize your own cognitive dissonance or unease with your involvement in this violent but unspoken carnist system. This can be a disturbing awakening, as it goes against our conditioning, and everything we have been told is normal and natural. But through discomfort, we grow and evolve. Your move towards a cruelty-free life is part of that evolution. As a *Rebel Vegan* it's our duty to challenge oppression and fight for justice and compassion.

THE ENVIRONMENT: INCONVENIENT SCIENCE

"We must change our diet.
The planet can't support billions of meat-eaters."
Sir David Attenborough[9]

Our current food system is simply not sustainable. Not because we can't produce enough food, as we learned above. Our food system is not sustainable because it literally consumes all our resources while destroying the planet we live on. Humanity's taste for flesh will make our children homeless. Animal agriculture is a main driver responsible for speeding up climate change. This is not a statement made up by Peta or a one-off environmental warrior. Eminent climate scientists have been sounding the alarm for decades. Their research shows that the most impactful thing we can do to halt the climate crisis is to reduce our reliance on animal products.[10]

While the greenhouse gas effect can be natural and beneficial, the fact is that the speed at which we increase the concentration of these gasses in our atmosphere is causing Earth's temperature to rise. The result is the climate disasters we are witnessing today. Cyclones devastated countries across southern Africa in 2019. At the same time, floods and landslides forced 12-million people from their homes in India, Nepal, and Bangladesh. Australia had the worst bushfire season on record in 2020. Hurricane after hurricane has swept through the southeastern United States, including the infamous Hurricane Ida,[11] while a vicious cycle of wildfires scorch the west.[12] And while it seems like water is an infinitely renewable resource, it's not. Droughts are leaving Central America's Dry Corridor without a successful crop season for the sixth year in a row, and the United Nations has announced that civilization will run out of freshwater by 2050 if we continue to waste this precious resource on animal agriculture. [13] [14]

The industry does not just waste water, it pollutes it beyond repair. Waste from the 70-billion animals raised in factory farms for slaughter each year,[15] consisting of antibiotic-resistant bacteria, hormones, bedding waste, antibiotic residues, chemicals, ammonia, nitrogen, heavy metals, and even dead animals, it runs off into our streams, rivers, and eventually our oceans. The result is ocean dead zones empty of their usual biodiversity. These zones also pose a risk to human health due to the toxic effects of red tides.[16] But why should we care about the biodiversity in the ocean?

In short, if the ocean dies... we die.

The ocean generates fifty percent of the oxygen we breathe. It helps regulate our climate, and it is the driving force of the global circulation system of water between land, sea, and the atmosphere. [17]

OUR HEALTH: LIES THE MEAT INDUSTRY TELLS US

"Everything in food works together to create health or disease."
T. Colin Campbell of The China Study[18]

Meat and dairy have been promoted as the pinnacles of a healthy diet and integral to our survival since the establishment of commercial food production systems. But the truth is we have all been misled and lied to. These foods aren't healthy - in fact, they are dangerous. They give us cancer, heart disease, obesity, and diabetes.[19] My mother taught me the truism that you are what you eat. Every time you eat, you either feed disease or fight it. You can consume vitality and health, or you can consume death or disease. Here I am reminded of the George Bernard Shaw quote: "I choose not to make a graveyard of my body for the rotting corpses of dead animals."[20]

Food is much more than simply fuel. There is truth in the old maxim that food is medicine, as it can either promote or worsen your health. It all depends on what you eat. Meat and dairy have been proven time and time again to cause inflammation, disease, and even death.[21] A plant-based diet of whole foods has been shown to not only prevent many chronic diseases, but may help treat some conditions, such as type 2 diabetes. Increasingly, the diet commonly prescribed to prevent, treat, and even reverse these diseases is a plant-based diet.

ANTIBIOTIC RESISTANCE: OUR FUTURE HEALTH UNDER THREAT

Meat and dairy also lead to antibiotic resistance. The Antimicrobial Resistance Global Report released by the World Health Organization (WHO) states that antimicrobial resistance is a:

> *"...widespread serious threat [that] is no longer a prediction for the future, it is happening right now in every region of the world and has the potential to affect anyone, of any age, in any country."*[22]

It is widespread and even necessary to misuse huge quantities of antibiotics on livestock, just so they can survive the brutal conditions of factory farming. It is estimated that worldwide 73% of all antibiotics are used on farm animals, not people. It became routine, as it enabled the animals to be kept in such appalling and unnatural conditions where disease would normally spread quickly. Even though the FDA banned the use of medically important antibiotics as growth promoters, the quantity of antibiotics sold for food-producing animals has been on the rise.[23] As a result, we are seeing an increase of antibiotic-resistant superbugs. Even our most commonplace and vital antibiotics, such as penicillin, are becoming obsolete. Without a massive shift in how we farm and produce food, we are heading towards another international health crisis.

The UK Government carried out an extensive study in 2019 and found that if we don't make changes to current farming practices, the number of deaths per year could increase to 10 million per year by 2050 - this would surpass the total deaths annually from cancer. This also has huge financial implications - with a cumulative cost of 11 trillion dollars. The World Bank estimates this would force 28 million people into extreme poverty.[24]

THE SOCIAL FACTOR:

"If you have men who will exclude any of God's creatures from the shelter of compassion and pity, you will have men who will deal likewise with their fellow men."

St Francis of Assisi[25]

"At his best, man is the noblest of all animals; separated from law and justice he is the worst."

Aristotle[26]

This is the least known reason for changing your diet and to rebel against the current food system. However, as little as we recognize it, meat production heavily influences our culture and how society functions. For instance, the animal agriculture industry is one of the factors contributing towards to social inequality. The industry provides jobs, but the treatment of their employees is comparable to modern-day slavery. The work is traumatizing, exploitative, hazardous, and grossly underpaid. And who is the industry giving these jobs to? Often it is destitute, the poor, and the illegal immigrants who have no voice, access to health care, and opportunities for advancement. They are stuck in this exploitative system.

People living near the slaughterhouses and factory farms are involuntarily suffering for our food choices as well. They have to endure air polluted with neurotoxins and chemicals that lead to respiratory conditions and even particles of feces.[27] The undesirable living conditions created by these factory operations often leads to them being located in impoverished communities where the people don't have the resources to fight back. They can't afford to fight, they can't afford to leave, and they certainly can't afford to treat the health burdens being forced upon them and their families.

If you care about equality and justice, then you care about vegan values.

COVID AND VEGANISM:

"What we eat matters all the more now."
British Medical Journal

It might be hard to see it at first, but Covid has put veganism on the map. It has exposed the old systems as dangerous and highlighted the urgent need for vegan values. And once you can see it, you can't unsee it.

Restaurants closing down and grocery stores facing scarcity of products allowed us the opportunity to pause, reflect, and prepare for what is being called the 'new normal'. More and more of us realize that we don't want to go back to our unsustainable or unhealthy ways, the effects of which are more prominent now than ever. We recognize that we need to move forward in a more mindful way, so we can avoid this happening again.

Covid has highlighted how essential our diet is in shaping our health. The brutal statistics have shown that people with high blood pressure, heart disease, diabetes, and obesity have a much higher risk of Covid-related mortality. We know that our standard Western diet is a huge factor in the development of these diseases. We also know that whole food, plant-based diets reduce the risk of all these health conditions, meaning changing the way we eat has never been more critical.

Beyond recognizing the seriousness of the health crises facing both ourselves and our planet, we recognized the need to not only prepare for future pandemics, but also to prevent them. Ending the exploitation of animals, and our intimate interaction with wildlife and mistreated factory-farmed animals through a plant-based lifestyle, is one of the biggest actions we can take to protect ourselves against future pandemics.

Animals in factory farms, backyard farms, and wildlife markets are held in horrifying conditions. Investigators from The Independent found animals living in pens with corpses in an advanced state of putrefaction, and containers overflowing with animal corpses covered in larvae. These are not isolated incidents, but a normal part of these operations. These conditions lead to the transmission of viruses between different species and humans, and could lead to another covid-like pandemic.[28]

Three out of four emerging infectious diseases come from animals. Every pandemic in recorded human history has come from our mistreatment of animals. Fifty-six zoonotic diseases are responsible for an estimated 2.5-billion cases of human illness, and 2.7-million deaths per year.[29] We have been relatively fortunate that covid wasn't more infectious or deadly.

This has given us a critical window of opportunity to rethink our food production and change our behavior. We need to learn these hard lessons. If we do not, the next pandemic could be much worse. And without a fundamental shift in the treatment of animals, it is not a question of if, but when.

If we want to protect our health, both individual and global, we must shift towards a diet that supports our immune systems while reducing the pressure on the planet.

I often say that the problem is on our plate. Luckily, so is the solution.

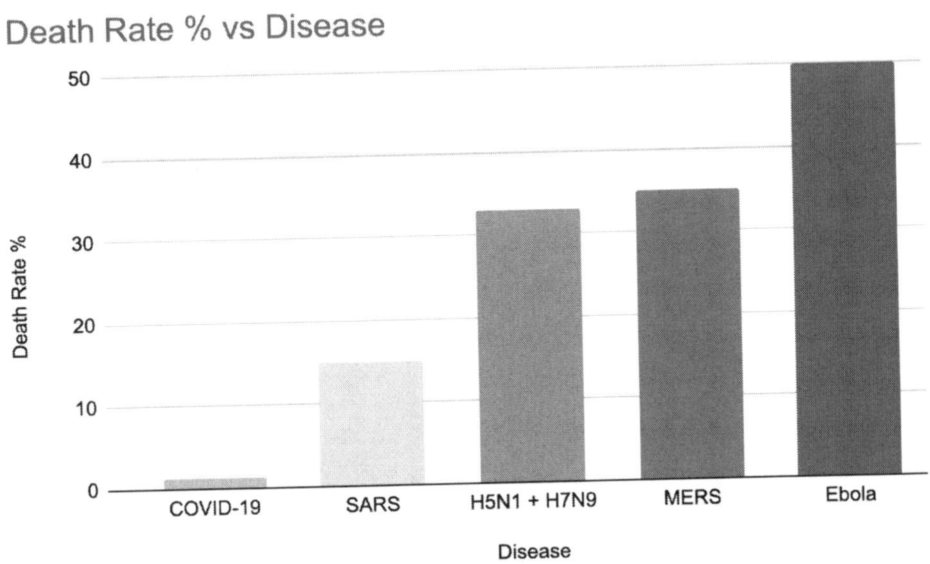

WHERE DO WE START?

With the science and warnings piling up, it becomes obvious that our diets and relationship with meat must change. It is an integral part of protecting our future. If you're anything like me, by now the voice in your head is probably screaming:

"But what can I do?"

I know I felt this way when I first learned the truth about the animal industry. I was enraged. I felt misled and disrespected. I wanted nothing to do with a system based on violence and inequality. It was time to rebel and fight for a brave new world.

We can protest, we can educate, we can fight through legislation—and we should. But there is something every person can do every day. Each day, you can save 1,100 gallons of water, forty-five pounds of grain, thirty square feet of forested land, twenty pounds of CO_2 in the atmosphere, and one animal's life.... Simply by choosing compassion, simply by going vegan.[29]

Rebel Vegan is a rally cry to forge a new, respectful relationship with other animals, with the planet, and ourselves. Throughout the pages of this book, I will help you take steps towards positive changes. I aim to arm you with everything you need to create your own compassionate revolution.

GET READY TO VEGANIZE YOUR WORLD ONE STEP AT A TIME.

B
12
K
V
C
B6

16

VEGANOMETRY
A PLANT-BASED HEALTH HANDBOOK

"The beef industry has contributed to more American deaths than all the wars of this century, all natural disasters, and all auto-mobile accidents combined. If beef is your idea of 'real food for real people' you'd better live real close to a real good hospital."

Dr. Neal D. Barnard[1]

"The most ethical diet just so happens to be the most environmentally sound diet and just so happens to be the healthiest."

Dr. Michael Greger[2]

FASTEN YOUR SEATBELTS.

This may shock you, it may disturb you, as it turns the long-accepted diet model on its head. According to medical scientists from Harvard University, the optimum amount of meat for a healthy diet is... **precisely zero.**[3]

The science regarding our current diet is in. It is overwhelming and unequivocal. The leading cause for premature death and disability in the United States is the standard American (or Western) diet.[4] This sobering statistic was the result of the largest ever study of risk factors for disease (the Global Burden of Disease Study), which examined deaths and their causes between 1990 and 2016.[5]

While it makes somber reading—after all, the study concludes that we've been making ourselves sick with every bite—it also offers hope. Because if our current way of eating has the power to make us unwell, then it also has the power to heal. If we veganize our diet, we can live longer, healthier lives... as well as be kinder to the environment and animals.

For your shift towards veganism to be successful, you need the tools and information to support your decision and a new way of life. If you're currently eating the standard Western diet—in which your meals are based around meat, dairy and eggs—simply removing animal products from your plate will likely leave you without enough calories or nutrients.

This is why many people who attempt a vegan diet return to eating meat, quoting tiredness and hunger as the main reasons. An understanding of what makes a healthy, balanced, plant-based diet will help you give your body everything it needs to thrive. So this chapter will give you that information so that you can begin to sustainably and successfully transition to a plant-based diet.

One of the oldest arguments leveled against veganism is the threat of malnourishment. The stereotype of the pale, thin vegan joylessly eating kale, lentils and brown rice for eternity is still present in many minds. The first question you've probably been asked if you've told anyone you're going plant-based is "but where will you get your protein/calcium/B12?"

Funny isn't it, how everyone becomes an expert, and people who have previously been unconcerned about any aspect of your diet suddenly become nutritionists when they find out you're vegan. Well, fear not, you can find all the nutrients your body needs in plants! And once you've finished reading this, you will be able to debunk any of the vegan nutrition myths that may be thrown your way.

Before we begin, I just want to explore and demystify the magical quality that seems to surround meat and dairy. Then, we'll get into the macro and micro-nutrients you need for health, and where you can find them. Plus, we'll see how veganism can help you get to your ideal body weight without counting calories.

WHY IS MEAT PROMOTED AS PART OF A HEALTHY DIET?

"Collectively the media; the meat, oil, and dairy industries; and our own government are not presenting accurate advice about the healthiest way to eat."

Dr. Caldwell Esselstyn[6]

If the science is in, telling us that plant-based nutrition is the healthiest option while meat and dairy contribute to disease, then why is there still such a strong reaction and skepticism around this topic? It turns out that this confusion is by design rather than by accident.

This is not the first time that powerful industries have attempted to pull the wool over our eyes. Fifty years ago, the tobacco industry used athletes, doctors, and soldiers as spokespeople to promote their products. Some of their adverts were even aimed at pregnant women (like Nico Time Cigarettes: "The smooth taste expectant mothers crave"). Among the claims were promises that smoking could calm an irritated throat, lessen coughing, and improve appetite management.[7]

When the harmful consequences of smoking began getting known, the tobacco industry funded its own studies to disprove any negative effects, while "proving" that smoking didn't actually cause cancer.[8]

These days, we would laugh if anyone tried telling us smoking is good for the body. The tide is turning on our diets too.

The industrial farming industry, large food corporations, and fast-food retailers use the same strategies as the tobacco industry did for decades to confuse the public about the dangers of their products. Backed by billions of dollars in profit and government subsidies, these industries are able to fund misleading studies, influence politicians, use celebrities to endorse their products, and put out clever marketing campaigns designed to keep the masses misinformed. What's more, their close ties to governments means certain foods remain on national nutritional guidelines, even though independent studies demonstrate that these foods cause disease and premature death.

I will give one example to illustrate this, but if you'd like to delve deeper into the murky world of industrial farming subsidies and corruption, head to Chapter 3 of the companion book, *REBEL VEGAN LIFE: A Radical New Take On Veganism For A Brave New World.*

In 2015, the World Health Organization (WHO) and International Agency for Research on Cancer (IARC) published a report on meat and cancer. They examined over 800 epidemiological studies and concluded that consuming meat poses a carcinogenic threat to humans. So much so that red meat was classified as a Group 2A carcinogen ("probably carcinogenic to humans") and processed meat as a Group 1 carcinogen ("carcinogenic to humans").[9] For comparison, tobacco and asbestos are both Group 1 carcinogens. Now, you might expect governments to take this information and act accordingly, for example, by publishing nutrition guidelines that help people reduce their consumption of animal products.

Another logical strategy would be to no longer advertise meat and dairy, or to put health warnings on fast food packaging, as they have done with cigarettes. Nothing of the sort has happened. In fact, US nutrition guidelines have remained largely unchanged for 15 years and still recommend a daily intake of meat and dairy.[10]

Clearly, it is up to us to do the research, challenge the status quo, and make the changes to create a just and sustainable future. That's what being a *Rebel Vegan* is all about.

THE DANGERS OF MEAT, DAIRY AND SEAFOOD

"The most ethical diet just so happens to be the most environmentally sound diet and just so happens to be the healthiest."

Dr. Michael Greger[11]

The accepted narrative and ingrained belief system are that animal products are essential for athletic muscles, strong bones, and a healthy brain. But while meat and dairy are still promoted as health-boosting foods, the reality is very different. Yes, they contain protein, B12, and heme iron, but they also contain saturated fat, cholesterol, and chemical residues from animal medications and feed.

These increase the risk of chronic non-communicable diseases, such as heart disease and cancer. Non-communicable diseases are lifestyle-related conditions. It is a sobering thought that our lifestyles are killing us over any virus, pandemic, or disaster. Today, more people will die from obesity than all the famines, wars, and car accidents in the world[12]. Often with little thought, we are making these potentially dangerous and important choices at every meal.

Here is a quick and dirty review of why meat, dairy, and even fish don't need to feature on your plate.

- Red and processed meat contain nitrates, saturated fat and other chemicals that increase the risk of colorectal cancer by 24%.[13] They also significantly increase the risk of cardiovascular disease, heart attacks and strokes.[14]
- Fish contain environmental pollutants such as methyl-mercury, polychlorinated biphenyls and mercury, which increase the risk of cardiovascular disease[15] and cognitive decline.[16]
- The FDA recommends that women of childbearing age should avoid fish because of mercury poisoning (a shockingly telling warning as far as I'm concerned!).[17]
- Dairy contains IGF-1 (insulin-like growth factor 1), which has been associated with an increased risk of cancer, diabetes, and chronic inflammation.[18]
- Dairy increases the risk of breast cancer by up to 80%.[19]
- Dairy increases the risk of prostate cancer by up to 65%.[20]
- Long-term consumption of eggs clogs the arteries and causes as much damage to blood vessels as smoking[21] (it is now illegal for egg manufacturers to advertise eggs as nutritious.[22])

CARDIOVASCULAR DISEASES:

Heart Diseases, Stroke, Heart Attack, Aorta Disease, Deep Vein Thrombosis.

Cardiovascular diseases are the leading cause of mortality globally, causing 32% of all deaths. Around 18 million people die because of heart disease (heart attacks and strokes) every year.[23]

Cardiovascular disease is caused by a build-up of fatty deposits (or plaque) in the blood vessels, which stop blood from flowing as it should to the brain or to the heart. One of the principal factors is diet–an excess of saturated fat and refined sugars, basically the two mainstays of the standard Western diet.

Diet is the cause of cardiovascular disease, and it can also be the antidote. A review of studies published in the journal *Trends in Cardiovascular Medicine* states that plant-based diets should be recommended as an environmentally sustainable dietary option to improve cardiovascular health.[24]

CANCER

Cancer is the second leading cause of death, causing 9.6 million deaths every year, or 1 in 6 deaths.[25]

It happens when normal cells begin to malfunction and mutate into tumors. While many still think that cancer is something that happens by accident or because of defective genes, the truth is that our lifestyle is mostly to blame.

According to a new study by the American Institute for Cancer Research, 42% of cancers are linked to risk factors we can control: excess weight, poor diet, and lack of physical activity.[26] Observational studies show that plant-based diets can reduce the risk of cancer by at least 10-12%.[27] Their protective effects come from the fiber, antioxidants and vitamins contained in vegetables, fruits, and other whole foods.

OBESITY

Worldwide obesity has almost tripled since 1975. According to the World Health Organization, 2 billion adults are overweight or obese, and at least 2.8 million people die each year as a result.[28] It is increasingly affecting children too - the proportion of obese or overweight 5-19 year olds has quadrupled from 4% in 1975 to 18% in 2016.[29]

Obesity is not a genetic disease. It is caused by an over-consumption of processed foods, low in nutrients, and high in fat and sugar. Ultimately, our current way of eating means that the population of the world's richest nations are simultaneously overfed but undernourished.

When it comes to weight management, shifting away from processed foods and towards whole plant foods is the best thing we can do. This is confirmed by a study published in the American Journal of Lifestyle Medicine, which states: "A diet centered on whole plant foods appears to be a safe, simple, sustainable solution to the obesity epidemic."[30]

TYPE 2 DIABETES

Around the world, 422 million people have diabetes. Tellingly, these are concentrated in wealthy nations with higher meat consumption rates. This disease causes 1.6 million deaths every year.[31]

Diabetes is characterized by high levels of blood sugar, which over time leads to damage to the nerves, blood vessels, eyes, kidneys, and heart. This happens when the body is unable to make enough insulin or becomes resistant to insulin, usually due to an excess intake of sugar. Diabetes is another disease that is both caused by–and preventable through–diet.

A study published in the European Journal of Epidemiology found that compared to meat-heavy diets, plant-based diets lower the risk of insulin resistance, pre-diabetes, and type 2 diabetes.[32]

DEMENTIA AND ALZHEIMER'S DISEASE

Worldwide, 50 million people have dementia, of which Alzheimer's is the most common form. There are around 10 million new cases of dementia each year.[33]

Dementia is a progressive disease that causes a deterioration in memory, thinking, emotional control, behavior, and the ability to live independently. While it mostly affects older people, it is not a normal part of aging. Studies show that diet-induced chronic inflammation and metabolic changes cause an acceleration of our cognitive decline.[34] Here again, our diet can either exacerbate or prevent this disease.

A study published by the *Journal Innovation in Aging* found that compared to non-vegetarians, people on a plant-based diet had a 38% lower risk of dementia.[35]

COVID-19

At the time of writing, there have been around 254 million cases and 5 million people have died from Covid.[36]

Covid-19 is not a chronic disease, but nonetheless, it has shone a spotlight on global health and the role of our diets. While questions still remain about exactly how the virus became a global pandemic, what we do know is that our ability to survive is in great part linked to our current state of health.

Studies show that people with obesity, diabetes, existing health conditions, or compromised immune systems are more likely to get Covid and to suffer complications. While diet alone cannot guarantee that you will avoid getting sick, a healthy diet does support a strong immune system–and a strong immune system is your body's defense against illness.

The science is clear when it comes to boosting immunity–a plant-based diet is the best solution. Centered around whole grains, beans, pulses, vegetables, fruits, nuts, and seeds, this diet is packed with nutrients that help the body stay healthy. And when your body is thriving, you are less likely to get sick.

In May 2021, a study published in the *British Medical Journal* compared the impact of different diets on Covid severity. Researchers found that plant-based diets and pescatarian diets were associated with a lower risk of moderate-to-severe Covid-19. They concluded that these types of diets can protect against severe Covid-19.[37]

"The beef industry has contributed to more American deaths than all the wars of this century, all natural disasters, and all automobile accidents combined. If beef is your idea of 'real food for real people,' you'd better live real close to a real good hospital."

Neal D. Barnard MD,
author of Foods That Fight Pain.[38]

IS JUST GOING VEGAN THE ANSWER?

Not entirely. And that's why it's so important to understand what makes a healthy diet. With big food producers bringing out vegan products, you can easily be a junk food vegan these days. And while this means you're not directly contributing to animal cruelty, it doesn't necessarily mean you're doing the best for your body.

Veganism is rooted in compassion—compassion for the animals, the planet, and fellow humans–and it's about trying your best to avoid inflicting harm. I think this should be extended to ourselves as well, and that means choosing foods that heal rather than damage your body.

The standard Western diet is characterized by a high intake of meat and dairy, but also a lot of sugar and processed foods—these foods harm the body. Plant-based foods, on the other hand, support health and longevity.

THE PROBLEM WITH SUGAR:
INFLAMMATION, OBESITY AND DIABETES

"History has demonstrated that a diet of specific vegan foods, eaten in a specific caloric ratio, will meet all our criteria. For healing inflammatory bowel diseases, other gut disorders and most other illnesses, I have learned which are the most beneficial foods of all. Those foods comprise what I call the Vegan Healing Diet."

Dr. David Klein[39]

We are consuming way too much sugar, and it is making us both fat and sick. Americans eat an average of 126g (30 teaspoons) of sugar a day.[40] The recommended intake according to the latest US nutritional guidelines is no more than 50 grams (12 teaspoons).[41] According to other health institutions, such as the NHS (the UK's National Health Service), this should be no more than 30 grams (7.25 teaspoons).[42] We are far from this ideal. Taking this into account, it is no wonder we suffer from so many preventable health problems.

There are two main ways that sugar damages your health. The first has to do with oxidative stress and inflammation. The second has to do with weight gain and diabetes.

Researchers have observed that excess sugar triggers a spike in free radicals.[43] Free radicals are chemicals that come from pollution and other toxins; they are also formed as by-products of your cells normal functioning (a little bit like exhaust fumes are a by-product of driving a car).

When there are too many free radicals circulating in the body, they cause something called oxidative stress. This process damages cell membranes, as well as causing DNA mutations that can trigger chronic disease.[44] Oxidative stress is one of the main factors in premature aging. Free radicals also increase inflammation in the body, and this increases your risk of chronic diseases (we'll look at inflammation in a moment).

When it comes to weight gain and diabetes, this has to do with how sugar is metabolized by the body. When you eat carbohydrates, your body breaks them down into glucose, which your cells can use as fuel. When glucose hits your bloodstream, your pancreas releases insulin–this is a hormone that signals to your cells to absorb the glucose.

When you eat too many carbohydrates or foods that contain a lot of sugar (such as processed foods and fizzy drinks), your pancreas has to pump out more and more insulin to try to get the glucose out of your bloodstream and into your cells. Over time, cells stop responding to the insulin–this is known as insulin resistance, which is the first step towards type 2 diabetes.

The other problem with insulin is that it also signals to the body to store any excess glucose as either glycogen (this is stored in your liver as readily available energy) or as fat (this happens when your glycogen stores are full). This is how sugar, which is technically fat-free (and, ironically, added to many no-fat or low-fat diet foods), actually causes excess body fat.

THE PROBLEM WITH PROCESSED FOODS:
CONVENIENT FOR YOUR SCHEDULE, NOT YOUR BODY

Processed foods are the ready-made foods we grab because it's convenient. According to a study by the British Medical Journal, over half of Americans' calories come from ultra-processed foods.[45] These are foods that have been taken apart and then put together again with added sweeteners, salt, oils, artificial additives and preservatives.

It wasn't that long ago that most people ate real food that was cooked at home from natural ingredients. These days, we just pick up something ready-made because it's faster. I mean, who has time to cook anyway? Programs like MasterChef have made us a little wary of stepping into the kitchen; we worry that cooking is a complex procedure that involves fidgety recipes, expensive gadgets, and hard-to-find ingredients. Ready-made meals are so much more convenient. But they are not convenient for our bodies.

As an example, let's take the average loaf of supermarket bread. It is made with a complex mix of refined flours, sugar, emulsifiers, preservatives, synthetic vitamins (which have to be added back in because the refining process strips the grains of their nutrients), and even dehydrated milk! On the other hand, homemade bread (or freshly made bread from a good bakery) contains whole grain flour, natural yeast, and water. The two will have a dramatically different impact on the body.

Processed food is any food that has been subjected to cleaning, heating, milling, chopping, pasteurizing, blanching, cooking, freezing, drying, dehydrating, mixing, packaging, or any other procedure that alters the original food source from its natural states, such as the addition of preservatives, flavorings, colors or other substances approved for use in food products.

I know what you're thinking—doesn't that mean most foods are processed? In a way, yes. We "process" foods when we cook them. So in effect, not all processed foods are bad—in fact, some are very handy to have in your kitchen because they make plant-based eating easier, such as canned beans.

Processed foods range from minimally processed to heavily processed:

- Minimally processed foods: such as roasted nuts, bagged salad, pre-chopped vegetables. These tend not to contain any additives.
- Foods processed to lock in nutritional value and freshness: such as canned tomatoes, canned vegetables and beans, plant milks, or frozen fruits and vegetables. Most of these do not contain added preservatives or ingredients (but you have to check the label, because some, particularly non-organic ones, contain added sugar, preservatives, and even artificial colors).
- Foods with added ingredients (like sugar, salt, oils, colors or preservatives) for flavor or texture: such as pasta sauces, salad dressings, cake mixes, sweetened yogurts, supermarket bread, sauces, dip, cheese slices, hot dogs, and processed meat products (like chicken nuggets).
- Ready to eat foods (these are the most heavily processed foods): such as crackers, biscuits, deli meats, crisps/chips, frozen ready-meals, microwaveable dinners, fizzy drinks, chilled desserts, sweets, candy.

When I say that processed foods should be avoided, I don't mean that you have to start preparing everything from scratch. Minimally processed foods (the first two bullet points) have a place in a healthy, balanced diet. For example, plant milk, frozen fruits and vegetables, roasted nuts and seeds, and canned beans do not have to be avoided. They contain nutrients that support health and help you move towards a vegan diet, while ensuring you give your body everything it needs.

So which processed foods should you avoid? They are easy to recognize. They tend to have a long shelf-life, and their ingredient label reads like a science experiment. They contain ingredients that sound like nothing you would have in your cupboards, such as:

- Monosodium glutamate: added to increase a food's umami flavor and to stimulate appetite. This additive has been linked to neurological issues and metabolic syndrome.[46]
- Erythrosine: added to make foods red. This additive has been linked to thyroid tumors.[47]
- Sodium nitrate: added to make processed meats salty and pink in color. This additive could increase the risk of stomach cancer.[48]
- Carrageenan: added as a thickener and preservative. This additive can trigger inflammation and digestive problems.[49]
- Sodium benzoate: added as a preservative, often found in fizzy drinks. This additive has been linked to ADHD[50] and cancer.[51]

As you can see, these ingredients are added to increase shelf life and to stimulate our taste buds so that we want to buy the product again (this is known in the industry as "repeat appeal"). Health and nutrition have little to do with it; it's more about profits and market share.

Another problem with ultra-processed foods is that they are empty calories. Empty, because they are devoid of nutrients. In other words, they do not contain the essential vitamins and minerals we need for optimum health. They just provide poor quality fuel (usually in the form of refined grains, sugars and fats) alongside a portion of chemicals that the body struggles to process and eliminate.

Let's compare a couple more foods, before we move on to the foundations of a healthy diet, and how you can begin to transition towards a way of eating that supports you while supporting animals and the planet.

The average ready-made salad dressing contains rapeseed oil, milk, eggs, sugar, artificial flavors and colors, ingredients that stress the body. On the other hand, you could very quickly throw together a simple salad dressing of olive oil, lemon juice, a pinch of salt, and maybe some parsley or mint - this would provide you with some healthy fats from the olive oil and inflammation-busting antioxidants from the lemon juice and herbs.

You could make a simple, filling meal in under 30 minutes by quickly stir-frying some vegetables and tofu, adding a splash of soy sauce and spoonful of peanut butter, and serve this alongside some buckwheat noodles or brown rice. This meal would provide you with antioxidants and fiber (vegetables), protein (tofu, peanut butter), healthy fats (peanuts) and complex carbohydrates (buckwheat noodles), which would fill you up and nourish you. Or you could buy a ready meal and pop it in the microwave, but because it is packed with sugar and made with refined ingredients, you're likely to feel hungry again within an hour.

Processed foods might look like the quicker, easier option–especially if you have a busy schedule– but they are not the smartest option when it comes to your health. I'm not saying that you must avoid all processed foods. After all, what is life without the occasional indulgence?

But it is about balance. I'm all about the 80-20 rule, which allows for a little deviation from whole foods. That means that most of your diet is made up of whole foods or minimally processed foods, with the occasional indulgence. The aim is not perfection, but to create the kind of diet you can sustain for life AND enjoy.

"When adopting a plant-based diet has been scientifically proven not only to stop the evolution of certain diseases, but it can also reverse them, we then have the moral responsibility to act upon and align our beliefs with our actions. Taking the courage to look the elephant in the eye."

Hayek Hospital goes plant-based[52]

MESSING WITH YOUR IMMUNE SYSTEM

Your immune system is your personal protection mechanism against disease and infection. Like a bodyguard, it patrols the body and destroys any chemicals, germs or parasites that put your health in danger. The immune system is able to recognize the cells that make up your body and eliminate anything unfamiliar or threatening. When you think about it, you are quite vulnerable. After all, we live in a toxic soup of microscopic bacteria, viruses, parasites, and toxins. These land on our skin, they're in the air we breathe, and the foods we eat. We survive thanks to our immune system, which works tirelessly to keep us safe.

This protective action can turn into a problem, for example, if your immune system reacts to something harmless (such as dust or pollen), or if it turns on itself (as is the case in autoimmune conditions). What makes the immune system over-react in this way? Chronic inflammation.

Chronic inflammation is something almost all of us struggle with to some degree, because of the way we live. Stress levels, polluted air, and processed food all cause an inflammatory response. While this response is normal and even desirable, it puts the immune system under stress. And we all know what happens when we become overwhelmed: we begin making mistakes.

FROM ACUTE INFLAMMATION TO CHRONIC INFLAMMATION - OUR DISRUPTED PROTECTION MECHANISM

Your immune system, or personal bodyguard, has several tools at its disposal to keep you safe. The one it uses most often is acute inflammation. You have no doubt experienced this in your life, if you've ever been bitten by a mosquito, sprained your wrist, or had a cold.

At the first sign of something being amiss—whether that's detecting a foreign substance (insect venom or virus) or damage (like a muscle tear)—your immune system springs into action. The symptoms of acute inflammation are easy to recognize:

- Redness: This is due to increased blood flow as the immune system sends white blood cells to the area.
- Swelling: This happens because of the extra fluids that carry immune cells to the site and carry away dead or damaged cells.
- Heat: Increased blood flow and fluids create more heat in the body.
- Pain: Caused by the by-products of these chemicals stimulating nerve endings.
- Timely: The symptoms last only until they're needed, usually between 2 days and 6 weeks.[53]
- If you have a cold, the symptoms you experience are due to your immune system's acute inflammation response. A red stuffy nose (swelling and redness), a fever (heat), and aching muscles (pain) are all signs that your body is working to get rid of the cold virus.

While acute inflammation is uncomfortable, it is a beneficial and healing process. Once the virus has been eliminated, the insect bite healed, or the muscle recovered, the symptoms disappear.

Chronic inflammation, on the other hand, is not beneficial. It is acute inflammation gone haywire. It happens when your immune system has too much to do. When your personal bodyguard is on constant high alert, it launches its inflammatory response constantly in order to combat substances that shouldn't be in your body.

Certain foods, particularly foods that contain excess sugar and artificial additives (meat, dairy, fish and processed foods, in other words), cause a temporary (acute) inflammatory response. If these foods are eaten regularly, this inflammatory response becomes chronic. When this happens, the effects go from being healing to being damaging. Chronic inflammation eventually damages healthy cells, tissues and organs, and leads to DNA damage, cellular disfunction and internal scarring. This then sets the scene for many chronic diseases—obesity, diabetes, heart disease, and cancer all have their roots in chronic inflammation.

According to the National Institute of Health, three out of every five deaths are due to diseases caused by chronic inflammation.[54] What's more, chronic inflammation makes it harder for your body to deal with illness or a virus. This is why people with a compromised immune system or those already struggling with inflammatory diseases are at higher risk of getting Covid or dying from it.

Stopping chronic inflammation in its tracks is a vital part of staying healthy and preventing disease. In order to do this, we must move away from the foods that cause inflammation, and move towards foods that actively fight inflammation and give the immune system what it needs to keep working effectively. We must transition to a diet that supports health.

What kind of diet is that? A whole-foods, plant-based diet. It's easier than you might think, once you know the foundations of a healthy, balanced diet. In the next chapter, we master the basics of a nutritious diet. Let's veganize our lives!

VEGAN DIET APPROPRIATE FOR ALL STAGES OF LIFE

The Canadian Dietetic Association, Dietitians of Canada, the British Dietetic Association and the American Dietetic Association have all come out in support of a vegan diet.

According to these recognized and respected institutions:

"Well planned vegan and other types of vegetarian diets are appropriate for all stages of the life cycle, including during pregnancy, lactation, infancy, childhood and adolescence."

They go on to say that plant-based diets offer:

"a number of nutritional benefits, including lower levels of saturated fats, cholesterol, and animal protein, as well as higher levels of carbohydrates, fiber, magnesium, potassium, folate, and antioxidants such as vitamins C and E and phytochemicals." [55]

THE CHINA STUDY: NO TURNING BACK FOR VEGANISM[56]

We have known for over two decades that a plant-based diet holds the key to our health and longevity. In 1998, the China study hit the headlines with groundbreaking findings: Our standard Western diet was killing us.

In the early 1980s, nutritional biochemist T. Colin Campbell from Cornell University set up a working partnership with the Chinese Academy of Preventative Medicine to study the connection between nutrition and disease. They called it the China Project. China offered a great opportunity to explore this because the population stayed in small areas and communities, and many regions relied on an almost entirely plant-based diet that was both low in fat and high in fiber–the exact opposite to the standard Western diet. This provided a great platform from which to compare the health of rural Chinese and the comparatively rich Americans.

Dr. Campbell's research was the first to highlight the need for a plant-based diet. His 20-year study looked at mortality rates from cancer and other chronic diseases in 65 counties in China, and found that the consumption of animal products and dairy increases the risk of chronic illnesses, such as cardiovascular disease, diabetes, breast cancer, prostate cancer, and bowel cancer.

Still today, this is considered one of the most comprehensive studies on nutrition ever carried out, and conclusively showed the dangers of a diet high in animal products, as well as the protective effect of a whole foods, plant-based diet. What shocked America and the world was how disturbing the comparison was between the health and weight of Chinese and American populations. Most assumed the land of plenty would have the superior diet and food system.

One of the study's biggest findings was the difference between how animal protein and plant protein behave in the body. It found that the proteins in animal foods cause both normal cells and cancerous cells to grow.

Animal proteins also trigger the production of growth factors (such as insulin-like growth factors), which increase the risk of cancer. On the other hand, plant proteins protect cells and do not promote cancer. The researchers' big takeaway was that cancer cells can be turned on or off simply by altering your diet and how much meat and casein proteins you eat.

Another important finding was that a whole foods, plant-based diet, does more than just prevent cancer – it is beneficial for a number of other diseases. During his study, Dr. Campbell realized how much the chronic diseases have in common. Because of these commonalities, it makes sense that proper nutrition both prevents disease and improves health. A plant-based diet can never be "bad" for you, only beneficial.

Ultimately, Campbell's book showed the West that it isn't necessary to eat meat. His book had such an impact that Bill Clinton became a vegan after reading it. To this day, the China Study is considered one of the most important studies into the connection between diet and health. There was no turning back!

"Nutrition that is truly beneficial for one chronic disease will support health across the board."
T. Colin Campbell

"Going vegan has kept me alive."
Bill Clinton

17

HOW VEGANISM CAN SAVE THE WORLD

BIOMASS: TRACKING THE RISE OF HUMANS VS THE FALL OF WILDLIFE

The natural world has been dangerously distorted and put under sustained threat after years of humans indiscriminately playing God.

One needs only to track the changing biomass of our planet over time to gain insight into how our current food systems and farming practices have drastically altered our natural world.

Biomass is an ecological term that accounts for all living matter—the mass of biological organisms alive in our ecosystem at any given time. Conveniently for us vegans, plants comprise most of the Earth's biomass. They are not under direct threat.[1]

But when we look at the changing animal biomass, we find alarming trends. Damningly, the most recent biomass study shows that 96% of the planet's mammals are now composed of domesticated animals.[2]

Once, a rich diversity of wild mammals roamed freely over our planet, making up most of the animal biomass. But chillingly, as we chart the rise of humans, we see the destruction of natural habitats and mass species extinction in our wake as the biomass index flipped on its head. We, and our ever-growing population of farmed animals, took over the natural world and started abusing its resources like they were infinite.

The biomass of wild animals has declined by 85% since the agricultural revolution, which saw humans domesticating certain wild animals and clearing the once-natural fertile plains and virgin forests for farmland. It seemingly went hand in hand; without the expansion and exploitation of much of the planet's natural resources, the rapid rise of humans would have been impossible. Add some greed into the mix; a storm of biblical proportions was building on our horizon.

Our industry leaders have brushed this off as the inevitable march of progress. But the biomass statistics are both sobering and catastrophic when you consider humans' brief timespan as masters of the universe. Although we only make up 0.01% of the Earth's total biomass, we have caused the loss of 85% of wild mammals, 80% of marine mammals, and 50% of plant life.[3]

It becomes even more incriminating when taken into account that half of those creatures are thought to have become extinct in the last fifty years. And, all the while, we continue to breed into existence farmed animals on an industrial scale. It is alarming to think we have destroyed so much rich life, unbalancing the natural order to such an extent, that the future of humanity itself is endangered.

This is the opposite of Darwin's natural selection theory; we have elevated ourselves to God. Today, the vast majority of surviving animals are bred for profit, not for the planet's wellbeing. Our fickle taste buds and greed are hastening the fall of the natural world.

But is there a way to turn things around? Are there viable solutions?

Ultimately, the only way to put things right is by reducing the amount of land we use in agriculture. Today, over half the world's habitable land surface is used in agriculture. The vast majority (80%) of this land is used for animal farming. Yet meat and dairy make up only 18% of the calories in our diets. This is dangerously inefficient and unsustainable.

Something has got to give. That something is us.

We already have the technology and means to produce enough food to feed the planet many times over on a plant-based diet. By transitioning to a primarily plant-based food system, we could produce enough food from a smaller land area, creating a better balance where wild animals could once again flourish.[4] From here, other benefits would flow. We would significantly reduce the risk of future pandemics or diseases, as we would have limited the opportunity for viruses to cross the species barrier into humans. The unneeded excess farmland could naturally rewild itself in no time, and much of our lost biodiversity would regenerate. This would lead to new animal life evolving and flourishing across the globe. Embryonic David Attenborough's would have new forests and species to track!

If we are serious about protecting what is left of wildlife, we need to stop destroying wild habitats, and the most powerful way to do that is to change our relationship with the other beings who share our planet. The biggest thing any of us can do, on a practical and individual level, is to alter our diets.

The problem is on our plates; luckily, so is the solution.

"Few problems are less recognized, but more important than, the accelerating disappearance of the Earth's biological resources.

In pushing other species to extinction, humanity is busy sawing off the limb on which it is perched."

Prof Paul K. Ehrlich, American Biologist and Author

18

COMPLETE NUTRITION

GETTING ALL YOU NEED FROM PLANTS

"People feel poorly because they are nourished by foods you wouldn't feed to your dog and cat. The rich western diet is full of fat, sugar, cholesterol, salt, animal protein — all the wrong foods for people."

Dr. John McDougall[1]

"Food is really and truly the most effective medicine."

Dr. Joel Fuhrman[2]

THE FOUNDATIONS OF A HEALTHY, BALANCED DIET

For optimum health, the body needs certain macro and micronutrients. Macro (meaning "big" in Greek) nutrients are the ones you need in large quantities: complex carbohydrates, protein, and healthy fats. Micro (meaning "small" in Greek) nutrients are those you need in smaller quantities: vitamins, minerals and antioxidants.

In this section, I'm going to break down why each of these nutrients is important for health, and where you can find them. In the next chapter, you'll find a step-by-step guide to begin putting this new knowledge into practice.

PROTEIN

I'll start with this one because it's the one most people are anxious about. There is a common misconception that you need meat for protein. The food industry has spent billions pushing that narrative, and it needs to be challenged. It's the first question every vegan must face: Where do you get your protein? We are a society obsessed with protein, but our obsession focuses on animal protein while ignoring or bypassing healthier (and often cheaper) plant proteins.

Protein is essential, and there is no denying that we need it; it is the building block of our cellular structures. Your body needs it to maintain and repair healthy tissues, bones, cartilage, and muscles. Proteins are made up of amino acids which the body uses to make enzymes (such as digestive enzymes that help you break down and absorb your food), hormones (such as epinephrine, which is important for muscle function and blood vessels; thyroxine, which is essential for thyroid function; and melatonin, which regulates your circadian rhythm).[3]

There are 21 amino acids the body needs for optimum health, nine of which are called essential because the body cannot make them, so they must be obtained from food. These essential amino acids are isoleucine, leucine, lysine, tryptophan, valine, threonine, histidine, phenylalanine and methionine. You'll find a list of these amino acids alongside food sources in the Appendix.

The reason we assume that animal products are the pinnacle of protein foods is that meat is classed as a "complete" protein because it contains all nine essential amino acids. However, it falls short in other areas: meat contains few vitamins, and no fiber or antioxidants.

But the good news is that you have options. Many plant foods contain these essential amino acids. And some contain all 21 essential amino acids. They are soybeans (edamame beans, tofu, tempeh), buckwheat, quinoa, hemp seeds and mycoprotein (mushroom protein, such as Quorn).

"Shifting the protein in your diet from animal meat to plant-based proteins is one of the most powerful measures someone can take to reduce the impact on our climate."

Leonardo DiCaprio

You can also combine certain plant food groups to obtain all nine essential amino acids:

- Combine grains and beans or legumes: for example peanut butter and oat crackers (peanuts are legumes, not nuts), rice and lentils, pasta and kidney beans, millet and black beans, couscous and chickpeas.
- Combine nuts or seeds with legumes or beans: for example pumpkin seeds and split peas, chickpeas and tahini (also known as hummus), sunflower seeds and black-eyed beans, almonds and lentils.

You can use the above to make quick, protein-rich side dishes or salads. For example, mixing canned lentils with toasted almonds, adding a drizzle of olive oil, squeeze of lemon and a pinch of salt. You can serve this alongside a grain (rice/pasta) and some veggies (roasted, stir-fried, or raw) and ta-dah! You've got a balanced, tasty and filling meal.

HOW MUCH PROTEIN DO YOU ACTUALLY NEED?

According to experts, sedentary adults need around 0.8 g of protein for every kilo of weight, or 0.43 g of protein per pound of weight, every day.[4] This equates to around 62 g of protein per day for an adult weighing 77 kilos / 170 pounds.

How does this translate in terms of food? Here are a few examples:

- 1 cup soybeans = 28.6 g protein[5]
- 1 Beyond Burger plant-based patty = 20 g protein[6]
- 1 Impossible Burger plant-based patty = 19 g protein[7]
- 1 cup cooked lentils = 18 g protein[8]
- 1 cup cooked split peas = 16.3 g protein[9]
- 1 cup cooked chickpeas = 14.5 g protein[10]
- 1 cup cooked quinoa = 11.4 g protein[11]
- 1/4 cup cashew nuts = 7.3 g protein[12]
- 1/4 cup sesame seeds = 6.4 g protein[13]
- 1 cup cooked buckwheat = 5.7 g protein[14]
- 1/4 cup almonds = 4.9 g protein[15]
- 2 tbsp flax seeds = 2.5 g protein[16]

But protein is not only present in beans, pulses, nuts and seeds. Grains and vegetables also contain some protein. For example:

- 1 cup cooked millet = 6.1 g protein[17]
- 1 cup cooked brown rice = 5 g protein[18]
- 1 cup broccoli = 3.7 g protein[19]
- 1 cup onions = 2.6 g protein[20]
- 1 cup mushrooms = 2.5 g protein[21]
- 1 cup cooked kale = 2.5 g protein[22]
- 1 cup cooked squash = 1.7 g protein[23]

You will find a handy table in the Appendix showing good sources of plant protein. The important thing to remember is that if you eat three good meals a day made up of plant-based whole foods, you will not struggle to get enough protein for your body.

The idea that meat is the best source of protein is a fallacy. Plant proteins are healthier (because they also contain fiber, minerals, and vitamins), cheaper, and better for the environment. In the last two years, Covid and a frightening sequence of climate disasters have sent many of us to the plant-based aisle. This has scared the meat industry, which has responded by pumping out articles aiming to push people back to meat by comparing "natural" beef burgers with "unnatural" plant-based options. But even this hasn't worked: nutritionists have come out in defense of plant-meats, stating that both the Beyond Meat and Impossible Burger contain more protein and less saturated fats than beef burgers.[24]

Plant-based meat substitutes are one way to easily adjust your diet to transition toward veganism.

Here are a few other ideas to get started:

- Use tofu or tempeh instead of chicken, pork, or beef in your stir-fries. Tofu is a blank canvas when it comes to flavor - you can marinate it with herbs or spices, and then fry, roast or bake it. Then serve alongside noodles, pasta, salads...
- Replace meat with lentils, beans, or plant-based mince in your chillies and curries.
- Add chickpeas or other beans to your salads for a protein kick.
- Try jackfruit, which has a texture similar to pulled pork or shredded chicken. Jackfruit can be marinated in whatever seasonings and sauces you enjoy. Jackfruit is a great meat substitute in curries - check out my *Rebel Vegan* recipes!
- Add hummus (or nut-based vegan cheese) to your sandwiches instead of deli meats or dairy cheese.
- Make scrambled tofu instead of scrambled eggs for breakfast.
- Try a chickpea omelet (made with gram flour) instead of an egg-based omelet.
- Try mashing chickpeas with vegan mayo or avocado for a mock tuna-mayo mix you can add to jacket potatoes or wraps.
- Fill your pittas with falafels (made from chickpeas) instead of meat or cheese.
- Try black beans instead of beef in your burritos.
- A marinated and baked portobello mushroom with avocado and vegan cheese is a delicious plant-based alternative to a beef burger.
- Have fun taste-testing the incredible variety of plant-based burgers to find one you love!

THE CONFUSION OVER CARBOHYDRATES

Carbohydrates are your body's main source of fuel. Your digestive enzymes break carbs down into glucose, which your cells convert into energy to carry out all their various functions–from moving your muscles to powering your thoughts (did you know your brain uses around 120 grams of glucose every day?[25]).

For the last decade or more, it has been increasingly fashionable to stay away from carbohydrates. This is a mistake. Not all carbohydrates are created equal–the trick is to choose the right ones. The three main types of carbohydrates are sugars, starches, and fiber. These can be split into two categories:

SIMPLE CARBOHYDRATES: The ones to limit

You'll find simple carbohydrates in fruit and cow's milk, as well as processed foods like fizzy drinks, cakes, sweets, ready meals, etc.

- Refined foods: such as white flour, white pasta, white bread, which are made from grains that have had their nutrients (such as the germ) removed.
- Added sugars: such as cane sugar, high-fructose corn syrup, glucose syrup.
- Naturally occurring sugars: fructose (found in fruits) and lactose (found in milk).

COMPLEX CARBOHYDRATES: The ones to indulge/good kind

You'll find complex carbohydrates in whole foods.

- Fiber–found in vegetables, whole grains, beans, legumes, fruits, nuts, and seeds.
- Starch–found in whole grains, root vegetables, beans, and pulses.

Simple carbohydrates are made up of one or two sugar molecules (mono-saccharides or di-saccharides), which are quickly absorbed by the body. Because of this, they tend to spike your blood sugar levels, disrupt insulin signaling, mess with your appetite, and increase the risk of disease.

In fact, scientists blame refined sugars for the current obesity, diabetes, and cardiovascular disease epidemics.[26] One reason for this is that diets high in refined carbohydrates cause an increase in c-reactive protein (CPR), a marker of chronic inflammation.[27]

On the other hand, complex carbohydrates are made up of three or more sugar molecules (oligo-saccharides or poly-saccharides), which are bonded together in a more complex chemical structure, and therefore broken down by the body more slowly. This means blood sugar levels remain stable, and the pancreas doesn't have to pump out a load of insulin.

Furthermore, complex carbohydrates contain vitamins and minerals that help the body stay healthy. Studies show that diets high in complex carbohydrates offer protection against many chronic diseases, including the ability to reverse existing diabetes and heart disease.[28]

Head to the Appendix to find a handy table with sources of complex carbohydrates.

FANTASTIC FIBER

The reason complex carbohydrates are better for you is that they contain plenty of healthy fiber. The fiber in whole foods helps with weight management, digestion, heart health, and even cancer prevention. Meat, fish, and dairy contain no fiber whatsoever. It is only found in plants. There are two types of fiber, both of which are beneficial: soluble and insoluble.

Soluble fiber soaks up water and turns into a gel (think about what happens when you mix water and oatmeal or chia seeds). It helps lower cholesterol because it prevents some dietary cholesterol from being absorbed. Over time, this can lower cholesterol levels. Soluble fiber also helps keep blood sugar levels stable, because it slows down the digestion of carbohydrates. What's more, it feeds the good bacteria in your gut, helping keep your digestive system healthy and your immune system strong.[29]

Insoluble fiber does not soak up water (think about what happens if you mix chopped kale with water). It acts like a broom, cleaning your digestive tract and ensuring things keep moving regularly. It adds bulk to your stools, which prevents constipation.

Although there is no fiber in meat or milk, you will find both soluble and insoluble fiber in varying proportions in all plant foods.[30]

People who eat a standard Western diet get on average 10 to 15 grams of fiber a day. This is far from the 40 grams recommended for health.[31] When you eat a plant-based diet, getting enough fiber is seldom a problem.

Carbohydrates are not the enemy, far from it! Studies show that people who eat a diet that contains plenty of complex carbohydrates from whole, natural foods (whole grains, beans, fruits and vegetables) are at a lower risk of obesity, type 2 diabetes and heart disease.[32]

Head to the Appendix for a full list of complex carbohydrates you can include in your diet.

Here are a few ways to start adding more complex carbohydrates and fiber to your day:

- Start your day with whole grains: for example, a bowl of steel-cut porridge oats (avoid instant porridge because this tends to be made from refined oats which have less fiber), granola or muesli made with whole grains, nuts and seeds (check the label and make sure that whole grains are the first ingredient and that there is little or no added sugar).
- Swap your bread for a whole grain variety: this is an effortless way to add more fiber into your day. Plus, whole grain loaves of bread are more satisfying and will keep you fuller than white bread.
- Swap your usual pasta or noodles for whole grain varieties: buckwheat noodles, whole grain spelt pasta, or even pasta made of beans or lentils, are an easy way to add more complex carbs into your life.
- Search beyond the bread aisle: Satisfy your carb craving with starchy vegetables like sweet potatoes, carrots and parsnips. They can be roasted and used in sandwiches, wraps or salads.
- Experiment with different grains: Branch out and try new things, such as quinoa, buckwheat, couscous, black rice, millet, barley. There are now tons of new and exciting bean kinds of pasta, and even couscous made from peas!

ARE FRUITS SIMPLE CARBOHYDRATES OR COMPLEX CARBOHYDRATES?

Both! Fruits contain simple carbohydrates (fructose), but they also contain fiber (especially in their skin and seeds) and other nutrients, such as antioxidants and fiber. So you can consider fruit a complex carbohydrate food, and an excellent addition to a balanced diet.

The best fruits are those that are colorful, low in sugar, and have edible peel and/or seeds (make sure you buy organic if you are not going to peel your produce), such as berries, apples, kiwis, watermelon, and papaya.

For optimum health and absorption of all the goodness in fruit, avoid juiced or fruit smoothies and eat the fruit whole. The basic rule is always to choose whole-foods over processed.

HEALTHY FATS

Before carbs were vilified, fats were held responsible for all our ills. The 80s brought us fat-free diets, but this did little to curb our globally expanding waistlines or reduce the number of heart attacks. This demonstrates that simply targeting one food group is not the answer.

Fat is not the enemy. Far from it. In fact, we need fat to function. The brain is made up mostly of fat. The protective layer around some neurons, known as the myelin sheath, is made up of fat. Cell membranes are made up of fat. Our liver needs fat in order to produce hormones.

But of course, just like carbohydrates and proteins, the quality of fat is important. Certain fats are best avoided, while others should take pride of place on your plate.

There are four main types of fat: saturated fats, trans-saturated fats, monounsaturated fats and polyunsaturated fats. The first two are usually solid at room temperature (like animal fat, butter or coconut oil), while the second two are usually liquid (like vegetable oil).

The accepted and over-simplified position is that saturated fats are bad because they increase cholesterol, while unsaturated fats are good because they can lower cholesterol. Both these statements are not as black and white as they seem.

When it comes to saturated fat and cholesterol, only 20% of the cholesterol in the body comes from food, the rest is produced by the body.[33] However, eating too much saturated fat causes a hike in LDL cholesterol (that's the "bad" cholesterol that increases the risk of heart disease and strokes). The standard Western diet contains a lot of saturated fat because of its high proportion of meat, dairy and eggs. That being said, not all saturated fats are bad–some are actually good for you. Coconut oil, for example, contains saturated fat alongside lauric acid, which increases HDL cholesterol (this is the good type of cholesterol that lowers the risk of heart disease).[34]

Looking at unsaturated fats, their health halo is not quite as bright as we might have been led to believe. Most of the unsaturated fats we consume come from vegetable oils like canola, corn, and soybean. These crops are either heavily sprayed with pesticides or genetically modified (in the US, 94% of soybean crops, 95% of canola crops, and 92% of corn crops are GMO[35]). As a result, the oils contain residues of pesticides and fertilizers, which have been shown to damage gut health[36] and are implicated in cancer (in 2015, the International Agency for Research on Cancer classified glyphosate, the most widely used herbicide in the world, as a Group 2A carcinogen[37]).

The way these oils are made doesn't bode well for their nutrient content either. Unlike olive oil or coconut oil, which can be obtained simply by pressing the fruit, vegetable oils have to undergo a lot of chemical processing (they have to be heated, mixed with solvents to extract the oils, then deodorized and treated to improve the smell, color, and flavor[38]). As we have shown, the more processing food has to go through, the less beneficial it is to health.

There's more. These oils are high in Omega-6. Which on the surface sounds good. We've all heard about the benefits of Omega-3 and Omega-6 fatty acids. We need both because the body does not produce either. Both are brain-healthy nutrients and are needed to help the body fight inflammation. But only in the right proportions.

The ideal ratio of Omega-3 to Omega-6 is between 1:1 and 1:3. In other words, we need to consume more or less the same amount of each, or just a little more Omega-6 than Omega-3. The standard Western diet, with its take-out foods and fried foods, is too rich in Omega-6. We're eating around twenty times more Omega-6 than Omega-3. The result is higher levels of chronic inflammation.

Your body uses Omega-6 and Omega-3 to make molecules called eicosanoids that are involved in the body's inflammation responses. The eicosanoids made from Omega-6 are pro-inflammatory, while those made from Omega-3 are anti-inflammatory. Both are needed because as we saw earlier, inflammation (when acute) is a beneficial action. But too much Omega-6 means more pro-inflammatory molecules are created in the body, and this can lead to chronic inflammation, which increases the risk of diseases such as cardiovascular disease, obesity, and Alzheimer's disease.[39]

To counter this, we need to reduce our intake of Omega-6 and eat more foods high in Omega-3. We'll take a closer look at Omega-3 in the Micronutrients section. In the Appendix section, you'll find a list of healthy fats to include in your diet.

Ways to add healthy fats to your diet:

- Swap your vegetable oils for cold-pressed olive oil, coconut oil, walnut oil, avocado oil, sesame oil, or flaxseed oil. Use coconut oil or avocado oil for cooking (both have a high smoke point, which makes them safe to heat at higher temperatures, and the others for making dressings or adding flavor to your dishes.
- Eat more avocados! Have it on toast, add to your salads, or blend with cacao powder and maple syrup to make a quick chocolate mousse.
- Snack on nuts and seeds.
- Roast nuts or seeds with spices or herbs, and add them to your meals for extra texture, flavor, and healthy fats.

CHOLESTEROL: GOOD OR BAD?

Cholesterol is a substance mired in misinformation. It isn't as simple as "cholesterol is bad." The truth is that the liver produces cholesterol to help build healthy cell membranes and hormones. But when too much cholesterol is obtained from our diet, problems arise.

There are two types of cholesterol: LDL (low-density lipoprotein) and HDL (high-density lipoprotein).

LDL cholesterol is known as "bad cholesterol" because it contributes to atherosclerosis (clogged arteries). HDL cholesterol is known as "good cholesterol" because it helps clear LDL cholesterol from blood vessels.

When cholesterol levels are measured, doctors will first look at total cholesterol, and then look at the ratio of LDL to HDL cholesterol to get a more accurate view of a person's health. A higher proportion of HDL cholesterol indicates a lower risk of heart disease. Ideally, total blood cholesterol should be less than 150 mg/dL (milligrams per deciliter) and the ratio of total cholesterol to HDL should be less than 4 to 1. However, the average American's ratio is 5 to 1, and almost 107 million Americans have cholesterol levels greater than 200 mg/dL. The average cholesterol level of coronary heart disease victims is 225 mg/dL.

The biggest source of cholesterol in our diet is animal products. Meat, dairy and eggs raise cholesterol levels and increase the risk of cardiovascular disease. On the other hand, whole plant-based foods do the opposite: their fiber slows the absorption of dietary cholesterol and reduces the amount of cholesterol produced by the liver, leading to a reduced risk of cardiovascular disease.[40]

ANOTHER PIECE OF THE PUZZLE: GUT HEALTH

No journey towards health is complete without addressing your digestive system and the bacteria that reside there.

Your gut is a foundational part of your health. We've talked about how your immune system can become disrupted and trigger chronic inflammation in response to certain foods. One of the best ways to improve health is to bring your immune system back into balance. And a key part of that is looking after your digestive system.

We see ourselves as complete and fully-formed humans, but that isn't the whole story. The body is made up of trillions of bacterial microorganisms. In fact, these cells outnumber human cells by 10 to 1.[41] While this might sound a bit crude, these bacteria should be celebrated because they work around the clock to keep you healthy. They are your first line of defense against disease.

Your immune system comes to life the moment you are born. When you passed through the birth canal, you became seeded with bacteria from your mother.

This bacteria, along with the bacteria in breast milk and the germs you naturally came into contact with in your early childhood, made up your unique bacterial fingerprint. From birth, these microbes taught your immune system how to respond to viruses, germs, and other threats. How well you can defend yourself against illness depends very much on having a strong population of bacteria.

The largest and most important concentration of bacteria is found in your gut. This is your immune system's piece de resistance – in fact, some scientists believe 80% of the immune system is located there. Gut microbes break down food into usable molecules, process indigestible carbohydrates (fiber) to produce essential vitamins, and trigger the appropriate immune-protective responses.

This means that if your gut is compromised, so is your immune system. The good news is that we know what damages the gut, and how to strengthen it.

Your gut lining is the barrier between your body and undigested food. When it is healthy, only food processed into useful molecules can pass through. If the gut lining becomes weak (a condition known as leaky gut or increased gut permeability), it can allow undigested particles to leak into your bloodstream. When this happens, your immune system recognizes these particles as foreign and launches an attack. The result is increased inflammation and changes in the gut's normal bacterial balance, which can lead to digestive problems and chronic disease.

Most people have leaky gut or bacterial imbalance to some degree, and our modern lifestyles are to blame. Here's how:

- Diet and inflammatory foods: The standard Western diet is high in sugar, fats, and processed foods that disrupt the gut's bacterial balance. Studies show that high meat diets cause gut dysbiosis[42] (a term that describes when bad bacteria outnumber the good bacteria).
- Pesticide residues: The chemicals used to grow our food has a negative impact on our gut. Research shows that even at allowed "safe" levels, glyphosate reduces good bacteria (particularly lactobacillus bacteria, which help fight inflammation), while increasing bad bacteria (such as prevotella bacteria, which is associated with overactive immune responses and low-grade inflammation).[43]
- Antibiotics: They're useful, but they destroy all bacteria, including the good ones.
- Ultra-sanitized environments: Our love of disinfecting everything means we are less exposed to naturally occurring bacteria.
- Lack of fiber: Fiber feeds the good bacteria in your gut. What's more, not eating enough fiber leads to constipation - and when waste lingers in the gut, this causes gut bacteria imbalances that weaken the intestinal lining.

DO YOU HAVE A LEAKY GUT?

Here are signs you could do with giving your gut a helping hand:

- Skin conditions such as acne, psoriasis, eczema
- Acid reflux
- Allergies
- Frequent illness
- Mood issues such as brain fog, anxiety, depression
- Fatigue
- Excess weight
- Swollen, red, or painful joints
- Digestive discomfort such as bloating, diarrhea, or constipation
- Trouble sleeping

It is possible to rebalance your gut.

It takes a simple, two-step process:

1. Avoid inflammatory foods: This means reducing your consumption of processed foods and avoiding meat and dairy. The good news is you've picked up this book at exactly the right time!
2. Include gut-friendly foods: This means foods that contain beneficial bacteria (fermented or probiotic foods) and foods that contain gut-friendly fiber (plant-based whole foods).

You will find a handy list of gut-friendly fermented foods, and tips to add them to your diet, in the Appendix.

Now that we know about the macronutrients you need to add to your diet to maintain your best health, let's take a look at which micronutrients will put a spring in your step.

MICRONUTRIENTS

These little powerhouses are essential for good health. Your body uses vitamins, minerals, and antioxidants to support many of its functions.

The first thing I will say about micronutrients is this: if you eat a diet made up of mostly plant foods, you will get the micronutrients you need for optimum health. That being said, when you switch to veganism, it is important to focus on certain key nutrients to ensure you get adequate amounts.

In this section, I'll tackle the main ones. In the appendix, you will find a table showing all the essential vitamins and minerals and where you can find them.

OMEGA-3

Omega-3 fatty acids are essential for maintaining and protecting cell membranes, particularly the brain, eyes, and cardiovascular system, as well as supporting your endocrine system (the network of glands that produce your hormones).[44] Your body uses Omega-3 to make molecules that help your immune system fight inflammation, making it a very useful tool to lower chronic inflammation and get your body back into balance.

Most people hear "Omega-3" and instantly think "fish oil." But did you know that fish get their Omega-3 from plants in the form of algae? The problem with prioritizing fish and fish oils to obtain enough Omega-3 is that these products also contain chemicals (heavy metals and pollutants like dioxin, mercury, and microplastics) that, ironically, put your health in danger. That's not to mention the environmental, ethical, and animal cruelty issues surrounding fish farming.

There are three Omega-3 fatty acids:

- Alpha-linolenic acid (ALA): found in plants such as flaxseed, which the body converts into EPA and DHA.
- Eicosapentaenoic acid (EPA): found in fish and fish oils
- Docosahexaenoic (DHA): found in fish and fish oils

Fish obtain their ALA Omega-3 from algae and then convert it to EPA and DHA. This conversion can be difficult for the human body, which is why some people insist that fish is essential to obtain enough Omega-3. Let me show you why this is not entirely true.

According to research from Cochrane University, EPA and DHA from oily fish and fish oil supplements have little or no effect on heart health.[45] On the other hand, a review of studies published in the British Journal of Nutrition found that ALA from plant foods helps reduce the risk of heart disease.[46] Put it another way: plant-based Omega-3 is better for you.

You can obtain your Omega-3 straight from the source (plants) instead of the middle man (fish). In fact, one study found that people on vegan diets obtain, on average, more than the recommended intake of Omega-3.[47]

Here are seven foods that are high in Omega-3:

- Chia seeds: 4,915 mg of Omega-3 per ounce (28 g)
- Hemp seeds: 6000 mg Omega-3 per ounce (28 g)
- Flax seeds: 6,388 mg of Omega-3 per ounce (28 g)
- Walnuts: 2,542 mg of Omega-3 per ounce (28 g)
- Algae oil supplement: Typically 300-500 mg of Omega-3 per capsule
- Perilla oil (made from perilla seeds, often used in Korean cuisine): 9,000 mg of Omega-3 per tablespoon (14 g)

Other plant foods also contain Omega-3, for example:

- Kidney beans: 300 mg per cup
- Brussels sprouts: 270 mg per cup
- Squash: 190 mg per cup
- Collard greens: 180 mg per cup
- Cauliflower: 210 mg per cup
- Chickpeas: 70 mg per cup
- Pumpkin seeds: 160 mg per cup
- Sunflower seeds: 120 mg per cup

Ways to add these to your diet:

- Make a chia pudding and have it for breakfast or a filling snack.
- Sprinkle chia seeds, hemp seeds, or flax seeds onto your breakfast cereal or other meals.
- Add chia seeds, hemp seeds, or flax seeds to your smoothies.
- Make energy balls or granola bars using chia seeds, hemp seeds, flax seeds, and/or walnuts.
- Toast walnuts and add to salads or have a handful as a snack.
- Use perilla oil instead of other oils (this would work well in a stir-fry or curry).
- Roast cauliflower or squash with curry spices and serve as a side dish, or blend them into a creamy soup.
- Sauté collard greens with a little garlic for a healthy side dish, or add to stir-fries.

B12

B12 is essential for the body's nervous system, red blood cells, and making DNA. Not getting enough can lead to megaloblastic anemia, where the bone marrow produces abnormal and immature red blood cells. If this happens, blood cells cannot deliver enough oxygen through the body. This leads to fatigue, lightheadedness, and irregular heartbeat. Left untreated, it can lead to irreparable nerve damage.[48]

This is the one nutrient vegans need to worry about because in today's world B12 is found exclusively in animal protein. This means you will need to get your B12 through supplementation. A B12 supplement is absolutely non-negotiable as you transition to a vegan diet. Check out the box below for the story of B12.

Thankfully, many vegan foods, such as soy products, plant-based milks, and cereals, are fortified with B12. The recommended intake of B12 is 2.4 micrograms a day, so check the label to see how much these foods provide. The simplest, most economical and convenient option is to take a good quality supplement.

Vegan sources of B12 include:

- Yeast extract (such as Marmite)
- Nutritional yeast (great for adding a cheesy flavor without dairy!)
- Breakfast cereals fortified with B12
- Plant milks fortified with B12
- Soy products fortified with B12
- ESSENTIAL: Good quality vegan multivitamin containing B12

Aim for a daily intake of 3 micrograms of B12 from food, or supplement at least 10 micrograms of B12 every day. While this is higher than the recommended intake, it will ensure you get enough of this nutrient. Your body only absorbs around 10 micrograms from a 500 microgram B12 supplement.[49]

For this reason, PETA recommends either eating enough fortified foods to obtain 3 micrograms per day or taking a daily cyanocobalamin B12 supplement (which your body converts to the two active forms of B12, methylcobalamin and adenosylcobalamin).[50]

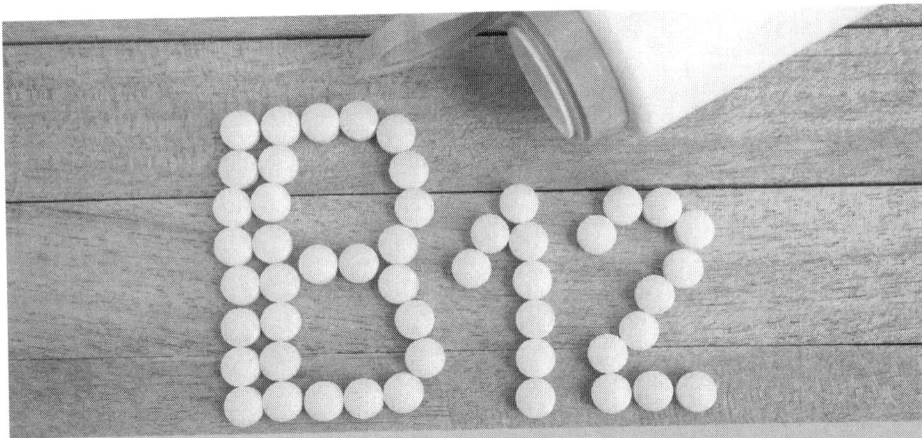

THE MISSING LINK: THE MYSTERY OF NATURE'S MISSING VITAMIN

The elusive and mysterious B12 is the only nutrient vegans cannot obtain from a fully plant-based diet. It's the missing link, and it has always bothered and intrigued me. I became curious how our mostly plant-based ancestors survived and evolved. I felt a little cheated by Mother Nature!

So I did a bit of digging and found interesting explanations, as well as a theory accepted by most historians for our ecosystem's glaring omission.

B12 is not made by plants or animals, but by bacteria that blanket the earth. Basically, it is in the dirt or topsoil. During most of human history, and before modern hygiene practices, traces of this bacteria from water, soil, and vegetables would get onto our fingers and into our mouths and guts, giving us the B12 we needed to survive and evolve—regardless of whether our ancestors had the methods or skills to kill wild animals (which they often didn't).

Our closest relatives, gorillas, get their B12 from accidentally eating soil (which contains bacteria) as part of their plant-based diet. Early humans got plenty of B12 from soil and from drinking water from rivers and streams that contain B12 producing bacteria. However, in today's sanitized world, water is commonly chlorinated to eliminate bacteria. This is positive, as we don't get cholera from our water supplies. But the downside is we don't get B12 either. What's more, due to intensive agricultural processes and over-farming, our soils no longer contain B12 producing bacteria. This is a problem facing both our farmed animals and us.

Cattle naturally get B12 from clumps of dirt around grassroots; chickens get their B12 from pecking soil for worms and insects. But factory farmed animals do not graze. They are kept indoors and never see the soil in their lifetime, so they would be deficient in B12 if it wasn't for supplementation. These artificial conditions make the "vegan is unnatural" argument seem somewhat ironic.

Did you know that 90% of B12 supplements are given to farmed animals? They are supplementing too.

In other words, people who eat meat simply receive B12 from the supplements given to the animals. Isn't it far better to simply take a B12 supplement and bypass the middle-man–or cow?

By the way, it's not just vegans who are at risk of B12 deficiency. The Framingham Offspring Study found that 39% of the population has either low or very low B12 levels. Interestingly, there was no difference between those who ate meat and poultry and those who didn't. The people with the highest levels of B12 were those who ate B12 fortified foods and those who took a B12 supplement.

The secret story of B12 exposes the hypocrisy and corruption of our broken food systems and modern farming.

CALCIUM

"The human body has no more need for cows' milk than it does for dogs' milk, horses' milk, or giraffes' milk."
Dr. Michael Klaper[51]

Calcium is vital for strong bones and much more besides. Your heart, muscles and nerves also require calcium in order to function properly. Calcium alongside Vitamin D (which your body needs to absorb calcium and make use of it) might even have a protective effect against cancer, heart disease, and high blood pressure.[52]

We have been repeatedly told that the only way we can build strong bones is by consuming dairy. It is time to shatter this myth. The reason milk contains calcium is that green plants pull calcium out of the soil through their roots and into their leaves.

Here again, cows are the middle-man; they eat the grass, we drink their milk. We have another option–we can go straight to the source. I don't mean to suggest you start eating grass, but leafy greens are a tasty alternative!

You need around 1,000 milligrams of calcium a day. Many vegan foods, such as plant-based milk, are fortified with calcium–many even contain more calcium than milk!

You can get all the calcium you need from leafy greens (like Swiss chard, broccoli, and kale), as well as other plant foods (listed below). This offers a double benefit: the calcium without the animal cruelty, and with added fiber and antioxidants that support health (whereas a cup of milk contains saturated fat that increases your risk of chronic disease[53]).

Plant-based sources of calcium include:[54]

- Tofu: 774 mg of calcium per 4 ounces (110 g)
- Collard greens: 267 mg of calcium per cup
- Swiss chard: 101 mg of calcium per cup
- Sesame seeds: 1404 mg of calcium per cup
- Kale: 93 mg of calcium per cup
- Bok choi: 158 mg of calcium per cup
- Almonds: 240 mg of calcium per cup
- Cabbage: 63 mg of calcium per cup
- Figs: 17 mg of calcium per medium fig
- Lentils: 37 mg of calcium per cup
- Bread and plant-based milk with added calcium (check the label for calcium amount)

Tips to add more calcium to your diet:

- Eat your greens: Include a portion of greens such as kale or collard greens in your day by adding them to stir-fries, sautéing them in olive oil and garlic, or steaming and adding to pasta for a filling green meal.
- Eat tofu: You can marinate it in maple syrup, ginger, and turmeric, or different spices, then fry, bake or roast and serve alongside vegetables and grains. Alternatively, add to your curries and stews, or try scrambled tofu instead of eggs. You can also add silken tofu to creamy soups and smoothies for an extra protein kick that will also deliver the calcium you need.
- Snack on dried figs and almonds.
- Make hummus by blending chickpeas, tahini (sesame seed paste), olive oil and garlic. Keep this in your fridge as a handy snack or tasty sandwich spread.
- Choose plant-based milk with added calcium (but check the label and avoid varieties with added sugar and preservatives).

IRON

Another nutrient we are told we need animal products for, and another nutrient we can get more efficiently from plants. Iron is essential for maintaining healthy blood by helping the body to produce red blood cells. If you don't get enough iron, the result is iron deficiency anemia. This condition affects between 4 and 5 million Americans every year and is the most common nutritional deficiency in the world.[55]

All animals get their iron from...you know the answer already: plants! Therefore, we can get iron from both plants and animals. But balance is key. Too much heme iron can trigger the production of free radicals, which damage cells, trigger disease, cause premature aging, and has been linked to several types of cancer.[56] To understand this better, let's look at the two forms of iron: heme and non-heme.

Heme iron is found only in animal products (meat, poultry and seafood). Non-heme iron is found in plant foods (whole grains, nuts, seeds, leafy greens, and legumes). The body absorbs heme iron from animal products regardless of its current level of iron. This means your body absorbs it from animal products, whether you need iron or not. Heme iron bypasses your body's attempts to control iron absorption. This can lead to high iron levels (and the formation of free radicals that I mentioned above, leading to a higher risk of premature aging and some cancers).

On the other hand, your body can adjust its absorption of non-heme iron depending on your iron levels–it is more absorbable when you need it, and less absorbable if your levels are too high. This means you can eat iron-rich plants without worrying about iron toxicity. And this is what gives non-heme iron a definite advantage over heme iron. Another win for plants. Now I know why my mother always said to finish my greens!

When it comes to iron supplementation, it is best avoided unless under the instruction of your doctor. You can get plenty of iron from a balanced plant-based diet. The recommended amount of iron is 8 milligrams per day for adult men and 18 milligrams per day for adult women.[57]

The richest sources of iron include:[58]

- Soybeans: 8.8 mg of iron per cup
- Lentils: 6.5 mg of iron per cup
- Spinach: 6.4 mg of iron per cup
- Sesame seeds: 21.6 mg of iron per cup
- Chickpeas: 4.7 mg of iron per cup
- Olives: 4.4 mg of iron per cup
- Kidney beans: 3.9 mg of iron per cup
- Swiss chard: 3.9 mg of iron per cup
- Black beans: 3.6 mg of iron per cup
- Pumpkin seeds: 2.8 mg of iron per cup
- Green peas: 2.8 mg of iron per cup
- Cumin: 2.7 mg of iron per 2 teaspoons
- Beet greens: 2.7 mg of iron per cup
- Asparagus: 1.6 mg of iron per cup
- Leeks: 1.1 mg of iron per cup

Ideas to include more iron into your diet:

- Use soybeans in your chillies, salads and stews.
- Toast pumpkin seeds and make a healthy trail mix (with roasted nuts and dried fruit) you can snack on.
- Make a cumin-flavored dish, for example by sprinkling cumin onto squash or sweet potatoes and roasting, or adding to hummus or bean dips for a spicy twist.
- Snack on olives or make an olive tapenade to snack on and add to your sandwiches.
- Add lentils to your lunchtime salad for extra protein and iron.
- Make a tahini (sesame paste) dressing and drizzle it on your salads or use it as a vegetable dip.

ZINC

Zinc is another essential nutrient for your health. It plays an important role in many processes, for example keeping your immune system strong (which is why you'll often find it in many over the counter cold remedies[59]), helping wound healing, and even sharpening your senses of taste and smell (very important for tasting and smelling the delicious plant-based food you'll be making as part of your journey towards veganism!). Zinc is also vital for a healthy pregnancy and helps growth and development during infancy.

This is another nutrient that we traditionally think of as only available from meat and dairy. However, a well-planned vegan diet provides adequate amounts of zinc. Researchers at the Medical Journal of Australia found that people on a plant-based diet can absorb and retain zinc better. What's more, their research indicates vegans are at no greater risk of zinc deficiency than non-vegans.[60]

The recommended daily intake of zinc is 11 milligrams per day for adult men and 8 milligrams a day for adult women.[61]

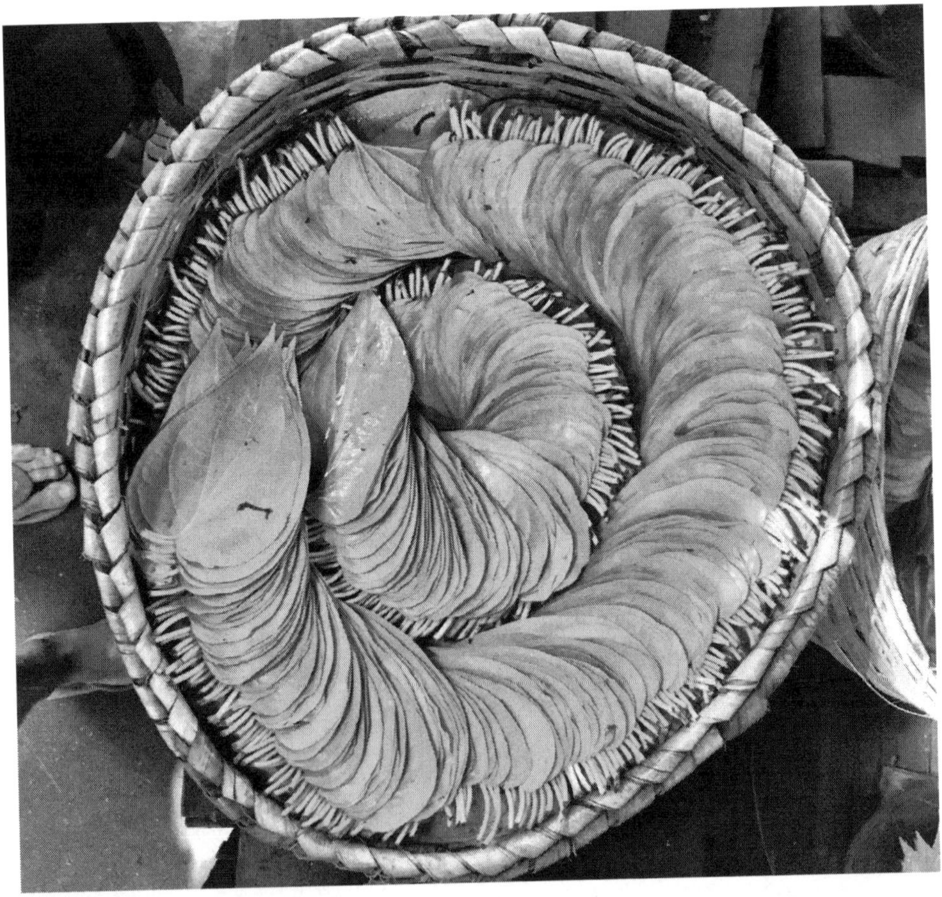

Plant-based sources of zinc include:[62]

- Spinach: 1.4 mg of zinc per cup
- Asparagus: 1.1 mg of zinc per cup
- Shiitake mushrooms: 2 mg of zinc per cup
- Sesame seeds: 11.2 mg of zinc per cup
- Quinoa: 2.7 mg of zinc per cup
- Pumpkin seeds: 10 mg of zinc per cup
- Chickpeas: 2.5 mg of zinc per cup
- Lentils: 2.5 mg of zinc per cup
- Cashew nuts: 9.2 mg of zinc per cup
- Tofu: 1.8 mg of zinc per 4 ounces (110g)
- Green peas: 1.6 mg of zinc per cup
- Oats: 6 mg of zinc per cup
- Squash: 0.7 mg of zinc per cup
- Broccoli: 0.7 mg of zinc per cup
- Swiss chard: 0.6 mg of zinc per cup
- Miso paste: 0.5 mg of zinc per tablespoon

Ideas to add more zinc to your life:

- Use shiitake mushrooms instead of chestnut mushrooms in your stir-fries and curries.
- Pan fry shiitake mushrooms with tamari sauce, soy sauce, or rosemary, and pile on top of sourdough bread for an epic zinc-boosting brunch dish.
- Prepare some homemade hummus using chickpeas and tahini - keep it in your fridge for a handy snack or just to dollop onto your salads and into sandwiches.
- Snack on roasted cashew nuts or pumpkin seeds.
- Try quinoa instead of brown rice or pasta.
- Start your day with a bowl of porridge, or add a handful of oats to your smoothies.
- Make a quick Asian-style dressing by mixing miso paste, a little water and a squeeze of lemon to liven up your veggies or use it to marinate tofu.

VITAMIN D

Also known as the sunshine vitamin, vitamin D is essential for many of the body's processes. For one, it is essential for strong bones because it helps your body absorb and use calcium. It also has a role in blood sugar control.

Some studies have found that vitamin D deficiency can increase the risk of developing diabetes, because it leads to impaired insulin control.[63] But perhaps even more important, vitamin D is essential for the body to produce mature and well-functioning white blood cells (these are your first line of defense against infection). A review of studies by the British Medical Journal found that vitamin D supplementation can protect against acute respiratory tract infections[64]--something that is particularly relevant right now to help fight Covid.

Very few foods naturally contain vitamin D, and most of them are animal foods, such as salmon, sardines, tuna, cow's milk and eggs. But even these foods do not deliver adequate amounts to save us from vitamin D deficiency.

In the US, where meat and dairy are consumed in large amounts, 41.6% of the population has vitamin D deficiency.[65] Humans naturally produce vitamin D when skin cells are exposed to sunlight. But with many of us staying indoors and wearing sunscreen, we rarely get enough sunlight to top up our levels.

So what's the answer?

Eating foods that are enriched with vitamin D, and taking a good-quality supplement. Make sure you choose a vegan brand because conventional vitamin D supplements are derived from lanolin (a fatty substance found in lamb's wool).

To avoid deficiency, the National Institutes of Health recommend an intake of 12 micrograms (or 600 IU - international units) per day for adults.[66]

SOURCES OF VITAMIN D:[67]

- White mushrooms (exposed to UV light to boost vitamin D concentration): 18.4 mg of vitamin D per cup
- Soy, almond, and oat milk fortified with vitamin D: 2.5 to 3.6 mg of vitamin D per cup
- Cereal fortified with vitamin D: 2 mg of vitamin D per serving (check the label)
- ESSENTIAL: Good quality vegan vitamin D supplement (check the label)

BEGIN PUTTING IT INTO PRACTICE

Becoming a *Rebel Vegan* involves challenging the dominant belief system and seeing through the profit-driven farming industry's claims about meat and dairy being healthy. I hope I've been able to convey to you in this chapter just how nutritious a plant-based diet can be.

Meat and dairy are not these magical foods that offer us everything we need for health–far from it. In fact, we can get everything we need from plant foods.

You might be wondering how this looks in practice. The trick here is to avoid overcomplicating it. As long as you make sure all macronutrients are present in your meals, you'll give yourself what you need for optimum health. A good way to visualize it is to fill half your plate with vegetables, and split the other half between complex carbohydrates and plant protein, then use healthy fats to flavor your dishes (for example by throwing on a handful of toasted seeds, or making a creamy dressing using nut or seed butters).

In the next chapter you'll find my handy 4-step program to transition to veganism. You've got the nutrition knowledge, now it's the fun part: putting it into practice. Let's start veganizing!

LOSING WEIGHT ON A VEGAN DIET

Q. What do you call someone who can't stick with a diet?
A. A desserter.

This is a guilt-free space, but... I think it won't come as a surprise when I tell you that we have put on weight during the pandemic (on average half a stone or 7 pounds[68]), because of extra stress and comfort eating. Not only is this bad for our morale, it also puts us in danger of getting sick.

Weight gain is one of the big factors in our global disease epidemics. Research shows people with excess weight are at a higher risk of diabetes, heart disease, cancer,[69] and the coronavirus. Even modest weight gain can lead to an elevated risk of hospitalization from Covid.[70]

The good news is that a vegan diet can help you shed excess weight and any Covid kilos you might have gained. Here's how:

MORE FIBER:

Fiber slows down the digestion of carbohydrates and sugar, which leads to more stable blood sugar levels and better appetite control. In other words, when you eat more plant foods, you won't feel as hungry between meal times, which leads to less snacking between meals and therefore better weight management.

PLANTS HELP YOUR BODY DETOX:

Your body is very clever. When there are too many toxins for it to process, because of pollution, stress and processed food, it stores them somewhere safe where they can do less damage–your fat cells. One of your main detoxification pathways is your digestive system. Thanks to increased fiber from plants, your bowel movements become regular, and this helps your body get rid of toxins. The result is gradual, sustainable, healthy weight loss.

ANTIOXIDANTS:

Plants are Mother Nature's medicines. Brightly colored fruits, vegetables, herbs, and spices are packed with plant pigments that act as antioxidants in the body. Antioxidants help your body neutralize free radicals and toxins. This helps your body release toxins and therefore helps you shed any excess weight.

IT'S A LIFESTYLE, NOT A DIET:

Diets don't work - they are rooted in short-term strategies that deliver short term results. The only thing we want to do when we're on a diet is to stop being on a diet. This diet mindset leads to disordered eating and disconnection with your body and your appetite.

A plant-based diet, on the other hand, is rooted in choosing foods that do your body, and the planet, good.

This is a game-changer.

It gives you the opportunity to create a diet that supports your body, tastes great, and helps you lose weight without counting calories or restricting.

I always say that veganism is not about restriction, but rather about BUILDING YOUR BEST LIFE.

WHAT ABOUT KETO?

We've all heard about the weight-loss benefits of a meat-centric ketogenic diet. But these results are inflated as a marketing tactic. The truth is that you'll lose more weight and be healthier by switching to a plant-based diet. This has been confirmed by a study comparing weight loss from a keto diet and a vegan diet. Participants who ate a carbohydrate-rich plant-based diet ate more food but lost body fat and retained muscle, while those who followed a meat-rich ketogenic diet ate less food but retained fat while losing muscle.

The researchers attributed these results to the fact that plant foods contain more fiber. Fiber helps keep you fuller for longer, improves your gut health, and supports one of your body's main detox pathways (your digestive tract), all of which helps you to release excess weight.[71]

So you see, a vegan diet is your friend when it comes to healthy, sustainable weight loss!

PRACTICAL WEIGHT-LOSS TIPS:

- **Fill up on fiber**. Satisfy your hunger by going for a second helping of greens or grains. The extra fiber will keep you full and help your body release excess weight.

- **Eat enough protein**. High-protein foods are the most filling foods and therefore help you manage your appetite. Add beans or tofu to your meals, snack on nuts or seeds, or add a scoop of vegan protein powder to your smoothies.

- **Start your day with a tall glass of water**. We often mistake thirst for hunger. Staying well hydrated ensures that you don't feel like snacking between meals. What's more, it helps your kidneys to flush out toxins, and this can help shift excess weight.

- **Limit processed food**. They contain a lot of sugar and fat which means we tend to over-eat them (because they taste good!) and then gain weight. Focus on whole foods instead. Go to the Appendix for a list of simple, tasty, healthy swaps to common processed foods.

- **Read the label**. Ingredients are listed in order of proportion. If sugar is the first, second, or third ingredient listed, leave that food on the shelf. If the ingredients sound like a chemistry experiment, it means the food is heavily processed and is best avoided.

- **Plan ahead**. Stock your fridge with healthy snacks you can quickly grab if a craving hits you. Hummus and vegetables, peanut butter and oat crackers, nuts and seeds, and homemade granola bars are all good options that will nourish you while helping you avoid processed foods.

- **Slow and steady wins the race.** You did not put weight on overnight, and it will take your body a little time to let go of the excess weight. Be patient and kind with yourself.

2
4
1
3

19

FOUR STEPS TO VEGAN

REBEL VEGINNER'S GUIDE

"You can't go back and change the beginning,
but you can start where you are and change the ending."
C. S. Lewis

Now for the fun part—putting your knowledge into practice. After all, knowledge is power, but only when it translates into action does it make a difference. Or, as I put it, compassion without action is just observation.

The Rebel Veginner's Guide introduces an easy and engaging program on how to get animal products out of your diet and embrace a life that is in line with your values. I have organized it so each step and meal time is supported with fun and simple recipes at the back of this book.

At each stage, please check out the corresponding recipes in Chapter 9 to help keep you motivated and inspire lasting change.

I always say veganism—like life—is a journey. So grab my hand, and let's start this new adventure. Let's veganize our lives!

LASTING CHANGE

Q: How many meat-eaters does it take to change a light bulb?
A: None. They prefer to stay in the dark!

The best way to make changes and stick to them is to go slowly, especially when you're changing something as integral as your diet. Gradually swapping one animal product at a time gives your body and mind time to adjust to new flavors and nutrients. I've designed the *Rebel Vegan* 4-week program to reduce your animal intake while remaining motivated, feeling supported and informed, and enjoying fabulous food.

While the steps are broken down into weeks, you have the option of going at your own pace–you're in the driver's seat. Some might race through, others might stop and pause while adjusting and finding their feet. Once you feel comfortable with each step, you can move on to the next one. In this way, you make sure you create your own journey towards the vegan you want to be.

With this unique approach, you can go as far along the vegan spectrum as you feel happy, and stop and start at any stage. You're in the driver's seat to fine-tune your diet and create your best life. If you are coming at this as a vegetarian, you only need to tackle the first step of this program to create a fully sustainable and cruelty-free life.

The goal of this guide is to be inclusive, flexible, and as guilt-free as possible. I developed this program for you to be emboldened and confident to find your own sweet spot. Although I encourage you to push yourself, only you can decide on your pace and how far you can go within your unique circumstances.

For change to last, you have to make it work for your lifestyle. There is a balance to be struck between your own driving forces, conscience, and circumstances. Of course, you have the option to go cold turkey, and while that works well for some, it doesn't sound gentle or cruelty-free!

When I first became vegan, I occasionally ate animal products at family events before my official "coming out." At home, I stopped stocking animal foods and gradually eliminated them from my kitchen cupboards and fridge. Slowly I got to know new recipes, new shops, and new restaurants. This is how I developed my unique and adaptable 4-week program. I was the first guinea pig!

Any effort you make to move further along the diet spectrum towards veganism to become more plant-based should be applauded. It will improve your health, reduce cruelty, and help create a more sustainable future.

You are becoming the change that you want to see.

BEFORE YOU BEGIN...

How many times have you started something (a diet, a health program, a course) only to give up before you've even got halfway? Don't feel bad, this happens to so many people, and all for one main reason: lack of proper planning. Yes, it's a cliché, but it's true—failing to plan is planning to fail.

And by planning, I don't just mean looking at your schedule and deciding when to go food shopping. I mean taking the time to fully connect with where you are now and where you want to be, to think about the potential challenges you will face so you can decide in advance how you will deal with them, and to start designing a routine that makes your new habits second nature.

Everyone has their preference when it comes to brainstorming. I get my best ideas by either walking or cycling in nature. Maybe you prefer to sit in front of an Excel spreadsheet, or to use a large piece of paper and lots of colored pens, or just record voice notes—whatever works for you.

Here are a few questions to think about before you embark on this 4-week transition.

- **Time management:** Block some time to begin your journey. Look at your weekly schedule and workout when you have spare time and when you have spare energy. Block these times in your diary - these are the moments when you'll be able to explore new aisles in the supermarket, try new recipes. Remember this is an adventure: make it fun!

- **Your current diet:** Now that you know more about the macro and micronutrients you need, how does your current way of eating measure up? How is the standard Western diet affecting you? (excess weight, tiredness, mood swings, diabetes, troubles sleeping, digestive issues...) Ask yourself what might happen if you don't make a change?

- **Your new diet:** Using the above answers as a guide, what benefits will veganism bring to you? How will you feel physically and emotionally thanks to this new lifestyle?

- **Preparing for and overcoming obstacles:** We all have triggers–what are yours? What situations might make you turn to habitual food patterns? How can you avoid this? For example, your trigger might be a looming deadline which sends you straight to the doughnut counter; or maybe you are a people-pleaser and worry that you might fall in with your friends' food preferences. Solutions might be that you keep some healthy vegan snacks in your office, or research vegan-friendly restaurants or cafes in your area. Thinking about how you would respond to possible triggers will help you stick to your plant-based diet even when the going gets tough.

- **Keep your "why" in mind:** Remember your driving forces. What are your hopes, dreams and goals as you transition to veganism?

WEEK 1
START THE DAY THE RIGHT WAY!

Let's jump in! Breakfast is the most important meal of the day, so let's start here and begin your day with plant-based goodness. If you are already vegetarian, this is your first and final step towards veganism. If you are coming to this from a standard Western diet, your first step is to cut out eggs and dairy.

Thanks to the rise of veganism, these foods are easy to replace. So this is a great place to begin. There is no cooking to adapt here, the only thing you need to do is change the aisle you walk down in the supermarket. Instead of heading to the dairy aisle, just head to the plant milk aisle. Simple! If you are really lucky, like me, you might even be able to get fresh oat milk delivered to your doorstep—it's worth checking.

MILK (OR "LIQUID MEAT" AS IT IS SOMETIMES CALLED!)

Ten years ago, you would have struggled to find a good alternative to cow milk, even in large supermarkets. It still bogles my mind that we don't question a massive industry that is essentially ferrying the body fluids of a new mother to our doors. Luckily, these days, you are spoiled for choice—you have oat, soy, almond, hazelnut, cashew, coconut, and even milk made from peas or potatoes!

The great thing here is that instead of being stuck with one type of milk for your tea, coffee, smoothies or cereal, you can now enjoy a wide selection of different flavors. For example, hazelnut milk works beautifully with coffee, pea milk adds a nice amount of protein to your smoothies, and almond milk adds nuttiness to your morning muesli (my personal favorite!).

CHEESE

This one is commonly quoted as the reason people can't possibly go vegan. But now there are many new and exciting vegan cheeses to try—both from big brands like Violife and smaller artisan vegan cheesemakers that are popping up all over the place to answer this need we have for cheesy goodness. You can also easily make your own simple herby vegan cheese (and I've included the recipe below).

Thanks to @strictlyrootsvegan

QUICK AND EASY VEGAN HERBY CASHEW SOFT CHEESE

INGREDIENTS:

- 1 cup cashew nuts (soaked overnight).
- 2 probiotic capsules (lactobacillus).
- 1 tsp Italian herb mix (or herbes de Provence).
- 1/8 tsp garlic granules (optional).
- Pinch of salt.

METHOD:

- Drain the cashews and place them in your high-speed blender. Blend until smooth. You might need to add a little water - try to add as little as possible because you want the mixture to stay quite thick (cream cheese consistency).
- Add the contents of two probiotic capsules and mix them in.
- Spoon the mixture into a bowl, cover it, and place in a warm dark place for 24 hours (for example an airing cupboard).
- When you check your mixture the next day, it should be aerated and smell slightly sour. If it isn't, leave it for another 24 hours.
- Mix in the herbs, garlic granules and salt.
- Spoon into a jar and store in the fridge. It will keep for 1 week.
- Spread on crackers, sandwiches, or use as a veggie dip.

HOW TO CHOOSE THE BEST PLANT-BASED DAIRY

Just like their dairy-based versions, some plant-based yogurts, cheeses and milk are basically just junk food: they are heavily processed and contain added sugar, preservatives and thickeners. A good place to start is to choose organic products, as these often contain fewer artificial ingredients and are less processed.

INGREDIENTS TO WATCH OUT FOR AND AVOID ARE:

- Sugar and other added sweeteners such as agave syrup, corn syrup, fructose, or sucrose. It's healthier to go for unsweetened yogurt and then add your own twist (for example fruit, dried fruit, oats, muesli, etc.)
- Thickeners are used to create the right yogurt consistency. But they are not created equal. Thickeners such as xanthan gum, guar gum, pectin and plant-based lecithin are safe. However, thickeners such as cellulose gum (carboxymethylcellulose), carrageenan, and polysorbate 80 can trigger digestive problems and are therefore best avoided.
- Additives such as titanium dioxide are sometimes added to make yogurt whiter. While it is generally recognized as safe by the FDA, I don't know how happy you feel about eating something that is also added to cosmetics and paint.
- Natural flavorings can also include unnatural flavorings made with chemicals, solvents, and preservatives. Go for unsweetened, unflavored vegan yogurt–you'll have a healthier starting point and can choose your own flavors to add.[1]

EGGS

Depending on how heavily eggs feature in your diet, you can cut them out here or wait until Week 4 when we eliminate all meat. There are plenty of great egg replacements available for recipes that traditionally call for eggs, or you can swap them for chia or flax eggs (simply mix 1 tablespoon of chia or flax with 3 tablespoons of warm water and voila—you have a healthy egg alternative).

If you enjoy baking, then research vegan recipes for your favorite cakes. I guarantee you will find several that can recreate your favorite baked goods without the animal products. Once you start veganizing, you'll be hooked.

YOGURT

If yogurt is an important part of your diet, you can swap it for coconut, almond, or soy-based yogurts instead. You can even make your own (you'll find a recipe for this below).

VEGAN YOGURT RECIPE

INGREDIENTS:

- 2 cups cashews (soaked overnight)
- 2 tsp organic raw apple cider vinegar
- 1 cup water
- 1 pinch of salt (optional)
- 2 capsules of probiotic supplement (lactobacillus works well)

METHOD:

- Rinse and drain the cashew nuts, then place in a blender along with all the other ingredients, except the probiotic supplements.
- Blend until completely smooth and creamy (depending on your blender, this will take between 1 and 4 minutes).
- Open the probiotic capsules and stir the powder into the blended cashews - use a wooden spoon or silicone spatula (metal spoons can stop the good bacteria from developing).
- Pour your cashew mix into a clean glass jar or bowl, and cover with a cheesecloth or clean and dry paper towel; use an elastic band to keep it in place and leave it somewhere safe.
- Wait 24-48 hours for the magic to happen. Taste the mix after 24 hours - if the flavor is slightly tangy, like yogurt, it's ready. If not, leave it for another 24 hours.
- Store your homemade vegan yogurt in the fridge and consume it within 5 days. You can also freeze it for up to a month.

OTHER OPTIONS:

- You can use a vegan yogurt starter - these are available in most health food shops. Simply follow the instructions.
- You can use 4 tablespoons of plain, unsweetened, organic vegan yogurt (simply mix this into the cashews once they are blended up).

ACTION PLAN FOR WEEK 1:

- Make your breakfasts plant-based. (See the Breakfast section of the Rebel Recipes for inspiration.)

- Invest in a good quality B12 supplement.

- Invest in a good quality vegan vitamin D supplement.

- Invest in a good quality vegan multivitamin.

- Explore new aisles: head to the supermarket and fill your trolley with plant-based goodies. Try a few types to find one you enjoy. Remember to check the label and focus on milk and yogurts that contain no added sugar, preservatives, artificial flavorings or colors.

- Embrace the new: change up your routine by trying out a new health food shop, buying an exotic fruit or unfamiliar vegetable and googling how to use it.

WEEK 2
THE FLEXITARIAN STAGE

The second step is to move to a flexitarian diet and cut out red meat. Also this week, your goal is to make both your breakfasts and lunches 100% plant-based. You can still have poultry and/or fish for dinner. This step might seem a little scary, but it's also exciting, as you can begin exploring all the tasty vegan options on offer. When I first tasted a Beyond Burger, I knew I could be a full-time vegan!

ACTION PLAN FOR WEEK 2:

- Make both your breakfast and lunch 100% plant-based. There is a whole section of lunch recipes in Chapter 9.

- Find your tribe! One of the main reasons ex-vegans fall off the wagon is because they feel isolated and unsupported.[1] Don't let this happen to you. There are plenty of great support networks out there, from Facebook groups to blogs. Join a local network and make some new plant-based buddies. Take a look at the Resource section at the end of the book for a list of good places to start.

- If you enjoy cooking, this is the time to invest in a good vegan cookbook (or more!) and start having some fun in the kitchen–after all, it is likely you've been stuck in a rut and eating the same foods day in and day out. This is your opportunity to rethink your dishes and start enjoying food all over again.

WEEK 3
DINNER - DOING THE PESCETARIAN

The third step is to go pescetarian. Cut out all land animals from your diet and begin making your dinners plant-based. Here, you can still "fall back" on seafood, but you should be reveling in your ongoing transformation and begin feeling healthier. Having massively reduced your consumption of animal products, your blood will be flowing better and your heart will be under less stress.[2] It's good to take stock and recognize your progression, improved health, and pat yourself on the back for coming this far.

ACTION PLAN FOR WEEK 3:

- Keep your breakfasts and lunches plant-based while cutting out all land animals from your dinner.
- Stay connected with your new vegan network. Don't hesitate to reach out for support, advice and inspiration.
- We all have one or two go-to dishes we love and can make and eat again and again. Choose two new go-to dishes that are vegan and easy to make. Keep it simple and fun! This is an adventure, so enjoy the journey.
- Stay motivated by reviewing your key driving forces for change. You can also reach out to your support network for recognition of how far you've come.
- If one of your driving forces is better health, this is a good time to check your blood pressure or jump on the scales - the results will incentivize you to keep going.
- If you are feeling shaky, review your driving forces from Chapter 1 and my tips to staying motivated and inspired later in Chapter 7

WEEK 4
MY NEW REALITY: COMING OUT

It's time to go fully plant-based! Cut out any remaining or lingering animal products from your diet. And if you didn't cut out eggs in Step 1, now is the time to do it. Your blood will be flowing at its best since you were a baby. Hopefully—like a dog let off a lead—you are eager and motivated to start your new healthy life.

Congratulate yourself and share the news with your vegan tribe and support networks. Tune into yourself: how are you feeling–physically and emotionally–now you've gone through these steps? Do you feel ready to come out into the world as a new vegan? Are you feeling lighter, do you have more energy, have you lost some weight? This is the week you can start resting easier knowing that you are living a cruelty-free life, making a difference to climate change, and improving your longevity.

ACTION PLAN FOR WEEK 4:

- Veganize and make all meals & snacks 100% plant-based!
- Try some of the easy dinner recipes at the back of the book.
- Research local plant-based-friendly restaurants, cafés, and communities.
- If you feel ready, now is the time to come out to close family and friends. Share your news with the people you trust. There is no need to be smug here - your glowing health and enthusiasm should be shared and will be celebrated by anyone who loves you.
- Gratitude and self-care: you are making brave choices so pat yourself on the back and be good to yourself!
- Coming out party! Mark this achievement with a special treat or a night out. I have included my favorite curry and desert in the Rebel Cookbook at the end of this book. Or you can celebrate at your newfound local vegan restaurant!
- And as an extra reward to celebrate your new life, I've included my two favourite vegan chocolate recipes on the next page. Go treat yourself! Congratulations!

MAKE YOUR OWN VEGAN CHOCOLATE! (2-INGREDIENT PEANUT CHOCOLATE FUDGE)

INGREDIENTS:

- 100g dark chocolate (choose an organic brand made with at least 75% cacao)
- 100g peanut butter (choose a brand made with peanuts and nothing else added)

METHOD:

- Chop the dark chocolate into small pieces, and place these in a bowl.
- Melt the chocolate over a bain-marie (place the bowl over a saucepan of boiling water).
- Once melted, add the peanut butter and mix until everything is combined.
- Pour into silicon molds or a container lined with parchment paper, and place in the fridge for an hour to set.
- Once set, store in an airtight container in the fridge. This will keep for at least 2 weeks (but mine never lasts that long!).
- Voila - easy healthy chocolate peanut fudge you can grab whenever you get a craving for something sweet.

EASY ALMOND & CHOCOLATE REBEL BITES

INGREDIENTS:

- 100g dark chocolate (choose an organic brand made with at least 75% cacao)
- 30g almond butter (choose a brand made with almonds and nothing else added)
- 50g roasted almonds (roughly chopped)
- Pinch of salt

METHOD:

- Chop the dark chocolate into small pieces, and place these in a bowl.
- Melt the chocolate over a bain-marie (place the bowl over a saucepan of boiling water).
- Once melted, add the almond butter and roasted almonds and mix until everything is combined.
- Pour into silicone molds or a container lined with parchment paper. Sprinkle it with salt and place in the fridge to set for an hour.
- Once set, store in an airtight container in the fridge.
- You can also get creative and use hazelnut butter and hazelnuts, or add granola instead of roasted nuts.

STAYING MINDFUL THROUGHOUT THIS JOURNEY

As you move along these steps, stay in touch with how you feel. By Week Four, you should notice quite a few changes. For one, you'll feel healthier. Most people lose unwanted weight and experience a surge in energy, as well as improved digestion. If you are diabetic, you should notice your blood sugar levels are getting better. Although it is less noticeable, the same will be true for your cholesterol levels and blood pressure.

You will also notice that your cravings change. As you eat more whole, plant-based foods, you will start hungering for the healthy over the harmful. The more you choose vegetables over animals, the more your tastebuds will adapt and begin to crave those foods.

This is why I advise you to stick to the process and give your body a proper chance to adapt and give this new lifestyle time to transform you. This is like a new superpower you never knew you could harness. Allow yourself to be excited by this adventure and the power you have to create a better future–not just for yourself but for animals and for the planet. It truly is life-changing in every aspect. I am proud of you and thrilled to welcome you as a *Rebel Vegan*!

WHAT TO DO ABOUT WITHDRAWAL SYMPTOMS?

We have all heard of withdrawal symptoms from things like caffeine, but did you know that you can get the same issue when you move away from the standard Western diet? A study published in the journal *Appetite* found that people who cut down on processed foods experience the same types of withdrawal symptoms as people who are addicted to drugs: sadness, tiredness, cravings, as well as increased irritability.[3]

This is hardly surprising when we remember that processed foods are packed with ingredients that hyper-stimulate the body—just like drugs, sugar and fat trigger a dopamine release that makes us feel good. This is why we turn to these foods again and again, especially when we need a lift. Whatever the guilty pleasure (whether it's French fries, pizza, donuts, or burgers), as we move away from these foods we have to find new ways to give ourselves the pleasure we crave.

According to the study, withdrawal symptoms lasted between two and five days, after which they cooled down somewhat. So the key thing to remember is that while you may experience cravings, it gets easier. You just have to stick with it. Another great way to navigate this is to plan ahead and have some fall-back foods ready in case a craving hits you.

Make a list of your guilty-pleasure foods and a counter-list of vegan versions that offer you the same flavor and texture experience without the addictive ingredients. Here are a few examples to get you started:

PROCESSED FOODS / ANIMAL PRODUCTS	**PLANT-BASED ALTERNATIVES**
Processed meats (ham, corned beef, chicken nuggets, burgers, sausages, etc.)	Marinated tofu or tempeh, Seitan (avoid this if you are sensitive to gluten), Soy chunks, Bean burgers or plant-based burgers, Quorn or soy sausages
Ice-cream	Vegan ice-cream made from cashews, coconut, almond or soy blended frozen banana (quickest, easiest ice-cream EVER)
Milkshakes	Peanut butter, banana and cacao smoothie, Blueberry, banana, almond milk smoothie, Mango, banana, coconut milk smoothie, If you have a blender, there are no limits!
Supermarket bread	Home-made bread or bread from an independent local bakery, made with whole grains.
Sugary breakfast cereal	Granola made with oats, nuts, seeds, coconut, and dried fruit, Overnight oats, Porridge topped with coconut yogurt and fruit
Cookies, biscuits, cakes, pastries	Home-made energy balls (a mix of dried fruits, oats, nuts and seeds), Home-made vegan and refined-sugar-free cookies, Home-made trail mix (for example with toasted almonds or cashews, pumpkin seeds, dried blueberries and cacao nibs)
Chocolate bars	Organic dark chocolate (at least 70%), Fruit & nut bars (choose brands made with no added flavors or sugar), Home-made vegan refined-sugar-free brownie
Crisps / chips	Kale crisps (simply mix kale with cashews and nutritional yeast and roast), Rice cakes or oat crackers with peanut butter, Vegetable crisps (beetroot, carrot, zucchini, parsnip…)
Energy drinks and fizzy drinks	Green tea or herbal tea, Kombucha, Coconut water, Sparkling water with a squeeze of lemon, crushed berries, or fresh mint
Pizza	Sourdough pizza with vegan cheese, Home-made pizza on a sprouted grain tortilla, Quick toastie with melted vegan cheese and sun-dried tomatoes and olives

It is easy to be a junk-food vegan–you can now find all your favorite ready meals and guilty-pleasures in plant-based form. While they don't contain animal-derived ingredients, these foods are as potentially harmful to your health as traditional processed foods. Having said that, they can be useful as you transition. What's more, I don't believe in denying yourself pleasure, that's why I'm a big fan of the 80-20 rule. This gives you some room for maneuver, particularly the first few weeks when you are navigating a new way of eating.

You will be surprised, once you begin, at just how easy it can be to move towards a diet where you're eating mostly whole plant-based foods that you prepare at home. This was part of the journey that I enjoyed the most: exploring new vegan foods and finding new recipes to try. Cooking new foods really opened up my world. Let it do the same for you.

YOUR VEGAN JOURNEY, YOUR RULES

"The vegan movement is one of the fastest growing social justice movements in the world today."
Dr. Melanie Joy

It is your journey, and yours to design in a way that works for you. From Meatless Mondays to "mostly vegan," it is up to you to design and align your diet to fit your values.

As much as I would love to see the whole world go vegan overnight, I accept that it is overly ambitious to expect everyone to adopt a plant-based diet instantly. Food is so intrinsically tied in with culture, traditions and habits that it is more realistic to accept everyone's unique path and inspire by example.

I have never felt better, more confident and stronger, then when I gave up meat and diary. And there is a beautiful sense of peace when you embrace a life that is in line with your values. I believe all of us has the power to make a huge difference just by opening ourselves up to a more plant-based diet and cruelty-free life.

Taking things one meal at a time, we can change the world.
I celebrate you for being here and being partof this global shift towards a more compassionate way of living.

You don't have to be vegan every day. But every single day you are, you save, on average:

ONE ANIMAL

40 POUNDS OF GRAIN

1100 GALLONS OF WATER

30 SQUARE FEET OF FOREST

Together, our 'one days' can add up to a massive change

For us, for animal welfare, and for our planet

@cowspiracy.com/facts & TheVeganCalculator.com

Welcome

20

EATING IN, EATING OUT, COMING OUT

"Living your best life is your most important journey in life."
Oprah Winfrey

Creating and maintaining a plant-powered life has its challenges, but it is also a great adventure that will bring huge rewards. This chapter is all about navigating that journey. Here are my practical guidelines and tips to help you implement a plant-based diet as effortlessly as possible.

EATING IN

PARTY IN MY PLANT-BASED KITCHEN!

BUDGET AND BULK-BUYING:

Many new vegans find that they actually save money on food bills, despite the often-mentioned argument that eating a healthier diet is more expensive. The great thing about a plant-based diet is that many staples are easy to stock and can be bought in bulk every month or so: canned tomatoes, beans, lentils, whole grains (rice, whole grain pasta, bean noodles, buckwheat noodles.) coconut milk, nuts, seeds, flour, spices, and dried herbs. Then all you need to do is buy fresh vegetables and fruits every week to create delicious, nutritious meals.

READING THE LABELS:

Many food companies proudly advertise their vegan products. Simply look for the little "V" mark that indicates the food is completely plant-based. If this mark is not present, it's about reading the label. You'll find a link to my favorite food label guide in the Resources section. While some foods are easy to identify as vegan (because of the "V" symbol), many foods you might think would be vegan actually contain milk, honey, eggs or gelatin–and you'll only find that out if you read the label.

NAVIGATING A NEW SHOPPING EXPERIENCE:

Shopping will feel different, especially in the beginning. You may need to give yourself more time to navigate aisles you've not walked down, and to read labels. Once you get comfortable with the products and brands you can trust, this will become much easier, but you'll still have to stay aware.

Get yourself online and look for recommendations by other vegans, for example foods known as "accidentally vegan." These are foods that weren't intended to be vegan, but don't contain any animal ingredients. A well-known example is Oreo cookies.

NAVIGATING A NEW COOKING EXPERIENCE:

A great way to learn how to structure your meals is to try vegan meal kits, such as those delivered by Purple Carrot, Daily Harvest, or Veestro (there are many more![1]). Each kit is a complete meal containing all the macro-nutrients you need. I didn't just learn some tasty recipes (the Purple Carrot burger is the best I've ever had), but also how to design nutritious meals. These kits can help you get into the rhythm and discover new dishes. An old-fashioned cookbook is also highly recommended!

TODD'S PANTRY LIST

WHOLE GRAINS	BEANS & LÉGUMES	OILS & SEASONINGS	BAKING & HEALTHY TREATS
Rice (brown rice, Venus black rice, wild rice) Buckwheat Quinoa Millet Polenta Oats Oat crackers Pasta or noodles made from brown rice, whole grain spelt, whole grain wheat, or buckwheat	You can buy canned for convenience and speed - make sure you choose brands with only beans and water, nothing else added) Chickpeas Black beans Kidney beans Cannellini beans Black eye beans Borlotti beans Mung beans (Adzuki beans Lentils (green or red) Split peas	Olive oil Coconut oil Avocado oil Sesame oil Flax oil Olives Sun-dried tomatoes Vegan mayonnaise Tamari sauce or soy sauce Apple cider vinegar Himalayan salt or other natural & unrefined salt Nutritional yeast	Whole grain spelt flour Whole grain wheat flour Rice flour Buckwheat flour Coconut flour Ground almonds Egg replacer Baking powder Vanilla essence or powder Dates Apricots Raisins Maple syrup, rice syrup, or vegan honey Cacao powder

SPICES & HERBS	NUTS & SEEDS	MILK & DAIRY ALTERNATIVES	CANNED GOODS
Cinnamon Turmeric Cumin Coriander Garam masala Ras el Hanout Italian herb mix or Herbes de Provence Mild curry powder Smoked paprika Oregano Rosemary Fennel seed Black pepper	Tahini Peanut butter Almond butter Cashew butter Hazelnut butter Pumpkin seeds Sunflower seeds Chia seeds Flax seeds Sesame seeds Hemp seeds Almonds Hazelnuts Cashew nuts Brazil nuts Coconut flakes or desiccated coconut Pine nuts	Almond milk Soy milk Oat milk Cashew milk Pea milk Hazelnut milk Tiger nut milk Silken tofu Soy cream Oat cream Almond cream Probiotic capsules or vegan starters (if you want to make your own vegan yogurt or cheese)	Canned tomatoes Canned jackfruit Canned coconut milk Canned beans (see beans & legumes)

A WELL-STOCKED PANTRY:

Give your kitchen cupboards a vegan make-over!

As you use up all the old packs of processed foods and animal products, you can begin restocking your pantry to make plant-based eating effortless. The trick here is to ensure you have all the ingredients you need to throw together vegan meals, simply with the addition of a few fresh vegetables or fruits.

Here is a snapshot of my pantry, to inspire you to create your own, based on the recipes you enjoy cooking. You don't have to have all these ingredients (indeed, stocking ten varieties of plant milk might be going a little over the top), but this table gives you an idea of what you need to start cooking healthy, tasty, easy vegan meals.

FROM VEGAN READY-MEALS TO VEGAN HOME-COOKING:

The best advice I can offer here is to start small and build from that.

Before you began your 4-week journey to veganism, you sat down with your schedule and worked out when you have free time and when you have spare energy—these are the moments you can dedicate to meal planning and meal prepping.

For example, say you have some spare time and energy on Sunday afternoon. You could spend a few hours getting food ready for the week. A case in point, by making a hearty pasta-bake or a big pot of curry, which can easily be portioned and frozen for later—then what you basically have is a ready-meal which contains only healthy ingredients, but is just as convenient and quick as supermarket meals. Meal prep does not have to be complicated—you just have to double, triple, or quadruple your ingredients, and voila! You've got ready-made food for the week.

It is also easy to batch-prepare things like chia puddings, energy balls, roasted nuts –all of which make tasty snacks. If you are taking lunches to work, you could prepare salad jars for a few days simply by cooking up a load of rice or other grains, and then layering the rice with beans and chopped vegetables (carrots, celery, radish, zucchini, sweet peppers, kale, etc.) in jars, and storing in the fridge.

You can also make hummus and salad dressings, which keep for about a week, and mean you'll always have something tasty to dip vegetables into or use as a sandwich spread. Once you start this process, you'll feel into the best method for your unique circumstances—whether you live on your own, work from home, or cook for your family.

As you begin, go easy on yourself. If you have to fall back on a vegan ready-meal every so often, that is okay. Remember the 80-20 rule. It's not about aiming for perfection, it's about creating a lifestyle you can sustain for the long term.

The more you cook from scratch, the more instinctive it will feel. You do not need to be a Masterchef candidate, nor spend hours in the kitchen to prepare tasty food. A well-stocked vegan pantry and a little bit of planning is all you need.

MAKE SURE YOU EAT ENOUGH AND EAT WHAT YOU LOVE:

If you feel hungry or are uninspired by what you're eating, then you will fall off the vegan wagon. That's why it is so important that you eat filling and flavorful food. When you are full and satiated, it is much easier to say no to temptations.

FIND YOUR FAVORITE VEGAN ALTERNATIVES:

Take the time to search for plant-based substitutes to your favorite animal products. You can make this a fun experience by buying several brands and then having a taste-test (maybe with some fellow vegan newbies, or curious friends). Gone are the days when there was just one option (soy milk!). These days most supermarkets stock at least three types of vegan cheese, countless plant milk varieties, not to mention vegan burgers.

BE THE FRIENDLY VEGAN IN YOUR SHARED HOUSE:

If you live in a house-share, changing your diet can feel daunting, but it doesn't have to be. It is usually easy to compartmentalize the kitchen and fridge space so that your shelves are kept vegan. Sit your roommates down and let them know you are making this change. Reassure them that you are not about to become "one of those vegans" who judge others for their choices, and that you're not going to bombard them with stats and facts while they're trying to enjoy their burger. This way, you will ensure there is no animosity in the household. After all, living together is an art form. The best thing you can do for the vegan movement is be kind and compassionate with others–they are on their own path!

CHOOSE MEALS YOU CAN EASILY ADAPT FOR YOUR NON-VEGAN LOVED ONES:

If you need to juggle different diets in your household, family, or relationship, this can be challenging. After all, meals are there to be shared. The easiest way to navigate this is to make meals that can be easily added to.

For example, you can prepare the joint meal in an assembly line style, and add the meat at the end. You can prepare the chicken/seafood/mince separately and add it at the last minute to the plate, stir-fry, curry, stew or casserole. As a rule, the defining flavor of a dish is the sauce, so you can experience and enjoy the meal together.

TAKE IT SLOW WITH BEANS, PEAS, AND LENTILS:

As you adapt from a diet high in saturated fats and animal products to a plant-based diet that contains a lot more fiber, you might find you get a bit too gassy. If this happens, it is a sign you need to give your body a little time to adapt to new foods.

As a general rule, beans and pulses are the main culprits when it comes to bloating and gas. The bloating comes from the indigestible fibers in the beans' shell. These become easier to digest if you soak the beans overnight and cook them thoroughly. Staying in tune with your body will help too—try different beans and lentils to see which ones you tolerate better, and go slowly.

EATING OUT: LET'S MAKE IT FUN!

"You are only confined by the walls that you build yourself."
REBEL VEGAN

Eating out is never just about the food. It's a social occasion, a way to catch up with friends and family, a moment we savor because we have our loved ones around us AND we won't need to do the washing up (win-win!). However, if your friends and family are meat-eaters, you might feel awkward asking about plant-based options. But fear not! These days, so many restaurants and cafes serve vegan options, and even those that don't have vegan options on the menu will help you out if you call ahead.

Better still, there's an app for that! Both *Happy Cow* and *Vanilla Bean* allow you to search by location, or use GPS to show you all the places near you that are either vegan or serve vegan options. It's time to challenge (if you feel comfortable to) and inspire your loved ones to try something new.

MY EATING OUT TIPS:

- **Get the apps:** *Happy Cow* is your best friend when it comes to exploring vegan-friendly eateries. You might be surprised at how many options there are locally.
- **Plan ahead:** If it's an organized event, you can contact the restaurant (by phone, WhatsApp or Facebook Messenger), get a copy of the menu, check the vegan options, and ask questions. With a little charm, it is usually easy to develop a rapport, and most restaurants will fall over themselves to be helpful. That way you can avoid any anxiety, just relax and enjoy the occasion.
- **Prepare for social events:** Most hosts are mindful and ask about dietary requirements, allergies, and likes or dislikes when they send out their invitation. Be polite but honest - the worst thing you can do is not tell a host you're vegan. You can also offer to bring food if you feel this would put the host under undue stress. Most hosts will refuse that offer and work with you to find a solution. If the event is a potluck dinner, bring your favorite vegan party food and share it with other guests (this is a great opportunity to showcase just how delicious plant-based food can be!). If you know there will be no vegan options at the event, eat a large meal beforehand and take some snacks with you.
- **Practice makes perfect:** If it's an impromptu event and you haven't had time to organize in advance, don't worry. With a little practice, you will soon be able to scan a menu and see what can be eaten or adapted. Until then, just fake it 'til you make it: turn on the charm and ask the waiter which dish can be made vegan. Don't be timid--you are a *REBEL VEGAN*! Be confident and comfortable. There's usually one or two dishes that can easily be modified to be vegan. Stir-fries are easily adaptable (for example, by removing chicken or prawns).
- **Ask for the secret menu:** Did you know that some restaurants have secret menus? Just ask. Often there is a vegetarian or vegan menu stashed away somewhere.

- **Get creative with side dishes:** A few sides of brown rice, beans and vegetables quickly add up to a balanced meal. Learn to laugh and pretend it's a tapas night.

- **Flirt:** Yes, a little gentle flirtation with the waiting staff will have them eating out of your hand. With the waiter on side, you'll be able to figure out some vegan options together.

- **Carry snacks:** If you think the options will be severely limited, then eat beforehand and/or during.

- **Go international.** Ethnic cuisines usually have the best plant-based traditions and options. Indian, Thai, Vietnamese, Mexican, or Mediterranean restaurants traditionally have many plant-based options.

- **Don't sweat the small stuff:** It might seem a challenge at first, but in the scheme of things it is only a meal. Focus on the occasion and the people, rather than the food.

- **Leave a review:** Especially if the restaurant has been super helpful. This is how we spread this compassionate revolution!

- **On the bright side, most alcohol is vegan.** But if you want to be sure, you can use the *Barnivore* website (you'll find the link in the resources section) to check whether your wine is vegan-friendly (some wines are filtered using animal products).

The main thing to remember is to be kind to yourself! Being vegan is not a competition. You're not going to be disqualified if you accidentally-on-purpose eat cheese or accept a slice of your grandmother's pumpkin pie! *REBEL VEGANS* make–and break–the rules, but always strive for compassion and justice.

VEGAN ON-THE-GO AND TRAVELING SNACK IDEAS:

- Peanut butter sandwiches (and the innumerable varieties: such as peanut butter and jelly, peanut butter and banana, peanut butter and chocolate spread...)

- Fruit and nut mixes: you can buy these ready-made or prepare your own at home (for example by roasting almonds, cashews, walnuts, pumpkin seeds, and adding dates, cranberries, raisins, coconut flakes, cacao nibs...)

- Hummus: it's easy to carry a little Tupperware of Hummus, bean dip, or guacamole you can eat with rice cakes or vegetable sticks.

- Granola bars: another very transportable snack. Here again, you can find good vegan granola bars or energy bars in most supermarkets (check the ingredient label and choose the ones made with whole foods only and no added sugar), or you can make some at home.

- For tips to stay vegan on the road, check out my *REBEL VEGAN* Travel Guide!

COMING OUT

SHOWING UP AS A *REBEL VEGAN*

"Accept who you are. Unless you're a serial killer."
Ellen DeGeneres[2]

As a REBEL VEGAN, you will need to find your inner strength to come out to your friends, your family, and the world. While we are trailblazers in an important social movement, we are also very misunderstood and often discriminated against.[3] This is known as vegaphobia. Yes, it is a thing!

In 2015, a study published in the Journal Group Processes & Intergroup Relations entitled "It ain't easy eating greens" found that vegans and vegetarians in Western societies experience discrimination on a par with other minorities.[4]

However, unlike other forms of bias (such as racism or sexism), negativity towards people who choose to eat plants over animals is not considered a social problem. In fact, it is both commonplace, largely accepted as "normal", and often left unaddressed.[5]

Be ready to navigate this new world with grace and poise. Learn to build your armor around you. Very often people react negatively towards vegans because of their own unconscious discomfort with their diet. After all, eating meat requires a cognitive dissonance of some kind. It requires people to shut their eyes and ears to the atrocities committed by the meat industry to animals and the planet.

When you show up as a *Rebel Vegan*, you shine a light on other people's choices, and this can be uncomfortable for them. So remember to smile and leave judgment at the door–just because they are judging your choices, does not mean you have to judge theirs. Remind them that your diet choices do not directly affect them—live and let live.

One of the big problems is this: you find yourself being lectured about why you "need" meat, usually by people who are not qualified nutritionists. Or people will assume you're surviving on a diet of carrots, celery and lettuce. Naturally, you will want to explain yourself (Chapter 12 of this companion book *REBEL VEGAN: A New Take on Veganism For a Brave New World*, delves deeper into this, and looks at the most common anti-vegan arguments and how to answer them with confidence). But when you do, you risk being labeled as "that vegan" who "doesn't shut up about veganism." It's almost like you can't win. But let me assure you—going vegan means you are winning and you're on the right side of history.

If you are confronted by sarcasm, simply be gently assertive in return. Try not to get sucked into arguments. With time, you will learn to recognize when you can have a sensible conversation about the topic, or whether the person in front of you is simply lashing out. If the conversation takes a turn for the more aggressive, you can simply state your truth and change the subject.

Don't let other people's opinions of your lifestyle choices affect you. When people judge, it's less about you, more about them. Just keep your focus on the positive changes you're making. Ultimately, you are not responsible for changing people's minds. We can only lead by example and focus on being the best versions of ourselves.

In this book, I share my coming out story. And, within this book, you have the tools to build your own unique journey towards veganism. Along the way, you will also find your confidence to come out and be a proud vegan. By embracing your inner rebel, you are living authentically, aligned with your core ethics, and being the change you want to see in the world.

My mantra:
If you can visualize it, you can veganize it.

VEGANISM ON THE ROAD: MY TRANSITION

When I went vegan, I was living and working on the road as an international tour manager in South East Asia. I would be living out of a suitcase for months at a time while taking groups through countries like Vietnam, Laos, Myanmar, and Cambodia. Some places were more accommodating than others. In Thailand, for example, there were bigger supermarkets where I could always stock up on vegan essentials - mine were soy milk and muesli. This way, I could always start my day with plant-based goodness and avoid the egg-based breakfasts that most hotels served. My backpack was always heavy with plant-based staples. While crossing over land borders dragging my heavy bags, I felt like a soy milk mule!

I learned to laugh at misunderstandings and enjoy eating sticky rice. I became pretty well known throughout South East Asia for taking over kitchens and street vendors and demonstrating first-hand what vegan cooking looked like.

After returning many times, I developed a bond with many restaurants in the region. I was trusted to go into the kitchen and help explain and cook vegan food with their staff. People in my groups would laugh and offer me a tip for cooking and delivering their food. A few of them jokingly called me the vegan Gordon Ramsey. But I like to think I was slightly more diplomatic!

After I ensured my group was fed, I would often stay and eat on the floor with my new friends in the kitchen. And I was continually surprised and impressed how the locals seemed to get veganism like second nature. It didn't cause as much tension as in the west and was instantly accepted as a perfectly logical lifestyle choice. They instinctively understood the philosophy of compassion, as it fits so seamlessly within their traditional values and Buddhist principles. These helped me realize my passion to veganize the world.

Veganism has opened up my world, never restricted it. I never saw it as a chore. Rather, it was a daily opportunity to engage with people and connect on a different level. Many were interested and receptive. The world is changing, and they want to be part of it. Some of my favorite moments were when I would return to these little towns and the owners would proudly present their new vegan menu with a wink. It felt like we were on the map.

Then, when I returned to the UK, I thought, how does this work? I remember walking down supermarket aisles I'd never noticed, searching for the "vegetarian" sign. There was a tiny section in the chilled meals section, and often only soy milk. But every time I returned to London, this section grew bigger. It was like coming back to a city under construction and witnessing the progress - new products, more options, a wider selection. Suddenly, all the supermarkets had their own plant-based range, and plant-based milks took over the health foods aisle. I still get excited each time I notice a new vegan range or product. It is my guilty pleasure to try them all. All in the name of research, of course!

My travels have always taken me back home to my vegan values that underpin everything I do. Veganism has given me the confidence and peace of mind to go out into the world as my authentic self. And this, in turn, has brought so many amazing people and places into my orbit. But there is no better feeling than coming home.

21

BEYOND DIET

VEGAN CHIC

"Traditional animal testing is expensive, time-consuming, uses a lot of animals and from a scientific perspective the results do not necessarily translate to humans."

Dr. Christopher Austin,
former director of the National Institutes of Health[1]

"The history of cancer research has been a history of curing cancer in the mouse. We have cured mice of cancer for decades and it simply didn't work in humans."

Dr. Richard Klausner,
former director of the National Cancer Institute[2]

What you have already braved and achieved is profound. I believe this knowledge is powerful, and we should use it wisely and ethically. We can transcend many of the global issues we face—species extinction, climate change, global pandemics, and disease epidemics—by going plant-based and cruelty-free. By transitioning to veganism, you have now lined up your beliefs and values with your lifestyle. Be happy and confident in your strong choices - you are making a positive impact on the world!

Now you have shifted your diet, you can explore other ways to build on your cruelty-free, sustainable life. Although I don't want to overwhelm you, I think it is important to consider the wider message of the vegan movement and use your awareness holistically.

A fully vegan lifestyle excludes all forms of exploitation and cruelty to animals, as far as practicable and possible. Diet is a huge part of that, but unfortunately animals are exploited in many other ways. Going fully vegan extends past dietary choices–it includes not going to zoos, wearing wool or leather, nor using cosmetics and products tested on animals.

I grew up beside a fox farm and have witnessed, in my lifetime, that whole industry implode as the top fashion houses ditched fur, and we all rethink what luxury is.

As you move along the spectrum towards veganism, you will feel empowered by your positive changes. If you feel emboldened to do so, you can become an ethical vegan and create a fully plant-based lifestyle. Going all the way means no honey or leather shoes. It feels fantastic to know you are living a fully cruelty-free life. So let's cast off those final carnistic shackles!

As your awareness increases and you remove animal products from your shopping trolley and kitchen cupboards, this inevitably brings up questions and uncomfortable realities around what you buy and wear. At this point, you can start to rethink your entire lifestyle: how cruelty-free are your fashion choices? Have your toiletries been tested on animals? This involves doing a little research to check the small print on everything from labels to the ethos of your go-to brands.

Just to reiterate, this is an optional final step, food for thought, planting a seed. I commend and support where you are right now. Just by questioning and changing your diet, you have made one of the most effective and positive impacts on the world!

If you would like to take it further, here are my tips for taking your veganism to the next level.

TOILETRIES AND HOUSEHOLD PRODUCTS

The thing to look out for first is the little "V" mark, which indicates the product is certified vegan. This means it doesn't contain animal-derived ingredients, and has not been tested on animals. If the little "V" is not present on the product packaging, you will need to check the brand's website to see whether they are cruelty-free or not.

Another thing to consider is the secondary effects of these products. For example, we know that products containing microplastic, solvents, and chemicals, are flushed down the drain and end up in all our water supplies. Even if these products are vegan, they harm aquatic life and pollute our planet.

If you want to take things to the next level, start phasing out your current products by finding vegan and green alternatives. The good news is it is easier than ever to find non-toxic, cruelty-free toiletries, make-up, and household products. Just head to your local health food shop and browse the household product aisle.

FASHION

Fast fashion is the second most polluting industry worldwide. According to the United Nations Environment Program (UNEP), the fashion industry is the second largest polluter of water globally. Every second, the equivalent of one garbage truck of textile is either landfilled or burned. If things continue as they are, this industry will use up a quarter of the world's carbon budgets. Fast fashion also uses plastic-derived textiles (polyester, for example), which accounts for around 9% of the microplastics in the ocean.[3] It takes 2,700 liters (713 gallons) of water to make enough cotton for just one t-shirt.[4]

There is also a human cost to the fashion industry. Most of us have heard about sweatshops and the conditions textile workers are forced to endure (low wages, long hours, unsanitary and unsafe working conditions), just so we can buy that cheap t-shirt.

Last but not least, animals experience torture and a violent death for wool, leather, suede, feathers, and fur. None of this is necessary, especially now that fake fur and vegan leather are so widespread and relatively easy to find.

We have gotten used to disposable fashion, but we can move away from it. Going vegan does not mean you have to exist in beige slacks and forget about being fashionable–far from it! But it requires a rethink of where you buy and how often you buy new clothes.

Here are a few ideas to help you create your cruelty-free wardrobe:

- Go second-hand! You'll be surprised just how much fun this can be. The buzz you get when you find the perfect outfit for a few dollars/pounds/euros is well worth rummaging around for.
- Have a clothes swap evening. Gather your friends for a (vegan) pot-luck dinner and clothing exchange. Everyone brings a dish and a few unwanted clothes, and everyone leaves with a new item. One person's garbage is another's treasure.
- Ask your network for recommendations: there are many ethical, vegan, cruelty-free fashion brands out there. So ask around and explore different options. You might just be surprised at how fashionable it can be to be vegan!
- Choose wisely: vegan leather is wonderful, but what materials have been used instead? Are they recycled plastics or virgin plastics? Is the clothing retailer really ethical, or have they just simply launched a "green" collection to greenwash their image?

ETHICAL BRANDS

This is where a little research is necessary. But as your awareness grows, you'll be able to sense whether a brand is ethical or not. And with a little practice, you'll also see through the green-washing and whether those brands who have jumped on the vegan bandwagon as lip-service and marketing rather than real compassion.

An example would be those global fast food giants. Yes, they now offer vegan options. But are they making a positive difference to the world, or are their practices destroying the planet and harming animals? Have they added a vegan option to their menu because they care about improving the state of the world, or because they've spotted an opportunity for increased profits? Unfortunately, I would say it's the latter. I'm not saying you shouldn't eat there, but it is worth thinking about the impact of the corporations we buy from.

Here are some questions to consider when choosing your new go-to brands:

- Are they sustainable? In other words, do they use sustainable materials or ingredients? Do they consider their impact on the environment and society? For example, by choosing local, independent supply chains, reducing their greenhouse gas emissions, or setting up local charities.
- Are they transparent? A really ethical company will be transparent about where and how they source their raw materials, how they treat their staff, and whether they test their products on animals. If you contact the company and don't get answers, it's a good sign that their practices are not ethical. Companies that care about their impact will be proud to share this with you. Look for clear, specific, and well-organized information.
- Do they have third-party certifications to confirm their positive impact? These aren't always foolproof, but it is a good place to start. For example, the Fair-trade certification is designed to help producers in developing countries get a fair price for their products and achieve sustainable, equitable trade relationships, but this isn't always the case. A study published by MIT Press found that benefits to producers were negligible because of an oversupply of certifications.[5] There are also question marks around whether Fairtrade can enforce fair trade standards. But there are certain certifications you can trust. For example, Certified B Corporations, which aim to use business as a force for good, balance purpose and profit, and are legally required to consider their impact on workers, customers, suppliers, community, and the environment.[6]

GREENWASHING AND HUMANE-WASHING

Talking nice about sun and wind and green jobs is just greenwash.
Dr James Hansen, NASA Scientist[7]

If something sounds a little too good to be true, it's usually worth digging a little deeper. Many brands use greenwashing to downplay their environmental impact and hoodwink consumers that their products are greener or less harmful than they truly are. When Shell or ExxonMobil launch adverts about their solar energy and wind turbines while staying silent about their more polluting practices (such as their plans to drill under the Arctic), this is greenwashing. Other strategies also include funding studies that mislead the public or confuse the climate change argument. Think of how the tobacco industry encouraged people to smoke by using doctors to recommend their products.

Humane-washing is similar to greenwashing. An increasingly desperate animal agriculture industry is using this new tactic to convince the public that their products are produced humanely, even as the evidence to the contrary becomes impossible to ignore. Cue images of well-fed, happy cows and cheeky chickens gently and lovingly herded by an attentive, friendly farmer. Most of the labels you will see on animal products, such as "free-range", "cage-free", "family-farmed", and "responsibly sourced", are misleading at best and fraudulent at worst.

Similarly, the powerful farming industry funds studies to proclaim that meat and dairy are "proven" to be healthy, while denouncing a vegan diet as "deficient." Meanwhile, a mountain of well-documented evidence shows the exact opposite. They are using the same dirty tactics as the cigarette corporations and trying to confuse and keep us hooked.

I am the ultimate vegan realist. Whether it's green or humane-washing, these labels are not there to protect the environment nor the animals, but to mislead you into thinking you're buying something sustainable. It's a cover-up to try to muddy the waters. Therefore, we have to scrutinize these false narratives and see through the marketing. This way, we defend truth and justice.

A *Rebel Vegan* needs to be able to recognize these deliberate distractions and see through these industry-driven studies and headlines about products that have been shown time and time again to be harmful to our health, animals, and the planet. These massive corporations have invested billions to mislead and convince the public they care. Therefore, we have to be vigilant and prepared to defend our values and wellbeing.

SPOTTING GREENWASHING AND HUMANE-WASHING:

- Does the brand's sustainability page answer your questions, or are you left with more questions than answers? If it's greenwashing/humane-washing, you'll just get lots of big statements and nice images, but nothing to back these claims up. If it's really ethical, you'll find information about their approach to materials, employees, emissions, and even what to do with their products once you've used them (for example, information on where to send old items for repair, donation, or recycling).
- Does the brand have any third-party certifications, and how do these certifications impact the brand's ethical and environmental responsibilities? Are the products themselves certified, or just the materials or factory used to make them?
- Who owns the brand? It is common for huge corporations with questionable ethics to buy independent brands or launch new brands under another name to conquer more of the market-place or attract eco-consumers. For example, Nestlé owns Haagen Dazs, Nespresso, and KitKat[8], while CocaCola owns Innocent Smoothies, and Honest Tea, among others.[9] You will usually find this information in the small print of their website.
- Check the small print: Who's funded the study? Do the researchers have any conflicts of interest? Are there studies that prove the exact opposite?
- Ultimately, beware of claims that sound too good to be true! Once you know what to look for, spotting greenwashing and humane-washing is pretty simple.

Once you're on the journey towards veganism and feel that increasing sense of contentment from being aligned with your ethics, it's not hard to build momentum.

Being a *Rebel Vegan* starts with diet, but inevitably goes further. Even if you do not feel ready to make these changes now, you'll notice that the longer you are vegan, the more you will be attracted to brands that take their social, environmental, and ethical responsibilities seriously. As you shift towards a kinder diet, you will naturally want to shift to a kinder, more sustainable, and compassionate lifestyle.

This is how we create a better world.
One step at a time - it starts with you.

B12
K
Aqua Faba
B6
C

22

11 SECRETS TO STAY MOTIVATED

"Put your heart, mind, and soul into even your smallest acts."
Swami Sivananda[1]

"The true secret of happiness lies in taking a genuine interest in all the details of daily life."
William Morris[2]

"The secret of your future is hidden in your daily routine."
Mike Murdock[3]

1. KEEP IT SUPER SIMPLE:

THE KISS PRINCIPLE

This is not about being a gourmet chef. If you overcomplicate your diet, or put too much pressure on yourself, you will likely become exasperated and give up. Focus on simple meals made with fresh ingredients. You're not practicing for MasterChef!

"Perfection is the enemy of progress."
Winston Churchill[4]

"Simplicity, patience, compassion.
These three are your greatest treasures."
Tao Te Ching - Lao Tzu[5]

ALBERT EINSTEIN 1879 - 1955
ITALIA
120
I.P.Z.S.-ROMA-1979
F. TULLI

2. OPEN YOUR MIND:

EXPAND YOUR VISION PAST THE HERE AND NOW

Everything you might want is available in vegan form these days—from cheese to sushi. Sure, it isn't 100% the same thing, but at least it is in alignment with your ethics. Open your mind to new flavors and experiences. I turned a corner when I discovered that plant-based burgers taste much better than their animal-based counterparts. I have learned to enjoy the adventure. And remember: your taste buds will soon adjust.

"Progress is impossible without change, and those who cannot change their minds cannot change anything."

George Bernard Shaw[6]

"The mind that opens up to a new idea never returns to its original size. The measure of intelligence is the ability to change."

Albert Einstein[7]

"An open heart is an open mind."

Dalai Lama[8]

3. PATIENCE IS A VIRTUE:

BE PATIENT WITH YOUR TASTE BUDS

They have a short memory—cravings for meat will soon pass as you begin tasting different foods and healthier flavors. Keep the faith, as eating plants will soon become both a habit and a preference. With a little perseverance and patience, you will never look back. Eventually, you will surprise yourself with new cravings for all things green.

"Genius is eternal patience."
Michelangelo

"Patience and perseverance have a magical effect before which difficulties disappear and obstacles vanish."
6th US President, John Quincy Adams[9]

"You will find that your taste buds have a memory of about 3 weeks."
Dr. Neal D. Barnard[10]

IMAGINE

4. BELONGING:

FIND YOUR TRIBE

Connect with positive, like-minded people who can help you grow in confidence. The power of belonging should never be underestimated. To successfully transform to a cruelty-free lifestyle requires support and understanding.

No vegan is an island! Going vegan is a great opportunity to meet new friends and find support and advice along the way from fellow Rebel Vegan. From Facebook groups to vegan dating apps, see this as an amazing opportunity to open up your world and create new friendships. For more detailed information, please explore our extensive Resources section at the back of this book.

"If you want to go fast, go alone.
If you want to go far, go together."
African Proverb

"You may say I'm a dreamer,
but I'm not the only one.
I hope someday you'll join us.
And the world will live as one."
John Lennon

"A dream you dream alone is only a dream.
A dream you dream together is reality."
John Lennon

5. TEMPTATIONS:

HAVE A BACKUP PLAN

Temptations and moments of weakness happen, so make sure you have a strategy ready. My weak point is the smell of bacon. As soon as it hits me, those old habits want to take over. My strategy is to have a word with myself and remember those images in Earthlings of baby pigs being taken away from their mother. I talk myself (almost bore myself) out of any notion of indulging.

Think about the driving forces that made you decide to go vegan—this will likely be the most effective safety mechanism when temptation hits. Sometimes it helps write down your reasons for going vegan and review the list when in need. Another strategy is to have a vegan friend on speed dial for those moments of weakness.

Warning: these strategies and your commitment will be especially tested when alcohol is involved.

"Start by doing what is necessary, then what is possible, and suddenly you are doing the impossible."
St. Francis Of Assisi[11]

"Weakness is giving in to temptation. Strength is resisting it."
Guillermo Del Toro[12]

"Where there is no temptation, there is no glory."
Italian proverb

Fighting

6. STAY YOUTHFUL & PRESENT:

EVERY CHILD'S WISH

If you have children, there is an extra onus and motivation to go plant-based and lead by example. A vegan diet won't just protect their health, but you'll also teach important values, such as preserving the planet and being compassionate towards other earthlings. And you'll also stay healthy and at your best for longer, which is what every child wants from their parents.

"I just decided that I was the high-risk person, and I didn't want to fool with this anymore. And I wanted to live to be a grandfather. So I decided to pick the diet that I thought would maximize my chances of long-term survival."
BILL Clinton[13]

"The most powerful leadership tool you have is your own personal example."
John Wooden, basketball coach and player[14]

"You will never look back on life and think, 'I spent too much time with my kids'."
Unknown

बापू
باپو
MAHATMA GANDHI
2 OCT 1869 30 JAN 1948
1 1/2 as
INDIA POSTAGE
COURVOISIER S. A.

7. ADAPT AND DEVELOP NEW SKILLS:

LEARN TO VEGANIZE

Both knowledge and charm are powerful tools. To make a lasting change, you need to feel confident in your choices and be able to respond to the skepticism and naysayers. This book's big sister, *REBEL VEGAN LIFE: A Radical Take on Veganism*, is the first deep dive into what makes vegan values so urgent in this post-pandemic world, and will prepare you for anything the skeptics throw at you.

If possible, find a vegan mentor. And, if you master the skill of veganizing, you don't need to say goodbye to your favorite restaurants or hangouts. Develop your skills to veganize with diplomacy and charm, and you will always find a tasty solution. You might even inspire your local restaurant to develop their menu, spread compassion, and inspire the next generation of *Rebel Vegans*.

"There is no end to education. The whole of life, from the moment you are born to the moment you die, is a process of learning."
Jiddu Krishnamurti[15]

"Live as if you were to die tomorrow. Learn as if you were to live forever."
Mahatma Gandhi[16]

"I think it's a great lifestyle for long-term stability. You also have to look at everything else in your regimen, what you're putting into your body, like supplements. I'm always learning."
Venus Williams[17]

"The Sooner You Step Away From Your Comfort Zone, The Sooner You'll Realize That It Wasn't Really All That Comfortable."
Eddie Harris[18]

MAYA ANGELOU
GHANA
c350
GREAT WRITERS OF THE 20TH CENTURY

8. RECOGNIZE INSPIRATION:

CELEBRATE YOUR IMPACT

You will impact more people than you realize by going vegan. Your bold choices and courage will be an inspiration. Even the naysayers will go away and reflect on their own behavior, and need to confront their cognitive dissonance and compliance in the system. And it is one of the kindest things you can do for your loved ones, because it inspires them to become aware and improve their diet. You might even save lives.

"Stand up straight and realize who you are, that you tower over your circumstances."
Maya Angelou[19]

"I am a firm believer in eating a full plant-based, whole food diet that can expand your life length and make you an all-around happier person."
Ariana Grande[20]

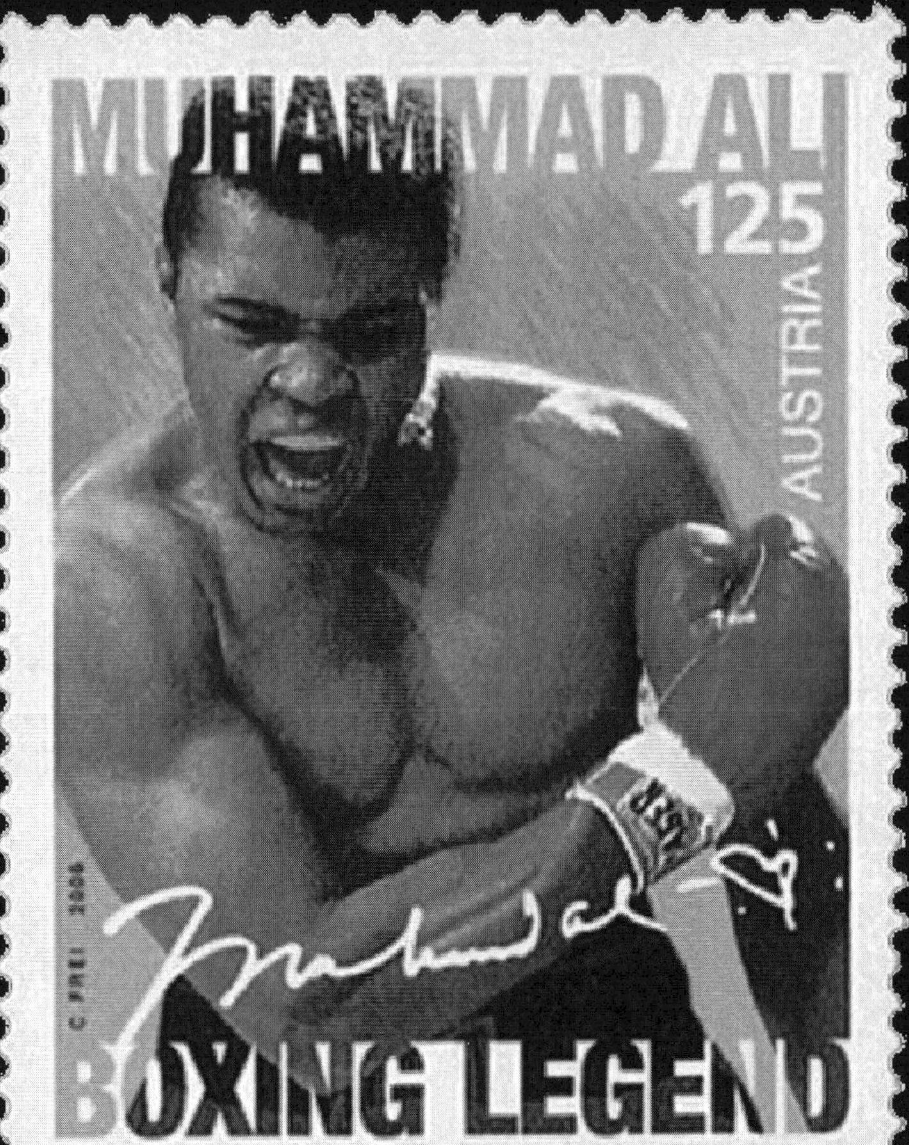
MUHAMMAD ALI
125
AUSTRIA
BOXING LEGEND

9. PAY IT FORWARD:

SUPPORT YOUR FELLOW *REBEL VEGANS*

Every vegan has unique circumstances and challenges, and has to make their own way. I believe we are stronger together, and our community should be welcoming. We share the same values, aspirations, and goals, so let's come together and celebrate each other and our movement. We are in this together, so let's make space at the table.

"Service to others is the rent you pay for your room here on Earth."
Muhammad Ali

"We rise by lifting others."
Robert Ingersoll

"There is no exercise better for the heart than reaching down and lifting people up."
John Holmes

"Unity Is Strength... When There Is Teamwork And Collaboration, Wonderful Things Can Be Achieved."
13-year-old poet, Mattie Stepanek[21]

10. KNOW THYSELF:

BELIEVE IN YOURSELF AND YOUR VALUES

It takes a real sense of self to challenge the status quo or dominant way of doing things. You might need to stand up for yourself and come out as a vegan many times. The secret is to have an unshakeable belief in your ethics and reason. I recommend writing down your personal drivers and reasons for choosing this lifestyle. You can return to them time and again. Hang them on your fridge, but ultimately, you need to know—and like—yourself!

"To know thyself is the beginning of wisdom."
Socrates[22]

"We must be the change we wish to see."
Mahatma Gandhi[23]

"With Every Experience, You Alone Are Painting Your Own Canvas, Thought By Thought, Choice By Choice."
Oprah Winfrey[24]

11. ULTIMATELY, GIVE IT YOUR ALL:

LIVE YOUR BEST LIFE

Whatever I do in life, I want to give it my all. It comes down to commitment and confidence in doing the right thing. Just don't forget to experiment AND have fun. Remember, like life, it's all about the journey and not the destination. Thank you for challenging and inspiring others with your brave choices.

"It's pretty amazing to wake up every morning, knowing that every decision I make is to cause as little harm as possible. It's a pretty fantastic way to live."
Colleen Patrick-Goudreau[25]

"As a new vegan, I'm enjoying exploring flavors from plants & plant-based proteins! Every journey is personal & deserves to be celebrated."
Lizzo[26]

"Once I started, I fell in love with the concept of fueling your body in the best way possible."
Venus Williams

23

FINAL THOUGHTS

COMMON VALUES

"If you don't have a seat at the table, you are likely on the menu."
Elizabeth Warren

Our lifestyles can either protect and strengthen us or send us to an early grave. The way we produce food and the way we eat are implicated in most of the grave but preventable crises we face today. The planet's delicate ecosystems are on the brink of collapse, chronic disease is the number one killer, and viral pandemics are increasing in both frequency and severity.

Humanity is at a crossroads. We have a choice. Continue with the current status quo, or rebel, and be a force for change–on a mission to create a better world.

When Covid hit, it offered us a unique opportunity to see what is right in front of us: health is a global issue, one that is intimately connected to the health of animals and the planet. The mounting science and studies show that the best way to stop future pandemics is to stop consuming animal products.I It is vital that we learn from Covid and make the necessary changes. This was a hard lesson, but also points towards the solutions.

Our individual health is also intimately connected to the way we eat. The standard Western diet is the biggest contributor to heart disease, cancer, obesity, diabetes, and other chronic illnesses.[1] These conditions are preventable and even reversible with a whole foods plant-based diet.[2]

Scientists have been warning for decades that our planet is suffering from the effects of our lifestyles, particularly our diet. Meat production causes deforestation, water wastage, and air pollution. Even if we stop using fossil fuels completely, we will exceed our 565-gigaton CO_2 limit by 2030, unless we drastically reduce our reliance on animal products.[3] No environmental solution will make a significant difference, unless it also includes a move away from meat production.

We must seize the small window of opportunity that we have to make real changes to the way we eat and produce food. This is our moment. We have seen through the lies: meat and dairy are not the health foods the food industry wants us to believe—quite the opposite. We can get all the nutrients we need from a well-balanced, plant-based diet. This guidebook is your springboard to a more compassionate way of eating—one that supports your health and longevity, is kind to the animals, is environmentally sustainable, and tastes amazing.

Everyone's unique journey towards veganism is like a pilgrimage home to our original, authentic selves; our empathetic and compassionate core. These are intrinsic values that we were born with, before our violent food system was normalized. Going vegan is a way to reclaim this birthright...and these are values that the world so desperately needs right now: compassion for ourselves and others, kindness towards all earthlings, and consideration for our planetary home.

Veganism is not just about eating more kale and avocados. It is more than just a diet; it's a shift in mentality away from a cavalier attitude to our planet, its resources, and other beings. What got us here in the first place!

Our intrinsic vegan values impel us to reshape our relationship with all the beings we share Earth's resources with. It is a rare and extraordinary opportunity to see the world afresh. It is the start of a new adventure to move through our lives in a way that causes the least harm. It is a way to connect with the world ethically, compassionately, and with dignity.

You have made the courageous, life-changing choice to become a *Rebel Vegan* and live in alignment with your core values. That's a big deal, because many won't make it, or even have the opportunity to do it—you did. By being your best and most authentic self, you will become a beacon of light.

Your rebellion is a gift, both to yourself, the animals, and the planet. Your bold choice to go vegan might be the missing link for someone else to make changes, question the status quo, and connect with their authentic selves; to embrace their core values. Your courageous example will challenge and inspire those around you. This is how we become a force for good and create a brave new world. Welcome home.

So as you start this adventure, remember to be kind to yourself, take it one day at a time, and savor every bite of your plant-based journey. I've saved you a seat at the table with all your fellow *Rebel Vegans*.

GEORGE BERNARD SHAW

ONE OF THE ORIGINAL REBEL VEGANS!

Born in Dublin in 1856, George Bernard Shaw became one of the world's greatest playwrights. He was a rebel in his own right. His plays dealt with social issues such as class privilege, inequality, education and healthcare, but his main focus was the exploitation of the vulnerable and working classes. He is the only person to be awarded both a Nobel Prize (for literature, in 1925) and an Oscar (in 1938, for his play Pygmalion, which was later turned into the film My Fair Lady).

At the age of 25, he became a strict vegetarian until his death 70 years later. He describes the vegetarian food scene in London and reports there were dozens of vegetarian restaurants, which he regularly frequented. If he were alive today, he would almost certainly identify as a vegan (the term vegan was first coined the year after he died).

He lived until the age of 94, which was almost unheard of in those days. His "extreme" diet was discussed and appraised in his obituaries around the world - probably the first time many people would have thought about this type of lifestyle.

Here are some of my favorite quotes by Shaw:[4]

"A mind of the caliber of mine cannot derive its nutriment from cows."

"The average age (longevity) of a meat eater is 63.
I am on the verge of 85 and still work as hard as ever.
I have lived quite long enough and am trying to die;
but I simply cannot do it.
A single beef-steak would finish me;
but I cannot bring myself to swallow it.
I am oppressed with a dread of living forever.
That is the only disadvantage of vegetarianism."

"Animals are my friends... and I don't eat my friends."

"You see things; you say, 'Why?'
But I dream things that never were; and I say 'Why not?' "
George Bernard Shaw, Back to Methuselah[5]

24

RECIPES

SAUCES, DIPS, SPREADS

NOTE:
YOU CAN FIND THE COLOR PHOTOS OF ALL THE RECIPES AND OUR OTHER IMAGES ON OUR WEBSITE AT **REBELVEGANLIFE.COM**

SERVES
1

SUNFLOWER CHIVES SPREAD

INGREDIENTS

4 tbsp chopped chives
1 small white onion
120g sunflower seeds
55ml sunflower seed oil
1 tbsp dried mixed herbs
¼ tsp nutmeg
Juice of ¼ lemon
Salt and pepper to taste

Optional: 1 clove of garlic

DIRECTIONS

- In a food processor or high speed blender, add sunflower seeds, oil, and the spices.
- Pour in enough water for everything to be covered, and blend until a creamy but slightly chunky paste forms.
- Chop up the chives and add to the mix with a finely chopped onion.
- Let set for about 20 minutes before serving.

Since this spread lasts at least 5 days in the fridge, it's a great staple for sandwiches, baguettes, etc.

SERVES
1

CAULIFLOWER CHEESE SAUCE

INGREDIENTS

200g Cauliflower
300g Potatoes
½ medium sized white onion
¼ tsp turmeric powder
½ tsp white pepper
½ tsp Dijon mustard
1 tbsp vegetable stock
6 tbsp nutritional yeast
Pinch of sugar
Water
Salt and pepper to taste

DIRECTIONS

- Peel the potatoes and add them, together with the cut cauliflower, to a medium size cooking pot.
- Roughly chop the onion, and throw it into the pot as well.
- Add enough water to cover the vegetables and add the vegetable stock.
- Cook until the potatoes and cauliflower are falling apart.
- Drain and keep save about 120 ml of the liquid.
- Add all the ingredients and spices into a blender and blend through until homogeneous.

This sauce is especially great for burgers, vegan mac and cheese, nacho platters, or in tacos!

SERVES
1

ARTICHOKE DIP

INGREDIENTS

125g Cashews
75g Firm Tofu
90g Artichokes from a jar
~200ml Plant milk of choice (I recommend oat or soy) – unsweetened
2 tbsp Nutritional yeast
½ tsp of each garlic and onion powder
1 ½ tbsp sweet paprika powder
2-3 tbsp sunflower seed or olive oil
Optional: Chili flakes

DIRECTIONS

- Soak the cashews in hot water (ensuring all the cashews are fully covered) for at least 1.5 hours.
- Rinse and drain them, and bring all the ingredients together in a high-speed blender.
- Blend until nice and smooth, and season with salt and pepper to taste.
- This is a great recipe to use for get-togethers, parties, or spontaneous picnics!
- Simply serve them with some vegan nachos or crackers on the side.
- And it also goes really well on bagels, sandwiches, or baguettes.

We love it combined with some fresh figs, dried tomatoes, and nuts.

WEEK 1
CUT OUT EGGS AND DAIRY AND START OFF WITH A VEGAN BREAKFAST

SERVES
1

AVOCADO BAGELS WITH MARINATED TOFU THINS

INGREDIENTS

Vegan bagel of choice
70g Smoked Tofu
½ Avocado
Fresh greens of choice (e.g. baby leaf spinach)
2-3 Walnuts
Juice of ¼ lime
Few slices of a small red onion

FOR THE MARINADE:

1 tsp soy sauce
½ tbsp Worcester sauce
1 tsp nutritional yeast
½ tsp of each garlic and onion powder
½ tsp smoked paprika powder
1 tbsp sunflower seed oil

DIRECTIONS

- Cut the tofu into equal sized slices that fit onto your bagel of choice.
- Prepare the marinade by mixing all the ingredients together, and let the tofu slices soak in it for at least 30 minutes.
- In the meantime, cut your bagel in half and toast until crispy golden brown.
- Mash the avocado together with lime juice and a pinch of salt.
- Grill the marinated tofu from both sides over medium heat and start assembling your bagel by starting with the artichoke cream, followed by greens, mashed avocado, tofu, onions, and walnuts. Enjoy!

SERVES
1 - 2

TOFU SCRAMBLE

INGREDIENTS

½ white onion

1 block firm tofu

3 tbsp nutritional yeast

1 tbsp sunflower seed oil or a slice of vegan butter

A pinch of each turmeric and garlic powder

Salt and pepper to taste

DIRECTIONS

- Cut the onion in rounds and slice in half.
- Add some oil to a pan and throw in the onion together with 1 block mashed (scrambled) firm tofu.
- Add all the spices and stir until homogeneous.
- Let the covered scramble cook for about 5 minutes over low-medium heat, mixing through every now and then.

SERVES
1

GF BANANA CHOCO MUFFINS

INGREDIENTS

165g oats or oat flour
200 ml plant milk (unsweetened)
1 tsp lemon or lime juice
1 ½ tsp baking powder
1 tsp baking soda
80g cane sugar
50-60g nut butter (e.g. almond)
½ tsp cinnamon powder
2 tbsp sunflower seed oil
2 small – medium size bananas (very ripened)

50g of dark chocolate (e.g. 70%)

DIRECTIONS

- Preheat your oven to about 180*C.
- Mix the milk together with lemon juice and set aside.
- If you're using oats for this recipe, make sure to first ground them into a flour.
- Mix the oat (flour) together with the rest of the dry ingredients, then add in the mashed bananas and milk.
- Chop up your chocolate and stir it into the batter.
- Grab your muffin tin or molds and fill them up before transferring them into the oven to bake for at least 30 to 40 minutes.

SERVES
1

BERRY SMOOTHIE

INGREDIENTS

1 large frozen banana
120g frozen mixed berries (or any other red berry)
220 ml almond milk
¼ tsp cinnamon
Optional: hemp seeds

DIRECTIONS

- Blend everything together in a high-speed blender and drink right away.

Smoothies are such a great "dish" as you can bring them with you wherever you go (as long as you keep them in an insulated jug/bottle)!

They're also a great way to add more greens or antioxidants into your diet!

SERVES
1

YOGHURT BOWL

INGREDIENTS

180g coconut yogurt
½ banana
Fruit of choice, e.g. figs, passionfruit
2 tbsp crushed or shaved nuts
1 tsp of each hemp and chia seeds
Optional: dark chocolate nibs

DIRECTIONS

- Add the yogurt to a serving bowl, chop up your favorite fruits, and add some nuts and seeds for healthy fats!

SERVES
2 – 4

CREPES WITH COOKED APPLES

INGREDIENTS

200g spelt flour
300 ml plant milk
2 tbsp cane or coconut blossom sugar
Pinch of salt
2 small apples
1 tsp coconut oil
Few raisins
1 tbsp cane or coconut blossom sugar
Pinch of each nutmeg and cinnamon

DIRECTIONS

- Prepare the crepes batter by simply adding all the dry ingredients into a mixing bowl before pouring in the milk.
- Whisk together and cook in a lightly greased pan over low-medium heat on both sides.
- Chop up the apples and transfer them into a small pot together with the raisins, cinnamon, nutmeg, coconut oil, and sugar.
- Cook down over low-medium heat and keep covered until you have finished the crepes batter.

SERVES 1–2

VEGANIZED ENGLISH BREAKFAST

INGREDIENTS

175g brown button mushrooms
Medium thick slice of vegan butter
Tofu scramble
Marinated smoked tofu
4 small tomatoes
150g white beans in tomato sauce

DIRECTIONS

- Cook mushrooms and tomatoes in a little bit of vegan butter for extra flavor!
- Then simply check out the recipes for the tofu scramble and for the smoked marinated tofu.
- You only have to prepare the marinade we have used for the tempeh medallions, cut your smoked tofu into slices and grill on both sides until crispy.
- Heat up the beans and assemble with some fresh bread on the side, and optionally, some freshly cut chives.
- Enjoy!

Not only is this a classic, it's also really healthy. It provides fiber, iron, proteins, and healthy carbs. It will keep you satiated for a long time!

WEEK 2
CUT OUT RED MEAT AND IMPLEMENT PLANT-BASED LUNCHES

SERVES
2

HARD-SHELLED TACOS WITH AVOCADO AND SALSA

INGREDIENTS

1 bell pepper
1.5 small red onion
2 cloves of garlic
100g tinned kidney beans
2 tsp tomato paste
1 tsp caraway
2 tsp smoked paprika
1.5 tbsp Worcester sauce
Olive oil
6-8 brown button mushrooms
1 Avocado
8 cherry tomatoes
Juice of ¼ - ½ lime
Salt and Pepper to taste
Fresh basil or coriander

DIRECTIONS

- Chop bell pepper, 1 clove of garlic, and onion into small cubes.
- Cook together with some olive oil in a medium size cooking pan over medium heat.
- Cover with a lid and let simmer until the peppers start to soften.
- Add in tomato paste, spices (except salt*), Worcester sauce, and mushrooms.
- Mix well and stir in kidney beans once the mushrooms are almost cooked.
- Turn off heat and keep covered with a lid while preparing your salsa!

FOR THE SALSA

- Start by chopping the tomatoes into small cubes.
- Do so with the other garlic clove and half of another red onion too.
- Mix it all together with some olive oil, salt and pepper, and fresh greens, such as coriander or basil.
- You can add some fresh chilies here for a bit of heat!
- Assemble as you please and enjoy together!

The artichoke dip is a great combination with this, as it's not too dominant in flavor, yet adds some creaminess.

The marinade of the tempeh medallions works great as a sauce for tacos and nachos too!

SERVES
1

HEARTY WALNUT PASTE ON BAGUETTE

INGREDIENTS

75g Walnuts
120g smoked tofu
½ red onion
1 tbsp soy sauce
1,5 tbsp tomato paste
1 tsp liquid smoke
½ tbsp smoked paprika powder
¼ tsp cumin
Pinch of garlic powder
2 tbsp sunflower seed oil
Fresh parsley to serve with

DIRECTIONS

- Add everything to a high speed food processor and blitz through
- (use the "pulse" setting here if your food processor has one).
- Make sure the texture remains chunky, but sticks together when pressed between your fingers.
- Store in fridge to keep fresh!

Serve it on the side of some fresh bread! We love a good French baguette or a rustic, crunchy dark bread with it.

SERVES
2

SWEET POTATO – BASIL PANCAKES

INGREDIENTS

80g shredded or shaved sweet potato
100g spelt flour
1 tbsp nutritional yeast
1 tbsp sunflower seed oil
½ tsp each garlic and onion powder
Pinch of nutmeg and turmeric
175 ml nut milk unsweetened (e.g. oat)
Few leaves fresh basil
6 medium size mushrooms
Handful fresh greens, e.g. arugula
100g soy yogurt
1 garlic clove
Squeeze of ½ lemon
Salt and pepper to taste

DIRECTIONS

- Mix the soy yogurt together with 1 clove of freshly minced garlic and lemon juice.
- Set aside.
- In a large mixing bowl, mix flour, spices, and plant milk.
- Add in the shredded sweet potato and whisk well.
- Add some oil to a pan over medium heat and bake the pancakes from both sides.
- Serve with fresh greens and your garlic infused lemon yogurt!

This is a great Sunday morning / brunch dish! It's hearty, fresh, and takes seconds to prepare.

Feel free to change up the toppings: marinated vegetables, sautéed spinach with mushrooms, etc.

ARUGULA CHICKPEA SALAD

SERVES
2

INGREDIENTS

3-4 handful fresh arugula
10 cherry tomatoes
175g precooked chickpeas
Kalamata olives
25g dried cranberries
2 tbsp sunflower or pumpkin seeds
2 tbsp olive oil
2-3 tbsp balsamic vinegar
Salt and pepper to taste

DIRECTIONS

- Wash and dry the arugula and transfer into a medium size mixing bowl.
- Chop tomatoes into quarters and olives in half – add to the salad.
- Throw in the rest of the ingredients and simply adjust with salt and pepper!

You can use this recipe as a main for a warmer day, or as a side salad to a soup as well!

SERVES
1

SANDWICH WITH MARINATED TOFU

INGREDIENTS

2 slices bread of choice
4 sundried tomatoes
75g firm tofu
2 leafs Roma salad
1 tomato
Grilled vegetables of choice (e.g. eggplant, bell pepper)
Cucumber
1 tsp Dijon mustard
2 tsp balsamic vinegar
1 tbsp liquid smoke
1 ½ tbsp maple syrup
½ tsp of each garlic and onion powder
Salt and pepper to taste

DIRECTIONS

- To marinate the tofu, mix all the liquids and spices in a mixing bowl, and let the tofu soak in it for at least 1 hour (you can also prepare this the night before and store it in the fridge).
- Cut your vegetables into Juliennes and grill them in a pan with a touch of oil.
- In the meantime, toast your bread and chop up the tomato and cucumber into rounds.
- Grill the tofu from both sides and assemble your sandwich together with the rest of the ingredients!

Such a good dish to take to work / school with you or to enjoy together on a picnic!

SERVES
2

LENTIL PASTA IN TOMATO SAUCE

INGREDIENTS

2 servings of pasta (of choice)
250-300g passata italiana / tomato sauce
1 tbsp tomato paste
2 garlic cloves
1 medium size white onion
150g cooked red or brown lentils
1 tsp dried Italian herbs
Salt and pepper to taste
2-4 tbsp pasta water

DIRECTIONS

- Cook two servings of pasta according to the directions on the package.
- To prepare the sauce, simply sauté the chopped up garlic and onion in a little bit of olive oil over medium heat.
- Once translucent add in tomato paste, herbs and mixed cracked pepper.
- Stir in the passata, followed by lentils.
- Pour a little bit of the pasta water into the sauce, then strain the pasta just a little before they're fully cooked (so they don't get too soft when being mixed with the sauce).
- Serve with some fresh herbs and nutritional yeast on top!

Pasta dishes are great to take to work or school as they can be enjoyed cold as well, don't take up too much space and can easily be reheated another time.

SERVES
2 – 3

CAULIFLOWER WHITE BEAN CURRY

INGREDIENTS

1 tin white beans
450g cauliflower
1 large white onion
2 cloves garlic
1 tbsp caraway
½ tsp nutmeg
1 tbsp smoked paprika
3 tsp yellow curry powder
2 tsp cane sugar
1,5 tbsp vegetable stock
150 ml water
Fresh ginger
Fresh coriander

DIRECTIONS

- Chop up onion and garlic and add to a large cooking pot with the oil and spices.
- Stir together and throw in the chopped up cauliflower.
- Pour in about 150ml of water together with the vegetable stock, and let it all cook down until the cauliflower starts to soften.
- Whisk in some thinly sliced ginger and the pre-cooked beans, and let sit for about 25 minutes without heat.
- Keep the pot covered and serve with rice and fresh lime on the side.

A lovely family dish that can be prepared in bigger batches in advance, so that you can simply freeze or store the rest in the refrigerator for another time!

WEEK 3
CUT OUT ALL LAND ANIMALS AND GO FOR VEGAN DINNERS AND SUPPERS

SERVES 4

REBEL VEGAN BURGERS

INGREDIENTS

Vegan Burger Buns
Tomatoes
Roma Salad
1 Red Onion
400g Firm Tofu
Optional: pickled cucumbers

FOR THE MARINADE:

2 tbsp Tomato paste
2 tbsp Liquid smoke
1 tbsp Sunflower seed oil
1 tbsp Worcester sauce
1 tbsp Nutritional Yeast
1 tsp White Pepper
½ tsp of each onion and garlic powder
Salt and Pepper to taste

DIRECTIONS

- Prepare the marinade by mixing all the ingredients together in a small mixing bowl (should be big enough for you to soak the tofu in).
- Note: You might want to use a little water if your marinade is getting too thick.
- Cut four equal sized rounds out of your blocks of tofu.
- Pat them dry and let them soak in the marinade for at least 1 hour. Flip and cover with marinade from both sides from time to time.
- Grill them in a pan from both sides over medium heat and keep it covered with a lid.
- Assemble your burgers as you please – done!

The Cauliflower – Cheese Sauce goes really well with this recipe!

Simply reheat the sauce over low-medium heat until warm enough, and drizzle over the patties while layering the ingredients.

SERVES
2 - 4

CHILI SIN CARNE

INGREDIENTS

1 Red Pepper
275g cooked kidney beans
1 large white onion
2 cloves of garlic
2-3 Tbsp Tomato Puree
250g tinned chopped tomatoes
2 Tbsp Vegetable stock
100-150 ml Water
1-2 Tbsp Olive Oil
1,5 Tbsp Smoked Paprika Powder
1 Tsp Miso Paste
1 Tsp caraway
Pinch of Sugar
1 Bay Leaf
Salt and Pepper to taste

DIRECTIONS

- Chop the onion into medium sized pieces and mince the garlic.
- Throw both together in a large cooking pot with some olive oil and sauté until translucent.
- Cut your pepper into bite size cubes and add to the pot with all the spices (including vegetable stock), miso, and tomato paste.
- Mix well, add the tinned tomatoes and water, and stir in the bay leaf.
- Cover with a lid and cook for about 10 to 15 minutes, or until the peppers start to feel a little soft.
- At this point, mix in your pre-cooked kidney beans so they heat up together with the rest.
- Turn off the heat and let everything sit for another 20 minutes (with the lid on).
- Serve with some fresh greens, such as coriander and parsley!

This is a really great party dish too, and I'm sure no one will taste the difference to a traditional chili con carne!

SERVES
2 – 3

STUFFED PEPPERS

INGREDIENTS

150g pre-cooked lentils
2 large bell peppers
1 serving rice (listed on the package)
1 medium sized carrot
1 medium sized white onion
2 cloves of garlic
1 – 2 tbsp olive oil
3 tbsp vegetable stock
2 tsp liquid smoke
1 tbsp smoked paprika powder
½ tsp caraway
1 tbsp tomato paste
Salt and pepper to taste
Juice of ½ lime
Water

DIRECTIONS

- Start by pre-heating your oven to about 200C.
- Cut open the peppers to remove their seeds, and glaze with a bit of oil. Sprinkle some salt before transferring them into the oven to grill while preparing the filling.

FILLING

- Slice the onion into rings, then cut in half.
- Chop the carrot into small cubes and mince the garlic.
- Add everything to a large cooking pan with some olive oil, and let simmer over low-medium heat with a lid on until onion and garlic start to lose color.
- Mix in your pre-cooked lentils together with all the spices, tomato paste, liquid smoke, and cooked rice.
- Whisk everything together, adjust with salt and pepper as you please, and turn off the heat.
- Add in the lime juice, then take the peppers out to stuff them.
- Transfer back into the oven for about 30 to 40 minutes.

Our Cauliflower-Cheese sauce goes really well with this recipe too!

SERVES
4

BROCCOLI ZUCCHINI LOAF WITH CHEESE SAUCE

INGREDIENTS

300g potatoes
300g broccoli
2 cloves of garlic
1 medium sized zucchini
1 medium sized white onion
1 tbsp smoked paprika powder
½ tbsp white pepper
2 tbsp olive oil
~ 100 ml plant milk unsweetened
Salt and pepper to taste

DIRECTIONS

- Preheat your oven to 185 C.
- Chop potatoes, broccoli, and zucchini into small cubes, making sure the potato pieces are a little smaller than the rest, as they take the longest to cook.
- Finely slice your garlic, chop up the onion and mix it all together in a large mixing bowl, together with the spices and oil.
- Add a little bit of plant milk to a casserole dish and transfer your vegetables into the oven for about 30 minutes – stir around every once in a while.
- After 30 minutes, pull out from the oven and pour the cheese sauce over.
- Let cook for another 20 minutes – done!

I recommend serving this with fresh greens, e.g. some flat leaf parsley or baby leaf spinach. It will add a nice crunch to it!

SERVES
1 – 2

TEMPEH MEDALLIONS ON GRILLED VEGETABLES

INGREDIENTS

200g tempeh
2 tbsp tomato paste
1 tbsp liquid smoke
2 tbsp Worcester sauce
1 tbsp plant oil (e.g. sunflower seed)
½ tsp Dijon mustard
2 tsp smoked paprika powder
1 tsp maple syrup
Optional: 1 tsp cayenne pepper
Water to dilute
½ large eggplant
2 peppers, e.g. red and yellow
1 medium size of both red and white onion
Salt and pepper to taste
Optional: freshly minced garlic

DIRECTIONS

- Mix all the listed ingredients together in a bowl, chop the tempeh into slices or rounds (depending on what shape it comes in) and marinade from both sides for at least 1h.
- Make sure you flip them every once in a while, so both sides are evenly covered and soaked.
- In the meantime, prepare your grilled vegetables by simply cutting them into Julienne strips and add them into a pan with a touch of oil.

SERVES
2

MUSHROOM TARTAR

INGREDIENTS

650g / 23 oz brown button mushrooms
3 shallots
2,5 tbsp sunflower seed oil
1 tsp lemon juice
1 tbsp freshly chopped parsley
1 – 2 tbsp freshly chopped
Salt and pepper to taste

DIRECTIONS

- Clean and gently wash the mushrooms, then chop into small cubes.
- Add some oil to a pan and grill the mushrooms until all liquids have evaporated.
- In the meantime, dice your shallots and add them to the pan just before the mushrooms are done.
- Finely chop up the fresh greens and bring all the ingredients together in a mixing bowl before seasoning with salt and pepper.
- Drizzle in some lemon juice and let sit for about 5 minutes before serving.

This dish goes great together with some fresh baguette and margarine!

It's also great for parties or as a starter!

WEEK 4
CELEBRATION DINNER!

SERVES
3 - 4

TODD'S CURRY

This is my party piece that I can whip up for unexpected guests in no time.

Each time I make it a little different with whatever veggies I have at hand.

If you need to feed more, simply add more coconut milk, chopped tomatoes, and veggies to fill it out. Everyone is welcome at my table.

INGREDIENTS

2 tbsp coconut oil
2 tins chickpeas
1 tin jackfruit
250g baby leaf spinach
½ tin coconut milk
½ tin chopped tomatoes
2 medium size white onions
2 medium size tomatoes
2 cloves of garlic
2 tbsp mustard seeds
2 tbsp cumin
1 tbsp garam masala
1 tbsp curry powder
1 tbsp turmeric
1 tsp freshly chopped ginger
Optional: 2 green chilies

DIRECTIONS

- In a large cooking pot, mix the coconut oil, chopped onions, minced garlic, and all the spices.
- Stir and cook until caramelized.
- Add in the ½ tin chopped tomatoes, freshly chopped tomatoes, and ginger.
- Let everything cook down over medium heat with a lid on.
- Stir every once in a while, then pour in ½ tin of coconut milk, 1 tin of each blended and unblended chickpeas and the jackfruit.
- Mix together and add the spinach afterwards.
- Cover with a lid, reduce the heat to low and let simmer for another 10 minutes.

SERVES
1

RAW VEGAN COCONUT BERRIES CAKE

INGREDIENTS

90g Cashews
2 tbsp Maple syrup
3 tbsp coconut yogurt
2 tbsp coconut oil
1 tsp vanilla extract
½ tsp rose water
Juice of ½ lemon

BASE

150g shredded oats
130g pitted dates
½ tsp cinnamon
Pinch of salt
1 ½ tbsp coconut oil

+ Frozen berries of choice

DIRECTIONS

- Soak the cashews in hot water for at least 1.5 hours.
- To prepare the base, mix all the ingredients (base) in a food processor until the mixture starts sticking together when pressed in between fingers.
- Press into a small ring baking tin with removable bottom and freeze for about 40 minutes.
- In the meantime, prepare the filling by draining the cashews and adding them to a blender with all the other ingredients.
- Pour onto the base and freeze for another 1,5h before decorating.
- Once you decorated the cake, freeze for another 40 to 60 minutes or until the filling is stiff enough.

Make sure to defrost the cake at room temperature for at least 10 minutes before cutting it so it doesn't break.

25

APPENDICES

APPENDIX 1: HANDY FOOD LISTS

ESSENTIAL AMINO ACIDS AND PLANT SOURCES[1]

ESSENTIAL AMINO ACID	PLANT FOOD SOURCES
Isoleucine	Tofu, lupin beans, lentils, oats, oat bran, buckwheat, lima beans, chickpeas, Swiss chard, whole wheat, pistachios, spinach, wild rice, quinoa, sunflower seeds.
Leucine	Tofu, oats, navy beans, adzuki beans, white beans, buckwheat, lentils, mung beans, broad beans, teff grain, kamut grain, pumpkin seeds, hemp seeds.
Lysine	Tofu, edamame beans (soy beans), green peas, lupin beans, navy beans, adzuki beans, lentils, lentil sprouts, white beans, split peas, buckwheat, oats, black beans, mung beans, quinoa, hemp seeds.
Tryptophan	Tofu, oats, buckwheat, pumpkin seeds, sea vegetables, whole wheat, walnuts, lentils, mung beans, chickpeas, sesame seeds, chia seeds, sunflower seeds, quinoa, potatoes, pine nuts, cacao.
Valine	Tofu, oats, buckwheat, navy beans, lupin beans, white beans, oat bran, adzuki beans, lentils, lentil sprouts, kidney beans, lima beans, black beans, peanuts, flax seeds, brown rice, spinach, cashew nuts.
Threonine	Tofu, lupin beans, oats, buckwheat, white beans, navy beans, lentils, adzuki beans, split peas, corn, chickpeas, soy sprouts, black eyed peas, broad beans, teff grain, hemp seeds, wheatgerm, pumpkin seeds, peanuts.
Histidine	Tofu, oats, buckwheat, lentils, white beans, kidney beans, adzuki beans, mung beans, pea sprouts, wild rice, chia seeds, almonds, sunflower seeds, whole wheat, peanuts.
Phenylalanine	Tofu, edamame beans (soy beans), oats, navy beans, lupin beans, white beans, kidney beans, pinto beans, buckwheat, lentils, lentil sprouts, mung beans, cornmeal, hemp seeds, peanuts, quinoa, millet, sunflower seeds, almonds.
Methionine	Tofu, oats, oat bran, brazil nuts, teff grain, wheatgerm, corn, buckwheat, hemp seeds, white beans, kidney beans, sesame seeds, lentils, green peas, sweet potatoes, millet.

ESSENTIAL MACRO-NUTRIENTS AND PLANT SOURCES

PLANT PROTEIN	COMPLEX CARBOHYDRATES	HEALTHY FATS
Lentils (brown, red, yellow, green) Chickpeas Black beans Black-eye beans Kidney beans Cannellini beans Butter beans Navy beans Split peas Snap peas Green beans Lima beans Pinto beans White beans Broad beans Mung beans Adzuki beans Peanuts Hemp seeds Chia seeds Quinoa* Buckwheat* Amaranth* Soy/tofu/tempeh Pasta and noodles made from beans or lentils	Root vegetables (sweet potatoes, carrots, celeriac, parsnips, beetroot, turnips, potatoes, yam, pumpkin, squash) Whole grains (amaranth*, barley, buckwheat*, rice, bulgur wheat, corn, polenta, kamut, millet, oats, quinoa*, rye, sorghum, spelt, teff, triticale, couscous) Pasta and noodles made from whole grains (wheat, spelt, wheat), as well as brown rice and buckwheat Sourdough bread or organic bread made from whole grains Oat crackers Fruits (especially ones with edible seeds like berries, apples, watermelon, papaya, kiwi)	Olive oil Coconut oil Avocado oil Walnut oil Sesame oil Flaxseed oil Almonds Hazelnuts Brazil nuts Cashew nuts Pecan nuts Macadamia nuts Pine nuts Pistachios Peanuts Pumpkin seeds Sunflower seeds Hemp seeds Chia seeds Sesame seeds Coconut (fresh, dried, or coconut milk) Avocado Omega-3: Seaweed and algae (sea salad, kombu, wakame, nori, spirulina) Chia seeds Hemp seeds Walnuts Flax seeds

* Amaranth, buckwheat, and quinoa are pseudo-grains - they are used like grains in cooking, but are actually seeds. This is why they are excellent sources of both protein and complex carbohydrates.

ESSENTIAL MICRONUTRIENTS AND PLANT SOURCES[2]

VITAMIN A
- Supports eyes and prevents age-related macular degeneration.
- Helps the body make antibodies that neutralize or fight pathogens.
- Needed to produce new red blood cells.

Sweet potatoes, carrots, spinach, kale, squash, Swiss chard, collard greens, squash, romaine lettuce, cantaloupe melon, bell peppers, parsley, broccoli, papaya, pink grapefruit, chives, apricots, tangerine, peaches, sour cherries, plantain

VITAMIN B1 (THIAMIN)
- Helps your body convert fat, sugars, and protein from food into usable energy.
- Has a role in brain cells' structure and function.

Sunflower seeds, sesame seeds, peanuts, black beans, peas, lentils, cabbage, navy beans, kidney beans, tofu, flaxseed, sweet potato, Brussels sprouts, yeast extract, spirulina, parsley, rice, oat bran, cornmeal, oats, barley, kamut

VITAMIN B2 (RIBOFLAVIN)
- Like all B vitamins, it helps the body convert food into useable energy.
- Helps recycle glutathione (the body's own powerful antioxidant).
- Helps prevent anemia.

Spinach, beetroot greens, mushrooms, sweet peppers, radish, yeast extract, parsley, chives, lychees, corn, wheat bran, soybeans, tempeh, almonds, sesame seeds, yeast extract (such as Marmite), spirulina

VITAMIN B3 (NIACIN)
- Essential for energy production.
- Protects against free radicals.

Mushrooms, green peas, potatoes, corn, asparagus, sweet potato, hot chili peppers, tomatoes, peanuts, brown rice, sunflower seeds, sesame seeds, wheat bran, buckwheat, spelt, wild rice, yeast extract

VITAMIN B5 (PANTOTHENIC ACID)
- Important for energy production, particularly from fats.
- Helps make anti-stress hormones and vitamin D.
- Maintains healthy skin and hair.

Shiitake mushrooms, portobello mushrooms, onions, avocado, sweet potato, potatoes, broccoli, cauliflower, papaya, squash, tomatoes, endive, dried apricots, lentils, peas, rye, rice, oat bran, wheat bran, amaranth, buckwheat, spelt, wheat, teff, sunflower seeds, sesame seeds, spirulina

VITAMIN B6 (PYRIDOXINE)
- Helps the body to produce red blood cells.
- Breaks down carbohydrates for energy.
- Required for the production of key neurotransmitters.
- Helps the liver eliminate toxins.

Cabbage, bok choi, sweet potato, potatoes, spinach, cauliflower, bell peppers, broccoli, squash, bananas, chives, shallots, prunes, apricots, garlic, pistachios, sunflower seeds, sesame seeds, wheat bran, rice, yellow corn, amaranth, buckwheat, yeast extract

VITAMIN B12 (COBALAMIN)
- Keeps the cardiovascular system healthy by helping blood carry oxygen to all your cells.
- Prevents homocysteine build up (an inflammatory marker linked with cardiovascular disease).
- Essential for DNA production.
- Keeps brain cells and nervous system healthy.

Small amounts found in some mushrooms and fermented foods (kimchi, sauerkraut, miso, kombucha) - however a good quality B12 supplement is recommended.

FOLIC ACID (FOLATE)
- Supports healthy brain and nervous system function.
- Reduces homocysteine levels and protects the cardiovascular system.
- Essential for fetus development during pregnancy.
- Helps form red blood cells.

Asparagus, spinach, leeks, edamame beans, radish, sweet peppers, parsley, avocado, black beans, kidney beans, wheat germ, enriched wheat flours, corn, rice, quinoa, wild rice, millet, lentils, pinto beans, chickpeas, yeast extract, agar agar seaweed, sunflower seeds, sesame seeds, hazelnuts, chestnuts

VITAMIN C
- Powerful antioxidant - protects the body against free radicals.
- Needed for collagen production and skin health.
- Required to make serotonin (our mood neurotransmitter).
- Supports a strong immune system and helps to fight infections.

Papaya, bell peppers, broccoli, strawberries, pineapple, oranges, kiwis, melon, cauliflower, parsley, kale, celery, Brussels sprouts, chives, mustard greens, red cabbage, lychees, red currants, lemons, grapefruit, peaches, papaya, strawberries, pineapple, apples, clementines, chestnuts, thyme, dill

VITAMIN D
- Helps the body absorb calcium to keep bones and teeth strong.
- Involved in blood sugar control (deficiency may be a factor in diabetes).
- Helps white blood cells mature and function.

Shiitake mushrooms, fortified breakfast cereals, plant milks, plant yogurts, and enriched flours - however, a good quality vegan Vitamin D supplement is recommended.

VITAMIN E
- Potent antioxidant - protects cell membranes against free radical oxidation.
- Reduces levels of bad cholesterol (LDL).
- Keeps skin supple.

Spinach, chard, avocado, peanuts, turnip greens, asparagus, sweet peppers, broccoli, fresh coriander, apricots, olives, brown rice, quinoa, rye, oat bran, whole grain wheat, agar agar seaweed, sunflower seeds, almonds, hazelnuts

VITAMIN K
- Needed for normal blood clotting.
- Helps keep bones strong.

Kale, spinach, collard greens, chard, parsley, broccoli, Brussels sprouts, radicchio, chicory greens, prunes, rhubarb, avocado, pears, pine nuts, pumpkin seeds, cashew nuts, soy beans, miso, natto (fermented soy), split peas, kidney beans, buckwheat, rye

CALCIUM
- Supports bone and teeth health.
- Critical for acid-alkaline balance of the body.
- Regulates nerve signals.

Collard greens, spinach, chives, radishes, leeks, kale, garlic, rhubarb, figs, tofu, sesame seeds, chia seeds, almonds, flaxseeds, carob powder, plant milks and tofu products fortified with calcium

CHROMIUM
- Keeps blood sugar levels balanced.
- Normalizes hunger, reduces cravings.

Broccoli, green beans, tomatoes, romaine lettuce, apples, grapes, whole wheat, barley, oats, brewer's yeast

IRON

- Helps take oxygen to all tissues and muscles.
- Supports cells' energy metabolism.

Spinach, olives, chard, sesame seeds, pumpkin seeds, sunflower seeds, cashew nuts, chickpeas, kidney beans, peanuts, soybeans, lentils, rice bran, wheat bran, amaranth, corn, rye, oat bran, parsley, chives, spirulina, agar agar seaweed

MAGNESIUM

- Keeps bones and teeth strong.
- Needed for energy production.
- Helps muscles to relax.
- Supports the nervous system.
- Reduces inflammation.

Spinach, chard, bananas, figs, prunes, apricots, watermelon (with seeds), soybeans, black beans, quinoa, rice, wild rice, wheat, buckwheat, amaranth, oat bran, teff, agar agar seaweed, spirulina, yeast extract, pumpkin seeds, flaxseeds, Brazil nuts, sunflower seeds, sesame seeds, almonds, cashew nuts

MANGANESE

- Important to keep bones, cartilage, tissues, and nerves healthy.
- Has a role in normal brain function.
- Helps balance blood sugar.
- Essential for insulin production.

Celery, lemongrass, leeks, raspberries, okra, lima beans, grapes, beetroot, garlic, peppers, pineapple, blueberries, rice, wheat, teff, rye, oats, agar agar seaweed, hazelnuts, pine nuts, pecans, macadamia nuts, chestnuts, pumpkin seeds, peanuts, soy beans

POTASSIUM

- Keeps muscles and nerves working properly.
- Supports heart and kidney function.
- Keeps blood pressure balanced.

Sweet potato, potatoes, tomato, beetroot, banana, butternut squash, parsley, sweet peppers, chives, apricots, bananas, peaches, lychee, prunes, raisins, medjool dates, figs, pears, avocado, plantain, grapefruit, apples, palm hearts, onions, shiitake mushrooms, rice, wheat, rye, buckwheat, oat bran, quinoa, amaranth, barley, black beans, soybeans, yeast extract, spirulina, agar agar seaweed, chestnuts, pumpkin seeds, sunflower seeds, flaxseeds, almonds, hazelnuts, brazil nuts, cashew nuts, pine nuts, pistachios

SELENIUM

- Needed for the production of glutathione, the body's own powerful antioxidant.
- Supports normal thyroid function.

Found in most plant foods but especially brazil nuts, sesame seeds, wheat, shiitake mushrooms, soybeans.

ZINC

- Helps the immune system fight infections.
- Keeps skin healthy - fights acne.
- Needed for sense of taste and smell.
- Important for male reproductive health.

Sesame seeds, pumpkin seeds, lentils, chickpeas, cashew nuts, quinoa, oats, wheat bran, wild rice, shiitake mushrooms, agar agar seaweed, watermelon seeds, soy beans, peanuts

PHYTONUTRIENTS AND ANTIOXIDANTS

- Neutralize free radicals.
- Slow down the aging process.
- Protect DNA.
- Reduce the risk of disease.

Brightly colored fruits and vegetables - Herbs: rosemary, coriander, oregano, parsley, mint, thyme - Spices: ginger, garlic, turmeric, cinnamon, cumin

APPENDIX 2:

GUT-FRIENDLY FOODS AND WAYS TO ADD THEM TO YOUR DIET

KOMBUCHA (FERMENTED TEA):

This is probably the easiest probiotic to add to your diet. Just drink a glass or two every day. When you buy kombucha, check the label to make sure it is raw, unpasteurized, and does not contain any artificial additives or added sweeteners.

SAUERKRAUT (FERMENTED CABBAGE):

You can make this at home or find it in health food shops. Make sure it is raw and unpasteurized, otherwise it won't contain beneficial bacteria. Sauerkraut is wonderful on top of a salad, added to a hummus wrap, or piled on top of a rice cake or oat cracker with smashed avocado.

KIMCHI (FERMENTED CABBAGE WITH GINGER, GARLIC, CHILI):

Like sauerkraut but with an Asian twist and plenty of heat. Complements stir-fried dishes, can be enjoyed added to salads, or added to your wraps and sandwiches.

COCONUT KEFIR (DAIRY-FREE FERMENTED MILK ALTERNATIVE MADE WITH KEFIR GRAINS):

You'll find coconut kefir in health food shops. Add it to smoothies, pour it on granola or fruit, or drink it on its own.

MISO (FERMENTED RICE PASTE):

Try white miso in dressings and marinades. It has a mild savory flavor that lifts ingredients out of bland and plonks them decidedly into tasty. You can also use miso paste to make Asian noodle dishes. Dark miso has a more pronounced savory flavor - a little goes a long way!

TEMPEH OR NATO (FERMENTED SOY BEANS):

Tempeh is delicious marinated in soy sauce, ginger, and garlic, and fried in a little coconut oil. You can also cut it into chunks and add it to stews and curries for extra protein. It has a subtle, slightly nutty taste. Nato has a very strong flavor and isn't for the faint-hearted.

PICKLES (LACTO-FERMENTED VEGETABLES):

Crunchy, sharp and tangy, pickled vegetables are great as a side to any meal, or added to wraps and salads.

MEAL IDEAS TO GET YOU STARTED

PLANT-BASED BREAKFASTS

Chia pudding made with almond milk and topped with berries	High in fiber, protein and healthy fats (chia seeds) High in antioxidants (berries) BONUS: can be made in batches for quick & easy breakfast.
Home-made buckwheat granola with coconut yogurt and fruit	High in fiber and protein (buckwheat) Good source of healthy fat (coconut) Good source of antioxidants (fruit) BONUS: can be made in batches for quick & easy breakfast.
Scrambled tofu, fried mushrooms, roasted tomatoes, home-made baked beans	High in protein and fiber (tofu, beans) Good source of vitamins and antioxidants (mushrooms, tomatoes)
Two slices of seeded sourdough bread with peanut butter and banana	Good source of complex carbs (seed bread, banana) Complete protein from combining seeds & legumes (seeds & peanut butter) Source of healthy fats (peanut butter)
Overnight oats topped with stewed apples and almond butter	Complex carbs and fiber (oats) Good source of antioxidants and fiber (apples) Healthy fats, fiber and protein (almond butter) BONUS: you can make enough for 2 or 3 breakfasts in advance.
Superfood smoothie with spinach, banana, apple, oats, hemp seeds, plant milk	High in fiber (oats, spinach, hemp seed) Complex carbs (oats, banana) Healthy fats and protein (hemp seeds) BONUS: you can go wild with your smoothies - try kale, berries, oats, tropical fruit, coconut milk, cacao, peanut/almond butter... the possibilities are endless.

PLANT-BASED LUNCHES/DINNERS

Buddha bowl: black rice, avocado, chickpeas, steamed broccoli, grated beetroot, tahini dressing	Healthy fats (avocado, tahini) Antioxidants (beetroot, broccoli) Protein (chickpeas) Fiber (all ingredients)
Buddha bowl: quinoa, grated carrot, diced celery, massaged kale, beetroot hummus, toasted seeds	Healthy fats (seeds) Antioxidants (carrot, kale, celery) Protein (hummus, quinoa, seeds) Fiber (all ingredients) BONUS: there's nothing easier than a Buddha bowl meal. Just freestyle with whatever veg you have in your fridge!
Stir fried vegetables (mange tout, mushrooms, tenderstem broccoli, leeks) with buckwheat noodles and a peanut tamari sauce	Antioxidants (broccoli, leeks...) Complex carbs (noodles) Complete protein (combination of buckwheat and peanuts) Healthy fats (peanuts) Fiber (all ingredients)

Parsnip tabbouleh (parsnip rice with finely diced cucumber, celery, mint, lemon juice, sunflower seeds)	Antioxidants (cucumber, celery, mint) Healthy fats (sunflower seeds) Complex carbs (parsnips) Fiber (all ingredients)
Tamari and ginger marinated tempeh with spinach and coconut black rice	Protein and fermented food (tempeh) Complex carbs (black rice) Antioxidants (ginger, spinach) Healthy fats (coconut) Fiber (all ingredients)
Lentil & coconut dhal with buckwheat	Protein (lentils, buckwheat) Complex carbs (buckwheat) Antioxidants (spices, ginger, garlic, onion) Fiber (all ingredients)
Bean & vegetable stew with polenta or whole grain pasta	Protein (beans) Antioxidants (onions, garlic, vegetables) Complex carbs (polenta or whole grain pasta) Healthy fats (olive oil) Fiber (all ingredients)
Roasted root veg (beetroot, sweet potato, parsnips...) and quinoa salad with lemon dressing	Complex carbs (root veg) Antioxidants (sweet potato, beetroot) Protein (quinoa) Healthy fat (olive oil dressing) Fiber (root veg, quinoa)

PLANT-BASED SNACKS

Oat, raisin & pumpkin seed cookie	Complex carbs (oats, raisins) Healthy fats and protein (seeds) Fiber (all ingredients)
Coconut, oat & ginger cookie	Complex carbs (oats) Healthy fats (coconut) Antioxidants (ginger) Fiber (all ingredients)
Energy ball - coconut & mango; oat, peanut & cacao nibs; almond & date...	Complex carbs (oats, dates) Healthy fats and protein (nuts, seeds) Antioxidants (cacao nibs) Fiber (oats, dates, seeds) BONUS: add a tablespoon of vegan protein powder or superfood powders like maca for added goodness.
Oat crackers with nut butter	Complex carbs (oats) Healthy fats (peanut butter) Complete protein (combining grains and legumes) Fiber (oats, peanut butter)
Home-made turmeric buckwheat granola with plant milk	Healthy fats (coconut oil, seeds) Complex carbs (oats) Protein (buckwheat) Antioxidants (turmeric) Fiber (oats, buckwheat)
Dark chocolate	Antioxidants and healthy fats (cacao)

RESOURCES

In my years of veganism and travel, I have collected a treasure trove of resources to help me along the way. I've done my best to share this knowledge and information with you in my Rebel Vegan series.

To help you quickly access this information while on the go, I have compiled all of the resources mentioned in this guide into one compact resource section. Feel free to dog-ear these pages and references when needed in your life and adventures.

WEBSITES

Save these websites to your Favorites Bar before preparing your next vegan vacation. These resources will make the planning process considerably easier.

- **Plant Based Health Online:** The top plant-based doctors in the UK offering healthcare and lifestyle advice to overcome chronic illnesses and certain cancers. ***PlantBasedHealthOnline.com***
- **HappyCow:** This website is helpful for finding vegan restaurants around the world. It is user-sourced, so you can add or update restaurants, as well as read customer reviews. Bonus, this website comes in app form too. ***HappyCow.net***
- **VegVisits:** The Airbnb for vegans. Book unique homestays and accommodations with locals in over 80 countries. ***VegVisits.com***
- **Vegan Meetups, Couchsurfing, and Traveling:** A Facebook community with 7,000 members. Vegan gatherings and open Couchsurfing opportunities are listed here. Members also discuss travel experiences and questions. You have to request membership for this group. ***facebook.com/groups/974772789309783***
- **Barnivore:** A searchable directory of wines, beers, and liquors denoting which are vegan-friendly. ***barnivore.com***
- **Vegan Travel Facebook Group:** The group currently has over 35,000 members. The content discusses all things vegan related, and many members are more than happy to answer your questions. ***facebook.com/groups/vegantravel***
- **Vegan Travel:** Virtual vegan community with reviews, blog posts, videos, and more for planning your vegan trips. ***VeganTravel.com***
- **Foundation for Intentional Community:** Want to live with other vegans? Interested in growing your own food? How about popping in for a weekend visit? Access a global directory of intentional communities where you can narrow the search to vegetarian/vegan communities. ***ic.org***
- **Food Labels Exposed:** Use this website put together by A Greener World to help you navigate the confusing world of food labels. ***aGreenerWorld.org/wp-content/uploads/2015/03/AGW-Food-Labels-Exposed-2017-EMAIL-SCREEN-8-31-2017.pdf***
- **Animal Welfare's Consumer's Guide:** The Animal Welfare Institute has put together a listing of all food labels and what they mean, explaining which are legal terms and which are made up by the food companies. ***awiOnline.org/content/consumers-guide-food-labels-and-animal-welfare***
- **Vegan Calculator:** Ever wished you could measure the impact you've made in your vegan or vegetarian journey? Now you can. Measure your impact at: ***VeganCalculator.com***
- **Book Different:** This website rates hotels in terms of their eco-friendliness. ***BookDifferent.com***

APPS

Download these apps on your phone ASAP! These resources will help you with just about everything - booking a hotel room, scoring a yummy vegan meal, communicating in a foreign language, and more.

- **Vegan Passport:** This is a digital food card available in various languages to help you explain your dietary preferences. The passport explains in detail which ingredients vegans do and don't eat in 78 different languages.

- **Google Translate:** You can speak or type words and phrases to be translated into over 100 languages. You can even point your camera at a block of text and have it translated for you in real-time. Be sure to download the language pack for the specific language you need, so that the app can be used offline as well.

- **AirVegan:** Use this app when heading to the airport. AirVegan shows how vegan-friendly an airport is. It lists all places that offer vegan options, and even tells you where they are located. Some of you may have encountered this app back when they only supported airports in the United States. Good news - the app went international with its listings back in 2018.

- **Food Monster:** This app provides the user with a database containing over 8,000 vegan recipes. While it isn't travel-related, it can aid you in your travels by providing quick and budget-friendly meals when you select the filters 'Less Than Five Ingredients' or 'Quick Meals'.

- **VeganXpress:** This app only works for travel in the US. It lists all vegan menu choices at 150 chain restaurants throughout the US. The database goes into great detail about all the possible vegan options. It also includes a food guide for supermarkets, and another guide for various alcoholic drinks.

- **V-Cards:** Vegan Abroad: V-cards, vegan cards in this case, are translation cards to help you order food abroad. This is a similar concept to the food cards offered up in the Hot Spots chapter of this guide, only they offer translations in over 100 languages on demand.

- **Veganagogo:** This is another translation app - because you can never have too many. Users choose from a list of pre-written questions and statements, making it easier to use than Google Translate in some scenarios.

- **Foodsaurus:** Standing in the grocery aisle at a foreign market completely unsure of what the ingredient list on the pre-made boxed meal lists? Whip out your phone and scan the ingredient list with Foodsaurus, and the app will translate the label to your language of choice.
- **Veggly:** Can't imagine dating an omnivore? Looking for a romantic partner that can hold you accountable in your vegan journey? Check out Veggly, a vegan dating app currently available in 181 countries.
- **Vegan Check:** This app double checks that products are entirely vegan before purchasing. It also includes services such as tattoo studios and salons.
- **Vegan Pocket:** Vegan Pocket scans barcodes to check if the product is vegan. No more reading confusing food labels! Just scan, and done.
- **abillion | Impact made easy:** This app lets you search for vegan brands and products near you, wherever you are around the world. After finding a vegan product on the app, you can even read customer reviews.

VOLUNTEERING

Want to get involved? Use these websites to find volunteer opportunities in the vegan community.

- **WWOOF:** Worldwide opportunities to volunteer on organic farms. Typically, room and board are offered in exchange. You must create an account for each country you would like to search for hosts in, and a subscription fee is required. ***wwoof.net***

- **WorkAway:** Worldwide opportunities to volunteer at organic and non-organic farms, homesteads, communities, non-profit organizations, and more. Room and board are typically offered in exchange. Sometimes hosts offer an hourly wage in addition to this. A small subscription fee is required. ***WorkAway.info***

- **HelpX:** HelpX is the same concept as WorkAway (above), without the opportunity for an hourly wage. Room and board are usually offered, and a small subscription fee is required. ***helpx.net***

- **Voluntouring:** This blog keeps an up-to-date listing of organizations looking for volunteers. The listing has a tab for listings that strictly adhere to vegan principles. ***voluntouring.org***

- **International Volunteering:** Facebook group listing international vegan-based volunteer opportunities. ***facebook.com/groups/217244375670902***

- **Grassroots Volunteering:** Database of international grassroots volunteer experiences. Search the site for vegan-centered opportunities, or contact hosts to see if vegans can be accommodated. ***GrassRootsVolunteering.org***

- **WorldPackers:** Volunteer experiences and programs for travelers in over 100 countries. ***WorldPackers.com***

VEGAN TOURS

These vegan tour guides and agencies take the work and planning out of your adventure, leaving nothing but fun and delicious plant-based food for you. Each has detailed websites listing all of their services and destinations! Even if you don't plan on booking with an agency, they are worth looking at for inspiration and ideas.

P.S. These are tour groups offering international opportunities. If you already have a destination in mind, do a quick Google search for vegan tour guides there. I bet you'll find even more resources!

- **Vegan Food Tours:** European Vegan City Tours. ***VeganFoodTours.com***
- **Vegan Adventure Tours:** Specializing in epic tours through Latin American and UK micro tours. ***VeganAdventureHolidays.com***
- **Intrepid Travel:** International tour company does several vegan tours annually. ***IntrepidTravel.com/vegan-food-adventures***
- **The Nomadic Vegan:** Website for Vegan Tours, Vegan Cruise, and Vegan-friendly tour operators. ***TheNomadicVegan.com/vegan-tours***

FESTS AND EVENTS

A great way to have fun and immerse in the vegan culture while traveling is to attend a festival or event. Below I list a number of resources for finding events in several destinations. This list is not exhaustive! Reference it, and then do further research to find even more fun items to add to your travel calendar.

- **Vegan Festivals Directory:** ***vegan.com/blog/festivals***
- **VegEvents International:** ***VegEvents.com***
- **International Listing:** ***vegan.com/blog/festivals***
- **Vegan Society International Listings:** ***VeganSociety.com/whats-new/events***
- **HappyCow International Listings:** ***HappyCow.net/events***
- **UK Vegan Events:** VeganEventsUK.co.uk
- **USA Vegan Events:** AmericanVegan.org/vegfests
- **Australia Vegan Events:** VeganAustralia.org.au/events

FILMS

- Cowspiracy (Netflix)
- Seaspiracy (Netflix)
- Earthlings (Free stream on http://www.nationearth.com/)
- The Game Changers (Netflix)
- What The Health (YouTube)
- Forks Over Knives (YouTube)
- The End of Meat (YouTube)
- Meat Me Halfway (YouTube/ Amazon Prime)
- Eating Our Way to Extinction (Amazon Prime)
- The Invisible Vegan (Amazon Prime)
- The Animal People (Amazon Prime)
- A Prayer for Compassion (Amazon Prime)
- My Octopus Teacher (Netflix)
- Okja (Netflix)

My Top Pic: Babe / Babe: Pig in the City (Amazon or Netflix)

BOOKS

CLASSIC READS:

- **Vegetable Diet: As Sanctioned by Medical Men, and by Experience in All Ages (1838) by William A Alcott:** The world's first book to advocate a vegetarian diet! It's been reprinted by The American Antiquarian Cookbook Collection and still in print today.

- **Diet for a Small Planet (1971) by Frances Moore Lappe:** A groundbreaking book arguing that world hunger is caused by the meat industry. It was the first time that meat was shown to be unhealthy and leading to global poverty.

- **Animal Liberation (1975) by Peter Singer:** This book is widely considered the founding philosophical statement of its ideas within the animal liberation movement. Singer claimed that industrial farming is responsible for more pain and misery than all the wars of history put together.

- **Main Street Vegan: Everything You Need to Know to Eat Healthfully and Live Compassionately in the Real World (2012) by Victoria Moran:** Holistic health practitioner Victoria Moran offers a complete guide to making this dietary and lifestyle shift with an emphasis on practical "baby steps," proving that you don't have to have a personal chef or lifestyle coach on speed dial to experience the physical and spiritual benefits of being a vegan.

- **The China study: The Most Comprehensive Study of Nutrition Ever Conducted and the Startling Implications for Diet, Weight Loss and Long-Term Health (2004) by T. Colin Cambell:** This novel takes the reader through a twenty-year study which looked at mortality rates from cancer and other chronic diseases from 1973 to 1975 in 65 counties in China. The China Study examines the link between the consumption of animal products (including dairy) and chronic illnesses such as coronary heart disease, diabetes, breast cancer, prostate cancer, and bowel cancer.

MODERN READS:

- **Why We Love Dogs, Eat Pigs, and Wear Cows by Melanie Joy:** The social psychologist who coined the word and hidden belief system of "carnism." (Her YouTube channel is good as well).
- **Beyond Beliefs: A Guide to Improving Relationships and Communication for Vegans, Vegetarians, and Meat Eaters by Melanie Joy, PhD:** This book is recommended for anyone living with or in close relationships with non-vegans.
- **We Are the Weather: Saving the Planet Begins at Breakfast by Jonathon Safran Foer:** This book explains how collective human action is the only way to save the planet, and as the title suggests, this begins with what is on our plates.
- **Eating Animals by Jonathon Safran Foer:** Part memoir, part investigative report. This book is a moral examination of vegetarianism, farming, and the food we eat.
- **Sex Robots & Vegan Meat: Adventures at the Frontier of Birth, Food, Sex, and Death by Jenny Kleeman:** This novel is an investigation into the forces driving innovation in the core areas of human experience.
- **Some We Love, Some We Eat, Some We Hate: Why It's So Hard to Think Straight About Animals by Hal Herzog:** A scientist in the field of anthrozoology offers a controversial exploration of the psychology behind the ways we think, feel, and behave towards animals.

Times are turbulent, and therefore dynamic.
Always check to ensure organizations are still in operation.

ACKNOWLEDGMENTS

Bringing together this special edition of my first published works has been a labor of love. They were always the yin and yang of a bigger story—the why and the how of veganism. Collectively, these works aim to restore balance and propel the growing movement for the vegan values of compassion and justice.

First and foremost, I must extend my deep gratitude to the monks who took me in and nursed me to health all those years ago. You started me on this incredible journey and put health and harmony at the center of my life. I bow to you, Namaste.

I am indebted to my editor, Gareth Clegg, whose creativity and patience kept me focused. He fine-tuned every aspect of this book and even found time to design the layout. Thank you for believing in this book and me from the beginning.

My family taught me the value of hard work, community, and love. I was always a rebel, but they accepted me and taught me to fight for what's right. Wherever I wander, you are my home.

Research and writing can be a lonely process. But, I was strengthened and sustained throughout it by my friends around the world. Charlie Brown always gave the best inspiration and ideas. Rachael freely gave the best feedback and corrected my grammar with a gentle nudge. Jason was there at every step to keep me focused, offering distraction when needed. My high school friends rallied and became my biggest cheerleaders. You are my dream team of rebels, and I love you all.

Writing this book involved many specialists in helping research and interpreting some of my medical and scientific research. Special thanks to my nutritionist, Mel—The Dopamine Chef— for patiently explaining all the health implications and becoming a friend in the process. I am also grateful for Dr. Laura Freeman's generous guidance, advice, and encouragement from Plant-Based Health Online.

I am incredibly grateful to my talented design team: Marco Montepulciano for designing my logo, Francesca Cook for bringing my book cover concept to life, and my dear neighbor, Cathy Brear, for her striking illustrations that give the book a cohesive beauty and impact.

My assistant, Damaris Russell, has become an integral part of my brand and a trusted friend. Thank you for your endless energy and helping me stay strengthened and motivated.

To Emma, who was my rock and held my hand throughout the process, I can't thank you enough. Without this foundation, every page in this book would be blank.

And finally, thanks to all my fellow rebels,
fighting for compassion and justice.

ABOUT THE AUTHOR

TODD SINCLAIR is the author of the
REBEL VEGAN LIFE series.

A passionate travel expert, activist, writer and speaker for the vegan cause, Todd currently lives his best Rebel Vegan Life in London.

His first book—*REBEL VEGAN LIFE: A Radical Take On Veganism*—won the best book of 2022 at the Vegan Choice Awards. VegfestUK named Todd the Best Vegan Author of 2023.

If not writing in his favorite city, you can find him exploring the world—perfecting his cooking in Southeast Asia, trekking volcanoes, or scuba diving—all while promoting plant-based living and putting veganism on the map.

Find out more about Rebel Vegan
at the website RebelVeganLife.com or on Social Media.

facebook.com/RebelVeganLife

instagram.com/RebelVeganLife

twitter.com/RebelVeganLife

ALSO BY TODD SINCLAIR

REBEL VEGAN LIFE:
A RADICAL TAKE ON VEGANISM FOR A BRAVE NEW WORLD

REBEL VEGAN LIFE:
A PLANT-BASED NUTRITION & BEGINNERS GUIDE

REBEL VEGAN LIFE:
VEGANISM ON THE GO

REFERENCE NOTES

VOLUME 1 - THE WHY OF VEGANISM

WHY VEGANISM MATTERS

1 https://www.vegansociety.com/
2 https://www.bmj.com/content/369/bmj.m2237

01 - RECLAIMING OUR HISTORY

1 https://www.nationalgeographic.com/foodfeatures/evolution-of-diet/
2 https://www.nationalgeographic.com/foodfeatures/evolution-of-diet/
3 https://www.tandfonline.com/doi/abs/10.1080/1751696X.2021.1903177
4 https://www.nationalgeographic.com/foodfeatures/evolution-of-diet/
5 https://www.nytimes.com/2002/02/26/science/when-humans-became-human.html
6 https://www.nytimes.com/2002/02/26/science/when-humans-became-human.html
7 https://www.nationalgeographic.com/science/article/chimps-humans-96-percent-the-same-gene-study-finds
8 https://blogs.scientificamerican.com/guest-blog/human-ancestors-were-nearly-all-vegetarians/
9 http://www.perseus.tufts.edu/hopper/text?doc=urn:cts:greekLit:tlg0007.tlg131.perseus-eng1:5
10 https://www.nationalgeographic.com/foodfeatures/evolution-of-diet/
11 https://www.nationalgeographic.com/foodfeatures/evolution-of-diet/
12 https://www.youtube.com/watch?v=i-dVlMdY-JQ
13 https://www.jewishveg.org/schwartz/quotations.html
14 https://www.huffpost.com/entry/are-buddhists-vegetarians_b_59c7c589e4b0f2df5e83af35
15 https://www.bbc.co.uk/religion/religions/christianity/christianethics/animals_1.shtml
16 https://www.milliondollarvegan.com/what-does-the-bible-say-about-veganism/
17 https://www.milliondollarvegan.com/what-does-the-bible-say-about-veganism/
18 https://biblehub.com/kjv/mark/16.htm
19 https://tamidnyc.org/113-tzar-baal-hachahim-caring-animals-2/
20 http://www.touregypt.net/featurestories/animalgods.htm
21 https://www.thoughtco.com/top-special-animals-in-greek-mythology-118586
22 https://www.independent.co.uk/life-style/who-were-the-world-s-very-earliest-vegans-a7668831.html
23 https://www.britannica.com/explore/savingearth/the-hidden-history-of-greco-roman-vegetarianism
24 https://www.ancient.eu/Pythagoras/
25 https://en.wikipedia.org/wiki/Apollonius_of_Tyana#cite_note-18
26 https://bulletin.hds.harvard.edu/the-secular-religion-of-plotinus/
27 http://www.perseus.tufts.edu/hopper/text?doc=urn:cts:greekLit:tlg0007.tlg131.perseus-eng1:5
28 https://en.wikipedia.org/wiki/Akhenaten
29 https://en.wikipedia.org/wiki/Emperor_Tenmu#Politics
30 https://fromgreens.com/galleryphoto/abraham-lincoln-quotes/
31 http://www.humanedecisions.com/benjamin-franklin-said-eating-flesh-is-unprovoked-murder/
32 https://vegsoc.org/about-us/world-history-of-vegetarianism/
33 https://en.wikipedia.org/wiki/George_Cheyne_(physician)#Vegetarianism
34 https://www.oxfordscholarlyeditions.com/view/10.1093/actrade/9780198205166.book.1/actrade-9780198205166-work-1
35 https://www.bl.uk/collection-items/p-b-shelleys-a-vindication-of-the-natural-diet
36 https://en.wikiquote.org/wiki/Donald_Watson
37 https://vegsoc.org/about-us/world-history-of-vegetarianism/
38 Vegetarian Messenger, 1923, 77, cited in Leneman, 221. And https://www.vegansociety.com/sites/default/files/uploads/Ripened%20by%20human%20determination.pdf
39 Vegetarian Messenger, 1935, 235 cited in Leneman, 221. And https://www.vegansociety.com/sites/default/files/uploads/Ripened%20by%20human%20determination.pdf
40 https://www.vegansociety.com/sites/default/files/uploads/Ripened%20by%20human%20determination.pdf
41 https://www.independent.co.uk/life-style/who-were-the-world-s-very-earliest-vegans-a7668831.html
42 https://www.theguardian.com/lifeandstyle/2021/oct/10/from-fringe-to-mainstream-how-millions-got-a-taste-for-going-vegan
43 https://www.vegansociety.com/about-us/history
44 https://wtvox.com/lifestyle/2019-the-world-of-vegan-but-how-many-vegans-are-in-the-world/
45 https://fridaysforfuture.org
46 https://www.bbc.com/future/article/20200122-are-there-health-benefits-to-going-vegan

02 - MEAT CORRUPTION

1 https://www.goodreads.com/quotes/8144295-the-world-will-not-be-destroyed-by-those-who-do
2 https://www.idtechex.com/en/research-article/the-meat-industry-is-unsustainable/20231
3 https://ourworldindata.org/meat-production
4 https://education.nationalgeographic.org/resource/development-agriculture
5 https://www.nationalgeographic.com/culture/article/neolithic-agricultural-revolution
6 https://en.wikipedia.org/wiki/Organicism
7 https://www.ncbi.nlm.nih.gov/pmc/articles/PMC2946087/
8 U.S. Food and Drug Administration. Letter to The Honorable Louise M. Slaughter: Sales of Antibacterial Drugs in Kilograms. Washington D.C.; 2010. And http://www.foodsystemprimer.org/food-production/industrialization-of-agriculture/
9 http://www.foodsystemprimer.org/food-production/industrialization-of-agriculture/
10 https://jia.sipa.columbia.edu/removing-meat-subsidy-our-cognitive-dissonance-around-animal-agriculture#6
11 https://jia.sipa.columbia.edu/removing-meat-subsidy-our-cognitive-dissonance-around-animal-agriculture#6 and David Robinson Simon, Meatonomics. Berkeley, California. Conari Press, 2013.]
12 https://www.aei.org/carpe-diem/farm-subsidies-gone-wild-cows-in-europe-earn-more-per-day-2-20-than-1-2-billion-poor-people/]
13 https://www.surgeactivism.org/articles/uk-farming-subsidies-and-brexit-explained and https://www.surgeactivism.org/animalagsubsidiesexplained
14 https://text.npr.org/790261705 and https://www.surgeactivism.org/animalagsubsidiesexplained
15 https://hal.archives-ouvertes.fr/hal-02891112/document
16 https://ourworldindata.org/grapher/meat-supply-per-person?tab=table
17 Source for pricing: www.walmart.com
18 https://www.who.int/bulletin/archives/78(7)902.pdf
19 http://www.spiegel.de/wirtschaft/ruegenwalder-muehle-verkauft-vegetarische-wurst-a-1023898.html
20 https://www.slowfood.com/become-a-beefatarian-the-absurd-eu-campaign-calling-for-an-increase-in-meat-consumption/
21 https://ec.europa.eu/chafea/agri/en/campaigns/proud-eu-beef
22 https://ec.europa.eu/commission/presscorner/detail/en/IP_21_3541
23 https://www.foodnavigator.com/Article/2020/08/28/New-campaign-champions-environmental-benefits-of-meat and www.sustainablebritishmeat.org
24 https://www.farminguk.com/news/-eat-balanced-meat-and-dairy-ad-campaign-goes-live_57292.html
25 https://cancerres.aacrjournals.org/content/43/5/2150
26 https://www.dietaryguidelines.gov/sites/default/files/2020-12/Dietary_Guidelines_for_Americans_2020-2025.pdf
https://health.gov/sites/default/files/2019-10/DietaryGuidelines2010.pdf
https://health.gov/sites/default/files/2019-09/2015-2020_Dietary_Guidelines.pdf
MyVeganPlate Image: https://www.vrg.org/nutshell/MyVeganPlate.pdf
https://MyPlate.gov

03 - MEAT THE FUTURE

1 https://www.spectator.co.uk/article/The--clean-meat--revolution-is-coming
2 https://www.spectator.co.uk/article/The--clean-meat--revolution-is-coming
3 https://sentientmedia.org/how-many-animals-are-killed-for-food-every-day/
4 https://blog.kerridgecs.com/10-inspirational-tech-quotes

04 - REBEL WITH A CAUSE

1 https://www.megainteresting.com/arts-culture/article/albert-einsteins-most-famous-quotes-601576757467
2 https://en.wikipedia.org/wiki/Western_pattern_diet
3 https://www.brainpickings.org/2016/06/17/albert-camus-the-rebel/
4 https://www.who.int/news/item/15-07-2019-world-hunger-is-still-not-going-down-after-three-years-and-obesity-is-still-growing-un-report

05 - LIVESTOCK

1 https://mainstreetvegan.net/veganism-and-martin-luther-king-jr-s-legacy-of-love-by-elisa-stone-mvlce/
2 "FAOSTAT". www.fao.org. Archived from the original on 11 May 2017. Retrieved 25 October 2019. And https://en.wikipedia.org/wiki/Animal_slaughter#cite_note-2
3 https://www.heromovement.net/blog/vegan-quotes/
4 https://en.wikipedia.org/wiki/Sentience
5 https://en.wikipedia.org/wiki/Ag-gag
6 https://www.theguardian.com/books/2015/sep/25/industrial-farming-one-worst-crimes-history-ethical-question
7 https://en.wikipedia.org/wiki/Ag-gag#cite_note-5
8 "Ag Gag: Safeguarding Industry Secrets by Punishing the Messenger" Archived 2014-07-18 at the Wayback Machine, Food Integrity Campaign, Retrieved June 25, 2013.
9 https://www.nrcs.usda.gov/wps/portal/nrcs/main/national/plantsanimals/livestock/afo/
10 https://en.wikipedia.org/wiki/Cattle
11 https://www.farmtransparency.org/kb/48-age-animals-slaughtered
12 https://www.peta.org/issues/animals-used-for-food/factory-farming/cows/cow-transport-slaughter/
13 https://www.nhes.org/animal-info-2/factory-farmed-animals-2/factory-farmed-cows/
14 https://www.peta.org/issues/animals-used-for-food/factory-farming/pigs/pig-transport-slaughter/
15 https://www.nhes.org/factory-farmed-pigs/
16 https://www.avma.org/sites/default/files/resources/swine_castration_bgnd.pdf
17 https://thehumaneleague.org/article/factory-farmed-pigs
18 https://www.wellbeingintlstudiesrepository.org/cgi/viewcontent.cgi?article=1042&context=acwp_asie
19 https://www.theguardian.com/books/2015/sep/25/industrial-farming-one-worst-crimes-history-ethical-question
20 https://www.weforum.org/agenda/2019/02/chart-of-the-day-this-is-how-many-animals-we-eat-each-year/
21 https://www.theguardian.com/environment/2016/apr/24/real-cost-of-roast-chicken-animal-welfare-farms
22 https://www.worldanimalprotection.org/news/10-facts-you-should-know-about-factory-farmed-chickens
23 https://www.britannica.com/explore/savingearth/the-difficult-lives-and-deaths-of-factory-farmed-chickens
24 https://www.theguardian.com/environment/2016/apr/24/real-cost-of-roast-chicken-animal-welfare-farms
25 https://thehumaneleague.org/article/factory-farmed-chickens
26 https://thehumaneleague.org/article/factory-farmed-chickens
27 https://www.latimes.com/archives/la-xpm-2003-nov-22-me-chipper22-story.html
28 https://www.peta.org/issues/animals-used-for-food/factory-farming/chickens/
29 https://grupojovenfl.files.wordpress.com/2019/10/peter-singer-animal-liberation-1.pdf
30 https://www.peta.org/issues/animals-used-for-food/factory-farming/fish/aquafarming/
31 http://www.fishcount.org.uk/published/std/fishcountexecsummary.pdf
32 "FAOSTAT". www.fao.org. Archived from the original on May 11, 2017. Retrieved October 25, 2019. And https://en.wikipedia.org/wiki/Meat#cite_note-27
33 The Vegan Calculator: https://thevegancalculator.com/animal-slaughter/ And Bite Size Vegan: https://bitesizevegan.org/ethics/quantifying-suffering-cruelty-by-the-numbers/

06 - ENVIRONMENT

1 https://www.theguardian.com/books/2019/sep/28/meat-of-the-matter-the-inconvenient-truth-about-what-we-eat
2 https://www.livekindly.co/inconvenient-sequel-overlooks-truth/
3 https://www.nrdc.org/stories/greenhouse-effect-101
4 https://www.theguardian.com/world/2021/jun/28/canada-hits-record-temperature-of-461c-amid-heatwave
5 https://www.theguardian.com/environment/2021/jul/30/greenland-ice-sheet-florida-water-climate-crisis
6 Journal: https://3209a1b2-3bad-4874-bf51-8fc2702ffa6c.filesusr.com/ugd/8654c5_7c6128c4df8741ad876709bc81afcfca.pdf page 156;
Article: https://plantbasednews.org/news/environment/animal-agriculture-responsible-for-87-of-greenhouse-gas-emissions/
7 https://www.sierraclub.org/michigan/why-are-cafos-bad#waste
8 https://www.sciencedirect.com/science/article/pii/S2212371713000024
9 https://ourworldindata.org/global-land-for-agriculture
10 https://journals.law.stanford.edu/stanford-environmental-law-journal-elj/blog/leading-cause-everything-one-industry-destroying-our-planet-and-our-ability-thrive-it
11 https://www.scientificamerican.com/article/earth-talks-daily-destruction/
12 www.savetheamazon.org/rainforeststats.htm
13 https://www.livekindly.co/inconvenient-sequel-overlooks-truth/
14 https://www.theworldcounts.com/challenges/planet-earth/forests-and-deserts/rate-of-deforestation/story
15 https://www.wri.org/insights/2021-must-be-turning-point-forests-2020-data-shows-us-why
16 https://www.theguardian.com/environment/2021/jul/14/amazon-rainforest-now-emitting-more-co2-than-it-absorbs
17 https://www.siwi.org/facts-and-statistics/6-food-agriculture-and-bioenergy/
18 https://unesdoc.unesco.org/ark:/48223/pf0000215492
and https://www.siwi.org/facts-and-statistics/6-food-agriculture-and-bioenergy/
19 https://waterfootprint.org/media/downloads/Report-48-WaterFootprint-AnimalProducts-Vol1_1.pdf and https://waterfootprint.org/en/water-footprint/product-water-footprint/water-footprint-crop-and-animal-products/
20 http://www.unesco.org/new/fileadmin/MULTIMEDIA/FIELD/Venice/pdf/special_events/bozza_scheda_DOW04_1.0.pdf and https://www.statista.com/statistics/1092652/volume-of-water-to-produce-a-liter-of-milk-by-type/
21 https://www.ciwf.com/media/1230930/CIWF-Strategic-Plan-2013-2017.pdf
22 https://www.nrcs.usda.gov/wps/portal/nrcs/main/national/plantsanimals/livestock/afo/
23 https://www.sierraclub.org/michigan/why-are-cafos-bad#waste
24 https://www.theguardian.com/environment/2017/aug/01/meat-industry-dead-zone-gulf-of-mexico-environment-pollution
25 https://www.nationalgeographic.com/environment/article/dead-zones
26 https://en.wikipedia.org/wiki/Dead_zone_(ecology)#cite_note-:12-2
27 https://www.theguardian.com/books/2015/sep/25/industrial-farming-one-worst-crimes-history-ethical-question
28 https://www.ipbes.net/news/Media-Release-Global-Assessment
29 https://www.ipbes.net/news/Media-Release-Global-Assessment
30 https://www.bbc.com/news/world-latin-america-41107862
31 https://en.wikipedia.org/wiki/Western_pattern_diet
32 https://en.wikipedia.org/wiki/Western_pattern_diet
33 https://www.sciencedirect.com/science/article/pii/S0048969720328709#f0005
34 https://www.nationalgeographic.com/foodfeatures/evolution-of-diet/

07 - GLOBAL HEALTH

1 https://www.sciencedirect.com/science/article/pii/S0014299918303595
2 Taylor LH, Latham SM, Woolhouse ME (2001). "Risk factors for human disease emergence". Philosophical Transactions of the Royal Society B: Biological Sciences. 356 (1411): 983–89. doi:10.1098/rstb.2001.0888. PMC 1088493. PMID 11516376.
3 Taylor LH, Latham SM, Woolhouse ME (2001). "Risk factors for human disease emergence". Philosophical Transactions of the Royal Society B: Biological Sciences. 356 (1411): 983–89. doi:10.1098/rstb.2001.0888. PMC 1088493. PMID 11516376.
4 https://www.theguardian.com/environment/2020/apr/08/human-impact-on-wildlife-to-blame-for-spread-of-viruses-says-study-aoe
5 https://en.wikipedia.org/wiki/Natural_reservoir
6 https://environmentlive.unep.org/media/docs/assessments/UNEP_Frontiers_2016_report_emerging_issues_of_environmental_concern.pdf
7 https://www.theguardian.com/world/2020/mar/28/is-factory-farming-to-blame-for-coronavirus
8 https://pubmed.ncbi.nlm.nih.gov/24531761/
9 https://www.ncbi.nlm.nih.gov/pmc/articles/PMC2720273/ and https://www.theguardian.com/commentisfree/2020/apr/16/coronavirus-covid-19-pandemic-food-animals
10 https://en.wikipedia.org/wiki/Bovine_spongiform_encephalopathy
11 https://www.nationalgeographic.co.uk/science-and-technology/2020/04/experts-warned-of-pandemic-decades-ago-why-werent-we-ready
12 https://www.ncbi.nlm.nih.gov/pmc/articles/PMC1963309/
13 https://www.theguardian.com/commentisfree/2020/apr/16/coronavirus-covid-19-pandemic-food-animals
14 https://www.worldometers.info/coronavirus/coronavirus-death-toll/
15 https://www.cidrap.umn.edu/news-perspective/2003/05/estimates-sars-death-rates-revised-upward
16 https://www.who.int/health-topics/middle-east-respiratory-syndrome-coronavirus-mers#tab=tab_1
17 https://www.who.int/news-room/fact-sheets/detail/ebola-virus-disease
18 https://www.theguardian.com/world/2020/mar/28/is-factory-farming-to-blame-for-coronavirus
19 https://www.worldometers.info/coronavirus/coronavirus-death-rate/
20 http://apps.who.int/iris/bitstream/handle/10665/112642/9789241564748_eng.pdf
21 https://www.fda.gov/animal-veterinary/antimicrobial-resistance/timeline-fda-action-antimicrobial-resistance
22 https://www.pewtrusts.org/en/research-and-analysis/articles/2020/01/16/antibiotic-sales-for-animal-agriculture-increase-again-after-a-two-year-decline
23 https://www.theworldcounts.com/challenges/consumption/foods-and-beverages/antibiotics-used-for-livestock/story
24 https://www.who.int/news/item/07-11-2017-stop-using-antibiotics-in-healthy-animals-to-prevent-the-spread-of-antibiotic-resistance
25 https://www.peta.org/issues/animals-used-for-food/factory-farming/cows/beef-industry/
26 https://www.cdc.gov/drugresistance/biggest-threats.html
27 https://www.who.int/news/item/07-11-2017-stop-using-antibiotics-in-healthy-animals-to-prevent-the-spread-of-antibiotic-resistance
28 https://www.who.int/mediacentre/news/statements/2011/whd_20110407/en/
29 https://www.worldometers.info/coronavirus/coronavirus-death-toll/
30 https://www.who.int/news-room/fact-sheets/detail/noncommunicable-diseases
31 https://en.wikipedia.org/wiki/Zoonosis
32 https://www.foodandwine.com/cooking-techniques/albert-einstein-genius-birthday-boy-vegetarian-vegan
33 https://en.wikipedia.org/wiki/Western_pattern_diet
34 https://www.ncbi.nlm.nih.gov/books/NBK493173/
35 https://en.wikipedia.org/wiki/Western_pattern_diet
36 https://pubmed.ncbi.nlm.nih.gov/30928934/
37 http://www.milkfacts.info/Milk%20Microbiology/Microbial%20Standards.htm
38 https://en.wikipedia.org/wiki/Western_pattern_diet
39 https://vegnews.com/2021/6/breast-cancer-study-meat-dairy
40 https://en.wikipedia.org/wiki/Western_pattern_diet
41 https://economictimes.indiatimes.com/magazines/panache/sugar-is-a-greater-danger-than-gunpowder-says-sapiens-author-yuval-noah-harari/articleshow/63574089.cms
42 https://www.who.int/news-room/fact-sheets/detail/obesity-and-overweight
43 https://www.ncbi.nlm.nih.gov/pmc/articles/PMC7721435/
44 https://www.ncbi.nlm.nih.gov/pmc/articles/PMC5507106/

45 https://www.nature.com/articles/s41591-020-01209-1
46 https://idf.org/aboutdiabetes/what-is-diabetes/facts-figures.html
47 https://www.who.int/news-room/fact-sheets/detail/diabetes
48 https://www.who.int/news-room/fact-sheets/detail/diabetes
49 https://www.ncbi.nlm.nih.gov/pmc/articles/PMC3173026/
50 https://www.sciencedaily.com/releases/2017/09/170905134506.htm
51 https://www.ncbi.nlm.nih.gov/pmc/articles/PMC2677007/
52 https://nutritionstudies.org/my-type-2-diabetic-patients-transformed-their-health-through-diet/
53 https://www.nih.gov/news-events/nih-research-matters/eating-red-meat-daily-triples-heart-disease-related-chemical
54 https://en.wikipedia.org/wiki/Western_pattern_diet
55 https://jamanetwork.com/journals/jama/fullarticle/2728487
56 https://www.ucsfhealth.org/education/cholesterol-content-of-foods
57 https://www.cdc.gov/heartdisease/facts.htm
58 https://www.pcrm.org/good-nutrition/nutrition-information/lowering-cholesterol-with-a-plant-based-diet AND Yokoyama Y, Levin SM, Barnard ND. Association between plant-based diets and plasma lipids: a systematic review and meta-analysis. Nutr Rev. Published online August 21, 2017.
59 https://www.ahajournals.org/doi/10.1161/JAHA.119.012865
60 https://acsjournals.onlinelibrary.wiley.com/doi/10.3322/caac.21660
61 https://www.who.int/news-room/q-a-detail/cancer-carcinogenicity-of-the-consumption-of-red-meat-and-processed-meat
62 https://www.who.int/news-room/q-a-detail/cancer-carcinogenicity-of-the-consumption-of-red-meat-and-processed-meat and https://publications.iarc.fr/Book-And-Report-Series/Iarc-Monographs-On-The-Identification-Of-Carcinogenic-Hazards-To-Humans/Red-Meat-And-Processed-Meat-2018
63 https://cancerdiscovery.aacrjournals.org/content/early/2021/06/11/2159-8290.CD-20-1656 and https://medicalxpress.com/news/2021-06-biological-links-red-meat-colorectal.html
64 https://www.pnas.org/content/116/32/16036 and https://health.ucsd.edu/news/releases/Pages/2019-07-22-evolutionary-gene-loss-may-help-explain-human-heart-attacks.aspx
65 https://vegnews.com/2021/6/breast-cancer-study-meat-dairy and https://pubmed.ncbi.nlm.nih.gov/33962395/
66 https://www.tandfonline.com/doi/abs/10.1080/10408398.2016.1138447?journalCode=bfsn20
67 https://jumdjournal.net/article/view/2892
68 https://www.ted.com/talks/samuel_cohen_alzheimer_s_is_not_normal_aging_and_we_can_cure_it/transcript
69 https://www.ncbi.nlm.nih.gov/pmc/articles/PMC6846186/
70 https://www.bluezones.com/2019/10/the-2-foods-that-combat-alzheimers-disease-other-lifestyle-factors-to-reduce-your-risk-of-cognitive-decline/#
71 https://www.bluezones.com/2018/11/a-greek-islands-ancient-secret-to-avoiding-alzheimers/#
72 https://www.cochranelibrary.com/cdsr/doi/10.1002/14651858.CD003177.pub3/full
73 https://pubmed.ncbi.nlm.nih.gov/29355094/
74 https://www.ahajournals.org/doi/10.1161/01.ATV.0000038493.65177.94
75 https://plantbasednews.org/your-health/faqs-and-mythbusting/fish-not-health-food-why/
76 https://epi.grants.cancer.gov/diet/foodsources/top-food-sources-report-02212020.pdf
77 https://epi.grants.cancer.gov/diet/foodsources/top-food-sources-report-02212020.pdf
78 https://academic.oup.com/ije/article-abstract/49/5/1526/5743492
79 https://www.eurekalert.org/pub_releases/2019-10/aoa-mcr101819.php
80 https://www.theguardian.com/lifeandstyle/2003/dec/13/foodanddrink.weekend
81 https://academic.oup.com/ije/article-abstract/49/5/1526/5743492
82 https://www.ncbi.nlm.nih.gov/pmc/articles/PMC6683061/
83 https://www.theguardian.com/lifeandstyle/2003/dec/13/foodanddrink.weekend
84 https://www.hsph.harvard.edu/nutritionsource/calcium/
85 https://en.wikipedia.org/wiki/Western_pattern_diet
86 https://www.nytimes.com/2012/10/28/magazine/the-island-where-people-forget-to-die.html
87 https://www.nationalgeographic.com/magazine/article/these-traditional-diets-from-the-blue-zones-can-lead-to-long-lives-feature
88 https://www.nationalgeographic.com/magazine/article/these-traditional-diets-from-the-blue-zones-can-lead-to-long-lives-feature
89 https://en.wikipedia.org/wiki/Western_pattern_diet
90 https://www.telegraph.co.uk/science/2018/04/26/third-early-deaths-could-prevented-everyone-giving-meat-harvard/

08 - SOCIAL INJUSTICE

1 https://www.ciwf.org.uk/media/7425974/industrial-livestock-production-the-twin-myths-of-efficiency-and-necessity.pdf
2 https://news.cornell.edu/stories/1997/08/us-could-feed-800-million-people-grain-livestock-eat
3 https://www.theguardian.com/news/2019/jan/28/can-we-ditch-intensive-farming-and-still-feed-the-world
4 https://www.aljazeera.com/economy/2021/5/25/bbin-2020-more-people-displaced-by-extreme-climate-than-conflict
5 https://news.un.org/en/story/2021/03/1087702
6 https://www.meatpoultry.com/articles/14493-study-quantifies-the-economic-impact-of-meat-industry
7 https://www.meatinstitute.org/index.php?ht=d/sp/i/47465/pid/47465
8 https://www.hrw.org/report/2010/12/11/rights-line/human-rights-watch-work-abuses-against-migrants-2010
9 https://mercyforanimals.org/blog/dairy-farm-worker-drowns/
10 https://foodispower.org/human-labor-slavery/factory-farm-workers/
11 "Concentrated Animal Feedlot Operations (CAFOs) Chemicals Associated with Air Emissions." Prepared by the CAFO subcommittee of the Michigan Department of Environmental Quality (MDEQ) Toxics Steering Group (TSG). 2006. http://www.michigan.gov/documents/CAFOs-Chemicals_Associated_with_Air_Emissions_5-10-06_158862_7.pdf (5/27/10) and https://foodispower.org/human-labor-slavery/factory-farm-workers/
12 Concentrated Animal Feedlot Operations (CAFOs) Chemicals Associated with Air Emissions." Prepared by the CAFO subcommittee of the Michigan Department of Environmental Quality (MDEQ) Toxics Steering Group (TSG). 2006. http://www.michigan.gov/documents/CAFOs-Chemicals_Associated_with_Air_Emissions_5-10-06_158862_7.pdf (5/27/10)
13 https://vegnews.com/2013/4/inside-the-life-of-a-factory-farm-worker
14 https://www.oxfamamerica.org/livesontheline/
15 https://vegnews.com/2013/4/inside-the-life-of-a-factory-farm-worker
16 Lewis, Cora (18 February 2018). "America's Largest Meat Producer Averages One Amputation Per Month". Buzzfeed News. Retrieved 23 May 2019. And https://en.wikipedia.org/wiki/Slaughterhouse
17 https://en.wikipedia.org/wiki/Slaughterhouse and Eisnitz, Gail A. Slaughterhouse. Prometheus Books, 1997, cited in Torres, Bob. Making a Killing. AK Press, 2007, p. 46.
18 https://www.theguardian.com/environment/2019/sep/18/us-moves-to-scrap-speed-limits-on-pig-slaughter-lines and https://abcnews.go.com/Health/wireStory/pork-group-asks-usda-support-faster-slaughterhouse-speeds-77897261
19 Baran, B. E.; Rogelberg, S. G.; Clausen, T (2016). "Routinized killing of animals: Going beyond dirty work and prestige to understand the well-being of slaughterhouse workers". Organization. 23 (3): 351–69. doi:10.1177/1350508416629456. S2CID 148368906. And https://en.wikipedia.org/wiki/Slaughterhouse
20 Fitzgerald, A. J.; Kalof, L. (2009). "Slaughterhouses and Increased Crime Rates: An Empirical Analysis of the Spillover From "The Jungle" Into the Surrounding Community". Organization & Environment. 22 (2): 158–84. doi:10.1177/1350508416629456. S2CID 148368906. And https://en.wikipedia.org/wiki/Slaughterhouse
21 https://www.peta.org/issues/animal-companion-issues/animal-companion-factsheets/animal-abuse-human-abuse-partners-crime/
22 Nadimpalli, Maya. "Persistence of livestock-associated antibiotic-resistant Staphylococcus aureus among industrial hog operation workers in North Carolina over 14 days." Occupational & Environmental Medicine, 72(2) (September 8, 2014). Retrieved May 31, 2018, from https://oem.bmj.com/content/early/2014/09/05/oemed-2014-102095.info and https://foodprint.org/issues/what-happens-to-animal-waste/
23 https://foodprint.org/issues/what-happens-to-animal-waste/ and US Environmental Protection Agency. "Basic Information about Nonpoint Source (NPS) Pollution. EPA, (n.d.). Retrieved May 31, 2018 from https://www.epa.gov/nps/basic-information-about-nonpoint-source-nps-pollution
24 https://www.doh.wa.gov/Portals/1/Documents/Pubs/331-214.pdf
25 http://animalstudies.msu.edu/Slaughterhouses_and_Increased_Crime_Rates.pdf and https://www.huffpost.com/entry/plight-of-factory-farm-workers_b_5662261
26 Carol J. Hodne, Concentrating on Clean Water: The Challenge of Concentrated Animal Feeding Operations, IA Policy Project (Apr. 2005), at 28, available at http://www.iowapolicyproject.org/2005docs/050406-cafo-fullx.pdf . And https://www.animallaw.info/article/detailed-discussion-concentrated-animal-feeding-operations
27 https://www.theguardian.com/us-news/2020/apr/28/trump-executive-order-meat-processing-plants-coronavirus
28 https://www.dol.gov/newsroom/releases/osha/osha20200428-1
29 https://www.theguardian.com/world/2020/may/02/meat-plant-workers-us-coronavirus-war
30 https://www.theguardian.com/world/2020/may/02/meat-plant-workers-us-coronavirus-war
31 Reported at the July 24-26 meeting of the Canadian Society of Animal Science, Montreal.
32 https://www.idtechex.com/en/research-article/the-meat-industry-is-unsustainable/20231
33 https://en.wikipedia.org/wiki/Western_pattern_diet

09 - LIFE ON THE SPECTRUM

1 https://www.independent.co.uk/life-style/food-and-drink/carnism-why-love-dogs-eat-pigs-wear-cows-leather-pork-dr-melanie-joy-vegan-psychology-a7932621.html
2 https://www.peta.org/about-peta/faq/what-is-speciesism/
3 https://en.wikipedia.org/wiki/Carnism
4 https://www.pure.ed.ac.uk/ws/files/24434085/Piazza_etal_A_2015_Rationalizing_Meat_Consumption_The_4Ns.pdf
5 https://www.pure.ed.ac.uk/ws/files/24434085/Piazza_etal_A_2015_Rationalizing_Meat_Consumption_The_4Ns.pdf
6 https://www.slowfood.com/press-release/slow-food-launches-the-worldwide-campaign-meat-the-change-to-change-peoples-meat-eating-habits/
7 https://en.wikipedia.org/wiki/Western_pattern_diet

10 - REBEL VEGAN STARTER KIT

1 https://www.wfp.org/zero-hunger
2 https://www.forbes.com/sites/jeffmcmahon/2019/04/04/meat-and-agriculture-are-worse-for-the-climate-than-dirty-energy-steven-chu-says/
3 https://news.cornell.edu/stories/1997/08/us-could-feed-800-million-people-grain-livestock-eat
4 http://shrinkthatfootprint.com/food-carbon-footprint-diet and https://www.cowspiracy.com/facts
5 Robbins, John. Diet for a New America, StillPoint Publishing, 1987, p. 352 and https://www.cowspiracy.com/facts
6 Oppenlander, Richard A. Food Choice and Sustainability: Why Buying Local, Eating Less Meat, and Taking Baby Steps Won't Work. Minneapolis, MN : Langdon Street, 2013. Print. And https://www.cowspiracy.com/facts
7 https://en.wikipedia.org/wiki/Western_pattern_diet
8 http://www.ncbi.nlm.nih.gov/pubmed/24717365 and https://nutritionfacts.org/video/do-flexitarians-live-longer/
9 https://en.wikipedia.org/wiki/Western_pattern_diet
10 http://www.ncbi.nlm.nih.gov/pubmed/21411506 and https://nutritionfacts.org/video/do-flexitarians-live-longer/
11 https://en.wikipedia.org/wiki/Western_pattern_diet
12 http://www.ncbi.nlm.nih.gov/pubmed/24524383 and https://nutritionfacts.org/video/do-flexitarians-live-longer/
13 https://www.cowspiracy.com/facts

11 - THE HOW

1 https://faunalytics.org/wp-content/uploads/2015/06/Faunalytics_Current-Former-Vegetarians_Full-Report.pdf
2 https://juniperpublishers.com/ctoij/CTOIJ.MS.ID.555906.php and https://jumdjournal.net/article/view/2892
3 https://v-dog.com/blogs/v-dog-blog/bramble-the-collies-secrets-to-living-to-age-25
4 https://www.ncbi.nlm.nih.gov/books/NBK80015/
5 https://pubmed.ncbi.nlm.nih.gov/19211820/
6 https://www.pcrm.org/good-nutrition/nutrition-information/soy-and-health
7 https://www.vegansociety.com/go-vegan/why-go-vegan/honey-industry
8 https://vegan.com/info/answers/#honey
9 https://www.vegansociety.com/go-vegan/why-go-vegan/honey-industry

12 - EMPOWERMENT

1 https://veganorigo.com/en/pages/famous-vegans/
2 https://metro.co.uk/2019/04/13/man-who-ate-raw-pigs-head-at-vegan-festival-stabbed-four-classmates-at-school-9184229/
3 https://london.eater.com/2019/7/23/20707059/squirrel-eating-pro-meat-anti-vegan-protest-soho-alt-right-youtube-channel
4 https://journals.sagepub.com/doi/abs/10.1177/1368430215618253 and https://www.theguardian.com/lifeandstyle/2019/oct/25/why-do-people-hate-vegans
5 https://www.peta.org/living/food/really-natural-truth-humans-eating-meat/
6 https://www.smithsonianmag.com/science-nature/where-do-humans-really-rank-on-the-food-chain-180948053/
7 Rizzo NS, Jaceldo-Siegl K, Sabate J, Fraser GE. Nutrient profiles of vegetarian and nonvegetarian dietary patterns. J Acad Nutr Diet. 2013 Dec;113(12):1610-9.
And https://gamechangersmovie.com/food/protein/
8 USDA Food Composition Databases and https://gamechangersmovie.com/food/protein/
9 https://switch4good.org/how-dairy-affects-childrens-health/
10 https://www.medicalnewstoday.com/articles/325425#nutritional-values
11 https://www.pnas.org/content/117/24/13596
12 https://www.independent.co.uk/news/world/asia/yulin-dog-meat-festival-explainer-what-it-when-start-banned-controversy-a8410426.html
13 https://en.wikipedia.org/wiki/Whaling_in_the_Faroe_Islands
14 https://www.humanesociety.org/resources/cage-free-vs-battery-cage-eggs
15 https://www.theguardian.com/lifeandstyle/shortcuts/2017/feb/28/what-does-free-range-actually-mean-its-complicated
16 https://en.wikipedia.org/wiki/Western_pattern_diet
17 https://www.bda.uk.com/resource/british-dietetic-association-confirms-well-planned-vegan-diets-can-support-healthy-living-in-people-of-all-ages.html
18 https://pubmed.ncbi.nlm.nih.gov/19562864/
19 https://pubmed.ncbi.nlm.nih.gov/12778049/
20 https://ods.od.nih.gov/factsheets/VitaminB12-HealthProfessional/
21 https://ods.od.nih.gov/factsheets/VitaminB12-HealthProfessional/

14 - APPENDICES

APPENDIX 2

1 https://www.statista.com/statistics/183785/per-capita-consumption-of-cheese-in-the-us-since-2000/ and https://www.ncbi.nlm.nih.gov/books/NBK45515/ (figure 4.4)
2 https://www.who.int/news/item/07-11-2017-stop-using-antibiotics-in-healthy-animals-to-prevent-the-spread-of-antibiotic-resistance

APPENDIX 4

1 https://www.sciencedirect.com/science/article/pii/S1198743X15010307
2 https://www.who.int/news-room/fact-sheets/detail/campylobacter
3 https://www.theguardian.com/world/2014/jul/23/-sp-revealed-dirty-secret-uk-poultry-industry-chicken-campylobacter
4 https://www.cdc.gov/campylobacter/index.html
5 https://www.theguardian.com/world/2014/jul/23/-sp-revealed-dirty-secret-uk-poultry-industry-chicken-campylobacter
6 https://en.wikipedia.org/wiki/Staphylococcus_aureus and https://www.intechopen.com/chapters/66903
7 https://en.wikipedia.org/wiki/Staphylococcus_aureus
8 www.sciencedaily.com/releases/2011/04/110415083153.htm
9 https://www.cdc.gov/drugresistance/biggest-threats.html
10 https://www.who.int/news-room/fact-sheets/detail/e-coli
11 https://www.ecdc.europa.eu/en/escherichia-coli-ecoli

VOLUME 2 - THE HOW OF VEGANISM

INTRODUCTION

1 https://www.azquotes.com/quotes/topics/truth.html
2 https://www.peta.org.uk/issues/animals-not-eat/meat-health/
1 https://freefromharm.org/animal-farmer-turned-vegan/howard-lyman-former-beef-and-dairy-farmer/ and https://www.youtube.com/watch?v=94QaCbytLEY

15 - COMPASSIONATE REVOLUTION

1 https://www.azquotes.com/quote/907397
2 https://quotlr.com/author/john-eliot
3 www.cowspiracy.com/facts
4 https://www.cowspiracy.com/facts
5 https://www.nationalgeographic.com/animals/article/animals-science-medical-pain
6 https://en.wikipedia.org/wiki/Western_pattern_diet
7 https://mercyforanimals.org/blog/pigs-are-intelligent-and-sensitive-so-why/
8 [Sources: Joy, Melanie (2011) [2009]. Why We Love Dogs, Eat Pigs, and Wear Cows: An Introduction to Carnism. Conari Press, p. 9. ISBN 1573245054. Andhttps://en.wikipedia.org/wiki/Carnism]
9 https://indianexpress.com/article/lifestyle/life-style/go-vegetarian-save-wildlife-planet-sir-david-attenborough-7148660/
10 www.livekindly.co/inconvenient-sequel-overlooks-truth
11 www.washingtonpost.com/climate-environment/2021/08/29/how-climate-change-helped-make-hurricane-ida-one-louisianas-worst/
12 https://apnews.com/article/fires-environment-and-nature-california-wildfires-a7df1b3939dfaa5114fb47d78cfea57f
13 www.siwi.org/facts-and-statistics/6-food-and-agriculture-and-bioenergy
14 https://www.undispatch.com/bad-news-world-will-begin-running-water-2050-good-news-not-2050-yet/
15 www.animalmatters.org
16 https://www.sailorsforthesea.org/programs/ocean-watch/ocean-dead-zones
17 https://seashepherd.org/2015/09/29/if-the-ocean-dies-we-all-die/
18 https://nutritionstudies.org
19 https://www.pcrm.org/good-nutrition/nutrition-information/health-concerns-about-dairy
20 https://www.goodreads.com/quotes/162579-i-choose-not-to-make-a-graveyard-of-my-body
21 https://www.ncbi.nlm.nih.gov/pmc/articles/PMC5035214/
22 http://apps.who.int/iris/bitstream/handle/10665/112642/9789241564748_eng.pdf
23 https://www.pewtrusts.org/en/research-and-analysis/articles/2020/01/16/antibiotic-sales-for-animal-agriculture-increase-again-after-a-two-year-decline
24 https://assets.publishing.service.gov.uk/government/uploads/system/uploads/attachment_data/file/773065/uk-20-year-vision-for-antimicrobial-resistance.pdf
25 https://www.goodreads.com/author/quotes/149151.Francis_of_Assisi
26 https://kidadl.com/articles/best-justice-quotes-to-fight-for-equality
27 https://foodprint.org/issues/what-happens-to-animal-waste/ and US Environmental Protection Agency. "Basic Information about Nonpoint Source (NPS) Pollution. EPA, (n.d.). Retrieved May 31, 2018 from https://www.epa.gov/nps/basic-information-about-nonpoint-source-nps-pollution
28 https://theecologist.org/2020/may/05/vegan-diet-can-stop-future-pandemics
29 www.cdc.gov/onehealth/basics/zoonotic-diseases.html

16 - VEGANOMETRY

1 https://www.heromovement.net/blog/vegan-quotes/
2 https://www.heromovement.net/blog/vegan-quotes/
3 https://www.health.harvard.edu/staying-healthy/cutting-red-meat-for-a-longer-life
4 The Standard American Diet (SAD), also known as the standard Western diet, is a pattern of eating is generally characterized by high intakes of meat, dairy products, eggs, fried foods, refined grains, and refined sugars, with low intakes of vegetables, fruits, whole grains, legumes, nuts and seeds.
5 https://pubmed.ncbi.nlm.nih.gov/29634829/ andhttps://www.hvst.com/posts/the-leading-cause-of-both-death-and-disability-in-the-u-s-is-the-american-diet-oNRTZkgk
6 http://www.dresselstyn.com/site/
7 https://www.google.com/search?q=tobacco+advert+for+pregnant+women&tbm=isch
8 https://www.thelancet.com/journals/lancet/article/PIIS0140-6736(12)62089-3/fulltext
9 https://www.who.int/news-room/q-a-detail/cancer-carcinogenicity-of-the-consumption-of-red-meat-and-processed-meat
10 https://www.dietaryguidelines.gov/sites/default/files/2020-12/Dietary_Guidelines_for_Americans_2020-2025.pdf https://health.gov/our-work/food-nutrition/previous-dietary-guidelines/2015;https://health.gov/our-work/food-nutrition/previous-dietary-guidelines/2010 andhttps://health.gov/our-work/food-nutrition/previous-dietary-guidelines/2005
11 https://www.heromovement.net/blog/vegan-quotes/
12 https://www.vox.com/science-and-health/2017/6/19/15819808/obesity-global-epidemic
13 https://www.ncbi.nlm.nih.gov/pmc/articles/PMC2121650/
14 https://www.jwatch.org/na52921/2020/12/23/red-meat-and-cardiovascular-risk-revisited
15 https://www.ahajournals.org/doi/10.1161/01.ATV.0000038493.65177.94
16 https://jamanetwork.com/journals/jama/fullarticle/200732
17 Sex Robots & Vegan Meat: Adventures at the Frontier of Birth, Food, Sex and Death - by Jenny Kleeman
18 https://epi.grants.cancer.gov/diet/foodsources/top-food-sources-report-02212020.pdf
19 https://academic.oup.com/ije/article-abstract/49/5/1526/5743492
20 https://www.eurekalert.org/pub_releases/2019-10/aoa-mcr101819.php
21 https://pubmed.ncbi.nlm.nih.gov/22882905/
22 https://www.fda.gov/media/136671/download
23 https://www.who.int/health-topics/cardiovascular-diseases#tab=tab_1
24 https://pubmed.ncbi.nlm.nih.gov/29496410/
25 https://www.who.int/health-topics/cancer#tab=tab_1
26 https://acsjournals.onlinelibrary.wiley.com/doi/full/10.3322/caac.21440
27 https://www.ncbi.nlm.nih.gov/pmc/articles/PMC3048091/
28 https://www.who.int/news-room/facts-in-pictures/detail/6-facts-on-obesity
29 https://www.who.int/health-topics/obesity#tab=tab_1
30 https://pubmed.ncbi.nlm.nih.gov/32922235/
31 https://www.who.int/health-topics/diabetes#tab=tab_1
32 https://pubmed.ncbi.nlm.nih.gov/29948369/
33 https://www.who.int/news-room/fact-sheets/detail/dementia
34 https://pubmed.ncbi.nlm.nih.gov/34214643/
35 https://www.ncbi.nlm.nih.gov/pmc/articles/PMC6846186/
36 https://www.worldometers.info/coronavirus/coronavirus-death-toll/
37 https://nutrition.bmj.com/content/4/1/257
38 https://www.goodreads.com/author/quotes/35040.Neal_D_Barnard
39 https://www.heromovement.net/blog/vegan-quotes/
40 https://www.thediabetescouncil.com/45-alarming-statistics-on-americans-sugar-consumption-and-the-effects-of-sugar-on-americans-health/
41 https://www.dietaryguidelines.gov/sites/default/files/2020-12/Dietary_Guidelines_for_Americans_2020-2025.pdf#page=31
42 https://www.nhs.uk/live-well/eat-well/how-does-sugar-in-our-diet-affect-our-health/
43 https://www.ncbi.nlm.nih.gov/pmc/articles/PMC4244242/
44 https://www.ncbi.nlm.nih.gov/pmc/articles/PMC3614697/
45 https://bmjopen.bmj.com/content/6/3/e009892
46 https://www.ncbi.nlm.nih.gov/pmc/articles/PMC5938543/
47 https://pubmed.ncbi.nlm.nih.gov/2836348/
48 https://pubmed.ncbi.nlm.nih.gov/22889895/
49 https://pubmed.ncbi.nlm.nih.gov/28507982/
50 https://pubmed.ncbi.nlm.nih.gov/22538314/
51 https://pubmed.ncbi.nlm.nih.gov/28229641/
52 https://www.euroweeklynews.com/2021/03/15/lebanon-introduces-worlds-first-hospital-serving-only-vegan-food/
53 https://www.sciencedirect.com/topics/engineering/acute-inflammation
54 https://www.ncbi.nlm.nih.gov/books/NBK493173/
55 Sources for footnotes:https://www.bda.uk.com/resource/british-dietetic-association-confirms-well-planned-vegan-diets-can-support-healthy-living-in-people-of-all-ages.html https://pubmed.ncbi.nlm.nih.gov/19562864/ https://pubmed.ncbi.nlm.nih.gov/12778049/
56 Sources:https://nutritionstudies.org/the-china-study-3-lessons-we-need-to-know/https://pubmed.ncbi.nlm.nih.gov/9860369/ andhttps://www.pnas.org/content/115/15/3804

17 - HOW VEGANISM CAN SAVE THE WORLD

1 https://en.wikipedia.org/wiki/Biomass_(ecology)
2 https://ourworldindata.org/wild-mammal-decline
3 https://royalsociety.org/-/media/policy/projects/biodiversity/Biodiversity---evidence-for-action.pdf
4 https://ourworldindata.org/global-land-for-agriculture

18 - COMPLETE NUTRITION

1 https://www.drmcdougall.com/
2 https://www.drfuhrman.com/
3 https://medlineplus.gov/ency/article/002222.htm
4 https://www.ncbi.nlm.nih.gov/books/NBK56068/table/summarytables.t4/?report=objectonly
5 http://www.whfoods.com/genpage.php?tname=foodspice&dbid=79
6 https://www.huffingtonpost.co.uk/entry/beyond-meat-impossible-burger-healthy_l_5d164ad1e4b07f6ca57cc3ed
7 https://www.huffingtonpost.co.uk/entry/beyond-meat-impossible-burger-healthy_l_5d164ad1e4b07f6ca57cc3ed
8 http://www.whfoods.com/genpage.php?tname=foodspice&dbid=52
9 http://www.whfoods.com/genpage.php?tname=foodspice&dbid=56
10 http://www.whfoods.com/genpage.php?tname=foodspice&dbid=58
11 http://www.whfoods.com/genpage.php?tname=foodspice&dbid=142
12 http://www.whfoods.com/genpage.php?tname=foodspice&dbid=98
13 http://www.whfoods.com/genpage.php?tname=foodspice&dbid=84
14 http://www.whfoods.com/genpage.php?tname=foodspice&dbid=11
15 http://www.whfoods.com/genpage.php?tname=foodspice&dbid=20
16 http://www.whfoods.com/genpage.php?tname=foodspice&dbid=81
17 http://www.whfoods.com/genpage.php?tname=foodspice&dbid=53
18 http://www.whfoods.com/genpage.php?tname=foodspice&dbid=128
19 http://www.whfoods.com/genpage.php?tname=foodspice&dbid=9
20 http://www.whfoods.com/genpage.php?tname=foodspice&dbid=45
21 http://www.whfoods.com/genpage.php?tname=foodspice&dbid=122
22 http://www.whfoods.com/genpage.php?tname=foodspice&dbid=38
23 http://www.whfoods.com/genpage.php?tname=foodspice&dbid=62
24 https://www.huffingtonpost.co.uk/entry/beyond-meat-impossible-burger-healthy_l_5d164ad1e4b07f6ca57cc3ed
25 https://www.ncbi.nlm.nih.gov/books/NBK22436/
26 https://www.ncbi.nlm.nih.gov/pubmed/17921363
27 https://pubmed.ncbi.nlm.nih.gov/28462631/
28 https://www.nature.com/articles/1602940
29 https://www.medicalnewstoday.com/articles/319176#what-are-the-benefits-of-fiber
30 https://www.helpguide.org/articles/healthy-eating/high-fiber-foods.htm
31 https://www.pcrm.org/good-nutrition/nutrition-information/fiber
32 https://www.pcrm.org/good-nutrition/nutrition-information/the-carbohydrate-advantage
33 https://www.health.harvard.edu/heart-health/how-its-made-cholesterol-production-in-your-body
34 https://pubmed.ncbi.nlm.nih.gov/27784848/
35 https://www.fda.gov/media/135274/download
36 https://pubmed.ncbi.nlm.nih.gov/31442459/
37 https://www.iarc.who.int/featured-news/media-centre-iarc-news-glyphosate/
38 https://en.wikipedia.org/wiki/Canola_oil
39 https://www.ncbi.nlm.nih.gov/pmc/articles/PMC3335257/
40 https://www.pcrm.org/good-nutrition/nutrition-information/lowering-cholesterol-with-a-plant-based-diet
41 https://www.nih.gov/news-events/news-releases/nih-human-microbiome-project-defines-normal-bacterial-makeup-body
42 https://pubmed.ncbi.nlm.nih.gov/32432868/
43 Mao, Q., Manservisi, F., Panzacchi, S., Mandrioli, D., Menghetti, I., Vornoli, A., Hu, J. (2018). The Ramazzini Institute 13-week pilot study on glyphosate and Roundup administered at human-equivalent dose to Sprague Dawley rats: effects on the microbiome. Environmental health: a global access science source, 17(1), 50. doi:10.1186/s12940-018-0394-x -https://www.ncbi.nlm.nih.gov/pmc/articles/PMC5972442/
44 https://ods.od.nih.gov/factsheets/Omega3FattyAcids-Consumer/
45 https://www.cochranelibrary.com/cdsr/doi/10.1002/14651858.CD003177.pub3/full
46 https://pubmed.ncbi.nlm.nih.gov/29355094/
47 https://www.jandonline.org/article/S2212-2672(13)01113-1/fulltext
48 https://rarediseases.org/rare-diseases/anemia-megaloblastic/
49 https://pubmed.ncbi.nlm.nih.gov/18606874/
50 https://www.vegansociety.com/resources/nutrition-and-health/nutrients/vitamin-b12
51 https://www.doctorklaper.com/
52 https://www.ncbi.nlm.nih.gov/pmc/articles/PMC3449318/
53 https://www.hsph.harvard.edu/nutritionsource/calcium/
54 http://www.whfoods.com/genpage.php?tname=nutrient&dbid=45

55 Le CH. The prevalence of anemia and moderate-severe anemia in the US population (NHANES 2003-2012). PLoS One. 2016 Nov 15;11(11):e0166635.https://journals.plos.org/plosone/article?id=10.1371/journal.pone.0166635
56 Nadia M. Bastide, Fabrice H.F. Pierre and Denis E. Corpet. "Heme Iron from Meat and Risk of Colorectal Cancer: A Meta-analysis and a Review of the Mechanisms Involved." Cancer Prev Res February. (2011): 177-184.
57 https://ods.od.nih.gov/factsheets/Iron-HealthProfessional/
58 http://www.whfoods.com/genpage.php?tname=nutrient&dbid=70
59 https://ods.od.nih.gov/factsheets/Zinc-HealthProfessional/
60 https://www.mja.com.au/journal/2013/199/4/zinc-and-vegetarian-diets
61 https://ods.od.nih.gov/factsheets/Zinc-HealthProfessional/
62 http://www.whfoods.com/genpage.php?tname=nutrient&dbid=115
63 https://pubmed.ncbi.nlm.nih.gov/15971062/
64 https://www.bmj.com/content/356/bmj.i6583
65 https://pubmed.ncbi.nlm.nih.gov/21310306/
66 https://ods.od.nih.gov/factsheets/VitaminD-HealthProfessional/
67 https://ods.od.nih.gov/factsheets/VitaminD-HealthProfessional/
68 https://www.bbc.com/news/health-57968651
69 https://pubmed.ncbi.nlm.nih.gov/9787730/
70 https://pubmed.ncbi.nlm.nih.gov/32788355/
71 https://www.nature.com/articles/s41591-020-01209-1

19 -FOUR STEPS TO VEGAN

1 https://foodrevolution.org/blog/plant-based-yogurt/?utm_source=sfmc&utm_medium=email&utm_campaign=blo-2021&utm_content=plant-based-yogurt
2 https://www.virtua.org/articles/prevent-and-reverse-heart-disease-with-a-plant-based-diet
3 https://www.healthline.com/health-news/quitting-junk-food-produces-similar-withdrawals-as-drug-addiction#What-junk-food-does-to-your-brain andhttps://www.sciencedirect.com/science/article/abs/pii/S0195666318306196
1 https://www.psychologytoday.com/us/blog/animals-and-us/201412/84-vegetarians-and-vegans-return-meat-why

20 -EATING IN, EATING OUT, COMING OUT

1 https://vegnews.com/2021/5/vegan-meal-kits
2 DeGeneres, Ellen - The Funny Thing Is... (2003)
3 https://www.researchgate.net/publication/317768313_Discrimination_Against_Vegans
4 https://journals.sagepub.com/doi/abs/10.1177/1368430215618253
5 https://journals.sagepub.com/doi/abs/10.1177/1368430215618253

21 - BEYOND DIET

1 https://www.peta.org/features/expert-quotes-reasons-animal-testing-unreliable
2 https://www.peta.org/features/expert-quotes-reasons-animal-testing-unreliable
3 https://www.unep.org/news-and-stories/story/putting-brakes-fast-fashion
4 https://www.worldwildlife.org/stories/the-impact-of-a-cotton-t-shirt
5 de Janvry, Alain; McIntosh, Craig; Sadoulet, Elisabeth (July 2015). "Fair Trade and Free Entry: Can a Disequilibrium Market Serve as a Development Tool?". The Review of Economics and Statistics. 97 (3): 567–573. doi:10.1162/REST_a_00512. S2CID 27543341. Andhttps://en.wikipedia.org/wiki/Fair_trade_debate
6 https://bcorporation.net/
7 https://grist.org/article/nasas-james-hansen-on-hacked-emails/
8 https://www.nestle.com/aboutus/overview/ourbrands
9 https://www.coca-colacompany.com/brands

22 - 11 SECRETS TO STAY MOTIVATED

1 https://www.brainyquote.com/topics/secret-quotes
2 https://www.brainyquote.com/topics/secret-quotes
3 https://www.brainyquote.com/topics/secret-quotes
4 https://winstonchurchill.org/resources/quotes/page/3/
5 https://www.goodreads.com/work/quotes/100074-d-o-d-j-ng
6 https://kidadl.com/articles/open-minded-quotes-to-open-yourself-up-to-the-world
7 https://kidadl.com/articles/open-minded-quotes-to-open-yourself-up-to-the-world
8 https://kidadl.com/articles/open-minded-quotes-to-open-yourself-up-to-the-world
9 https://en.wikipedia.org/wiki/John_Quincy_Adams
10 https://libquotes.com/neal-d-barnard/quote/lbx9r7i
11 https://www.goodreads.com/author/quotes/149151.Francis_of_Assisi
12 https://www.greatsayings.net/sayings-about-not-giving-into-temptation/
13 https://healingwithplants.us/2018/02/former-president-bill-clinton-healed-heart-disease-with-a-plant-based-diet
14 https://getlighthouse.com/blog/john-wooden-quotes-leadership-manager/
15 https://www.growthengineering.co.uk/55-quotes-about-learning/
16 https://www.growthengineering.co.uk/55-quotes-about-learning/
17 https://www.futurekind.com/blogs/vegan/10-vegan-celebrities
18 https://www.garyfox.co/inspirational-quotes/
19 https://www.azquotes.com/quote/811759
20 https://www.futurekind.com/blogs/vegan/10-vegan-celebrities
21 https://www.garyfox.co/inspirational-quotes/
22 https://www.goalcast.com/socrates-quotes
23 https://elated.co.za/vegan-quotes/
24 https://www.garyfox.co/inspirational-quotes/
25 https://www.azquotes.com/author/19347-Colleen_Patrick_Goudreau
26 @lizzo/tiktok

23 - FINAL THOUGHTS

1 https://www.ncbi.nlm.nih.gov/pmc/articles/PMC7721435/
2 https://pubmed.ncbi.nlm.nih.gov/31728489/
3 https://www.worldwatch.org/node/6294 andhttps://mercyforanimals.org/blog/this-new-study-is-further-proof-that-going/
4 https://ireland-calling.com/george-bernard-shaw-quotes-vegetarianism/
5 https://www.goodreads.com/quotes/13287-you-see-things-you-say-why-but-i-dream-things

25 - APPENDICES

APPENDIX 1

1 Information sourced from https://nutritiondata.self.com/
2 Info sourced from http://www.whfoods.com andhttps://nutritiondata.self.comht

Printed in Great Britain
by Amazon

33685593R00227